DIVINITY III

HEROES OF
THE GLORIOUS
STALINVERSE

JEFF LEMIRE | MATT KINDT | JOE HARRIS | SCOTT BRYAN WILSON | ELIOT RAHAL
CLAYTON CRAIN | JUAN JOSÉ RYP | CAFU | ROBERT GILL | FRANCIS PORTELA

CONTENTS

Assistant Editors: Danny Khazem
(BLOODSHOT, ARIC, ESCAPE, "Origin of...") and
Charlotte Greenbaum (ESCAPE)
Editors: Kyle Andrukiewicz (SHADOWMAN) and
Warren Simons (BLOODSHOT, ARIC, ESCAPE,
"Origin of...")
Editor-in-Chief: Warren Simons

Collection Cover Art: Stephen Segovia
with Elmer Santos

VALIANT.

Peter Cuneo
Chairman

Dinesh Shamdasani
CEO & Chief Creative Officer

Gavin Cuneo
Chief Operating Officer & CFO

Fred Pierce
Publisher

Warren Simons
Editor-in-Chief

Walter Black
VP Operations

Hunter Gorinson
VP Marketing & Communications

Atom! Freeman
Director of Sales

Andy Liegl
Alex Rae
Sales Managers

Annie Rosa
Sales Coordinator

Josh Johns
Director of Digital Media and Development

Travis Escarfullery
Jeff Walker
Production & Design Managers

Kyle Andrukiewicz
Editor and Creative Executive

Robert Meyers
Managing Editor

Peter Stern
Publishing & Operations Manager

Andrew Steinbeiser
Marketing & Communications Manager

Danny Khazem
Charlotte Greenbaum
Associate Editors

Benjamin Peterson
Editorial Assistant

Shanyce Lora
Digital Media Coordinator

Ivan Cohen
Collection Editor

Steve Blackwell
Collection Designer

Rian Hughes/Device
Original Trade Dress & Book Design

Russell Brown
President, Consumer Products,
Promotions and Ad Sales

Caritza Berlioz
Licensing Coodinator

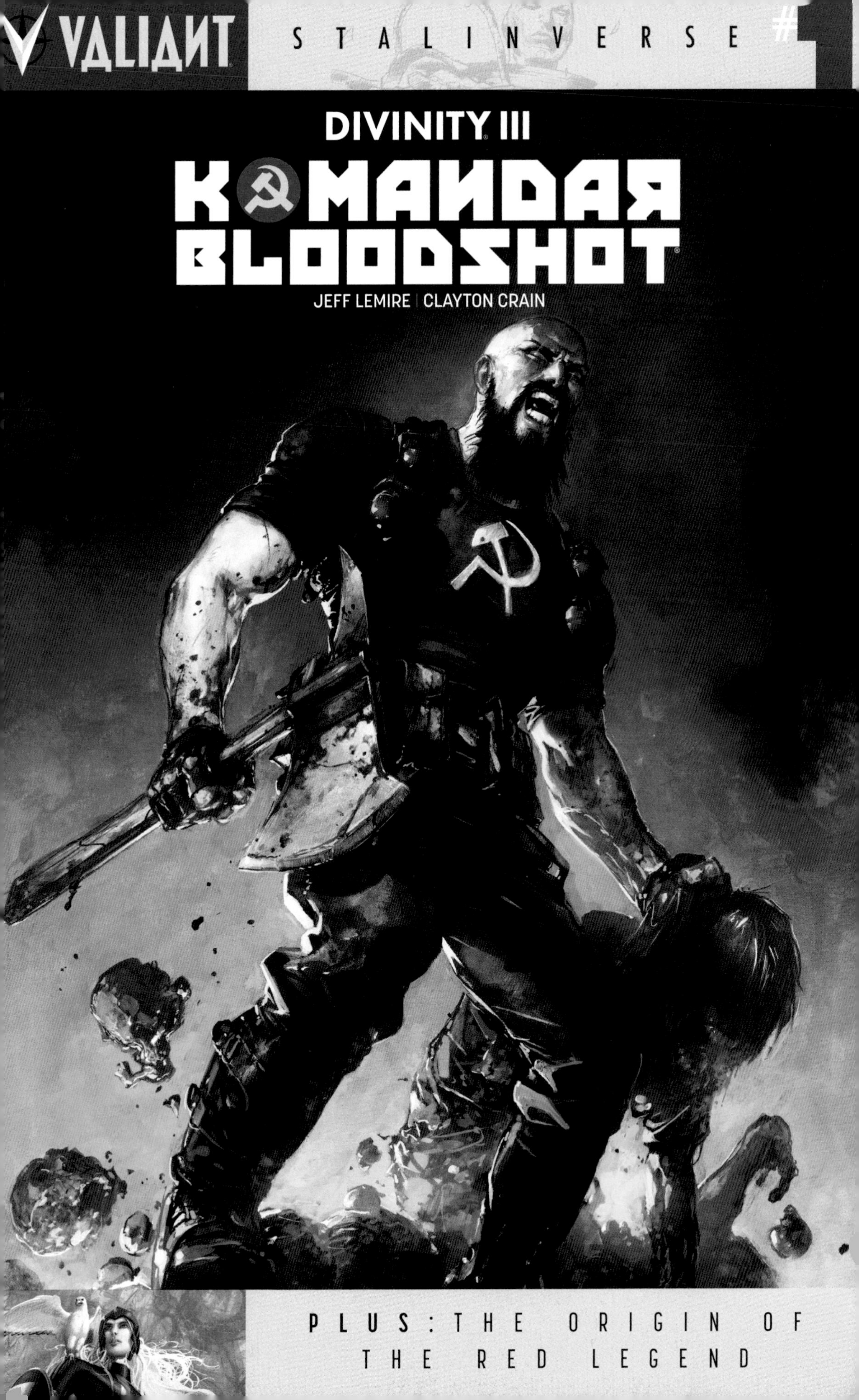
VALIANT
STALINVERSE #
DIVINITY III
KOMANDAR BLOODSHOT
JEFF LEMIRE | CLAYTON CRAIN
PLUS: THE ORIGIN OF THE RED LEGEND

1922 JOSEPH STALIN ASSASSINATES VLADIMIR LENIN AND BECOMES LEADER OF THE SOVIET UNION.

1934 RUSSIA FORMS THE SOVIET UNION BY ANNEXING THE BALTIC STATES AS WELL AS POLAND, HUNGARY, GERMANY AND FRANCE.

1939 GREAT PATRIOTIC WAR OF EUROPE BEGINS.

1945 SOVIET UNION EMERGES TRIUMPHANT AFTER THE GREAT PATRIOTIC WAR.

1946 SOVIET UNION ENVELOPES ALL OF EUROPE EXCEPT FOR GREAT BRITAIN.

1947 BATTLE OF BRITAIN. ENGLAND, SCOTLAND, AND IRELAND FALL UNDER SOVIET RULE.

1948 WAR FOR ASIA BEGINS.

1949 SOVIET UNION DROPS ATOM BOMB ON TOKYO, ENDING THE WAR FOR ASIA.

1951 USSR INSTALLS JOSEPH McCARTHY AS PUPPET PRESIDENT OF THE UNITED STATES.

1960 SOVIET UNION ACCELERATES DEEP SPACE EXPLORATION.

1963 SINO-SOVIET PACT SIGNED.

1968 AMERICAN CIVIL WAR II BEGINS.

1969 THE FIRST BATTLE OF LOS ANGELES.

1972 SOVIET UNION ANNEXES SOUTH AMERICA AND NORTH AMERICAN WEST COAST.

1973 AMERICAN REBEL LEADER, JOHN KENNEDY, IS ASSASSINATED OFF THE COAST OF CUBA.

1987 COSMONAUTS BEGIN MAPPING NEIGHBORING GALAXIES.

1993 THE SECOND BATTLE OF LOS ANGELES.

1994 SEATTLE PEACE ACCORDS ARE SIGNED.

1995 THE AMERICAS OFFICIALLY BECOME SOVIET COLONIES. MASS INSURGENCIES CONTINUE.

2012 ARIC, SON OF THE REVOLUTION, APPEARS IN ROMANIA.

2016 THE RED BRIGADE IS FORMALLY ANNOUNCED AS WORLD SECURITY FORCE.

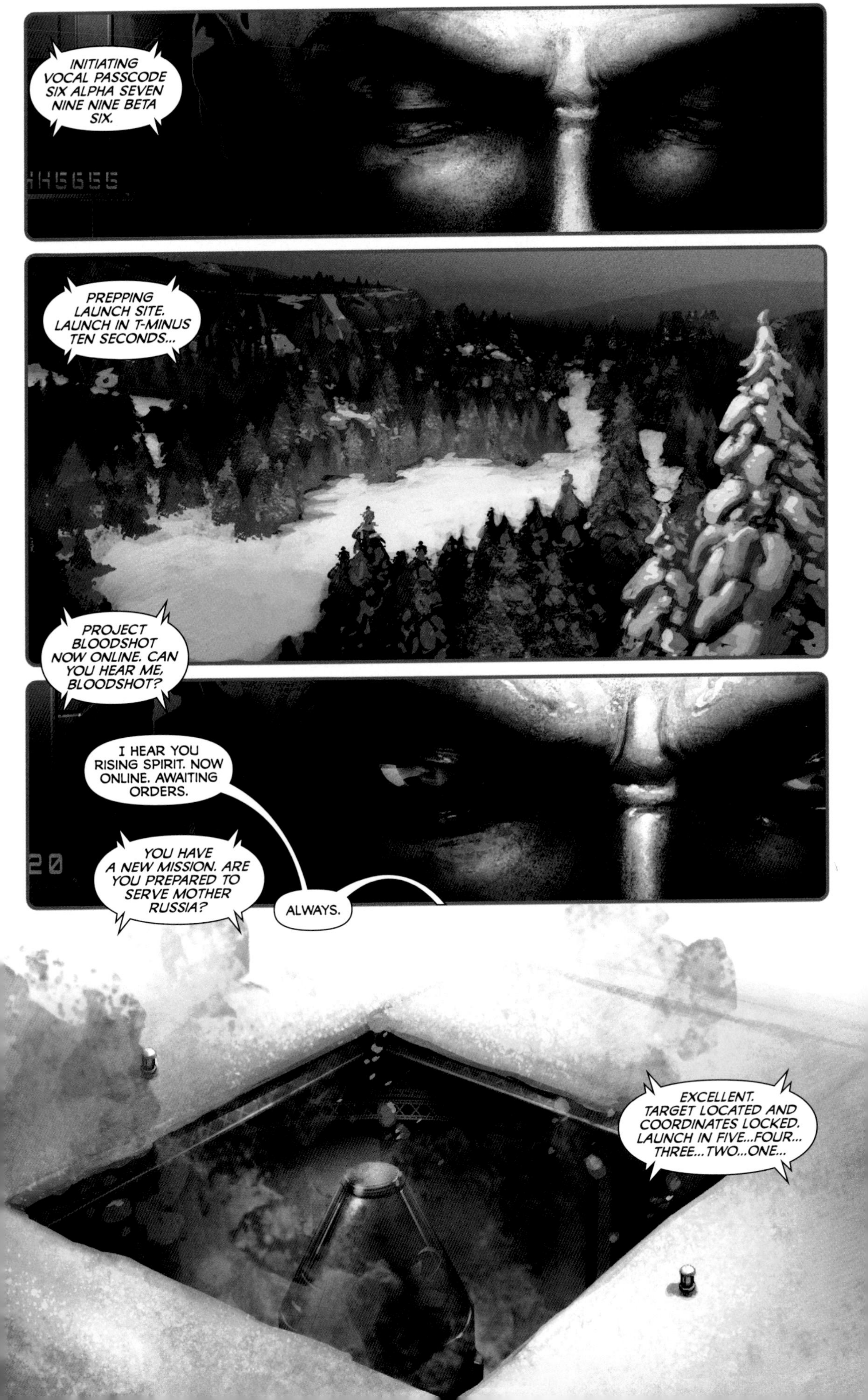
INITIATING VOCAL PASSCODE SIX ALPHA SEVEN NINE NINE BETA SIX.
PREPPING LAUNCH SITE. LAUNCH IN T-MINUS TEN SECONDS...
PROJECT BLOODSHOT NOW ONLINE. CAN YOU HEAR ME, BLOODSHOT?
I HEAR YOU RISING SPIRIT. NOW ONLINE. AWAITING ORDERS.
YOU HAVE A NEW MISSION. ARE YOU PREPARED TO SERVE MOTHER RUSSIA?
ALWAYS.
EXCELLENT. TARGET LOCATED AND COORDINATES LOCKED. LAUNCH IN FIVE...FOUR... THREE...TWO...ONE...

BLAST OFF. LAUNCH SUCCESSFUL. WARHEAD NOW LEAVING SIBERIAN AIRSPACE.
MISSION DEBRIEF INITIATED...WE HAVE RECENTLY UNCOVERED THE LOCATION OF A TERRORIST CELL DEEP IN THE NORTH AMERICAN CONTINENT.
THIS IS NO GROUP OF MINOR REBELS OR MERE DISSIDENTS. WE HAVE REASON TO BELIEVE THAT THIS CELL IS THE HEART OF THE WEST COAST INSURGENCY.
THEY HAVE A BUNKER DEEP IN THE MOUNTAINS OF COLORADO AND WE EXPECT THAT THEY WILL BE HEAVILY ARMED AND MAY EVEN BE IN POSSESSION OF WEAPONS OF MASS DESTRUCTION. THIS IS AN ALPHA LEVEL THREAT TO THE STATE.

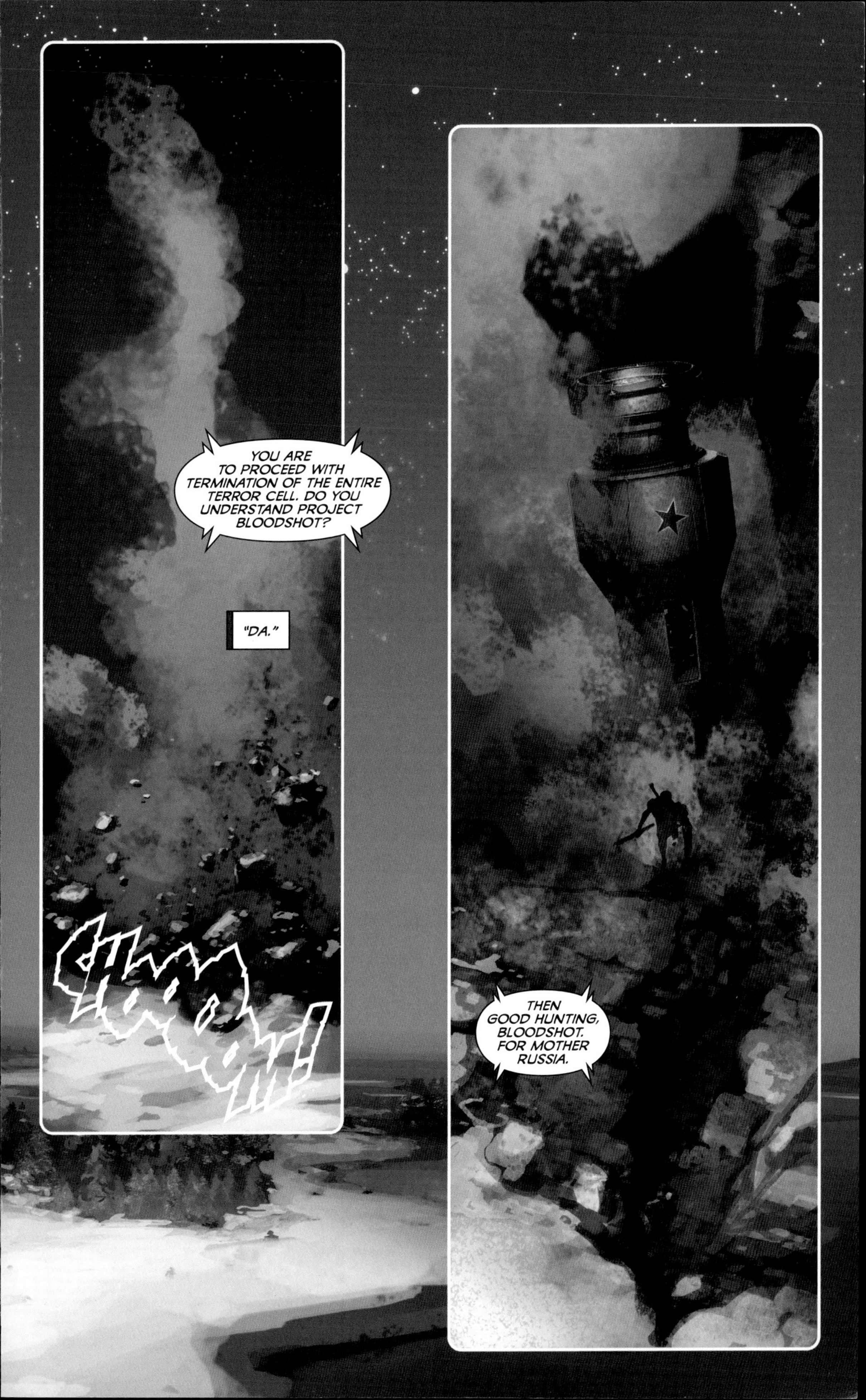
YOU ARE TO PROCEED WITH TERMINATION OF THE ENTIRE TERROR CELL. DO YOU UNDERSTAND PROJECT BLOODSHOT?
"DA."
THEN GOOD HUNTING, BLOODSHOT. FOR MOTHER RUSSIA.

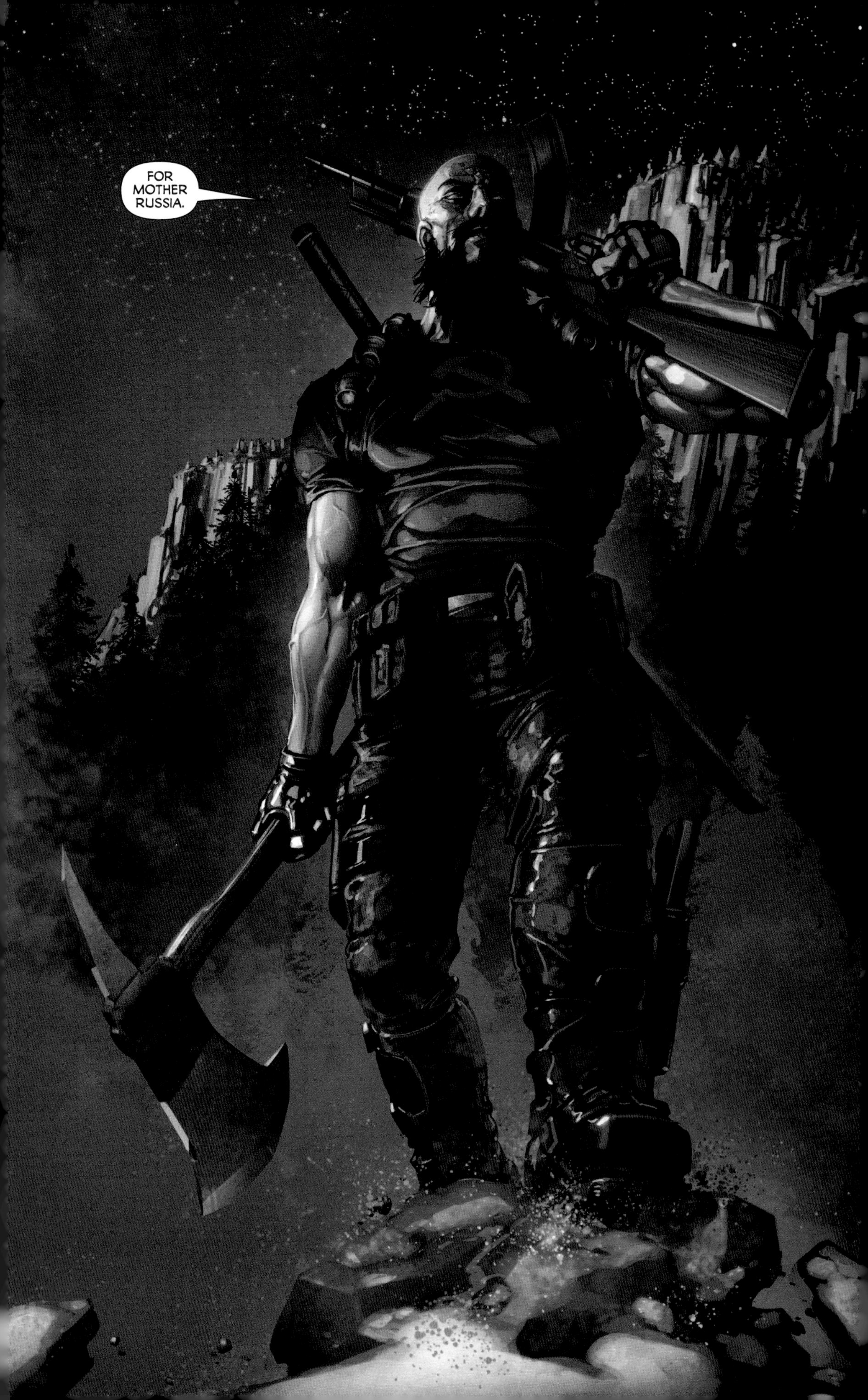
FOR MOTHER RUSSIA.

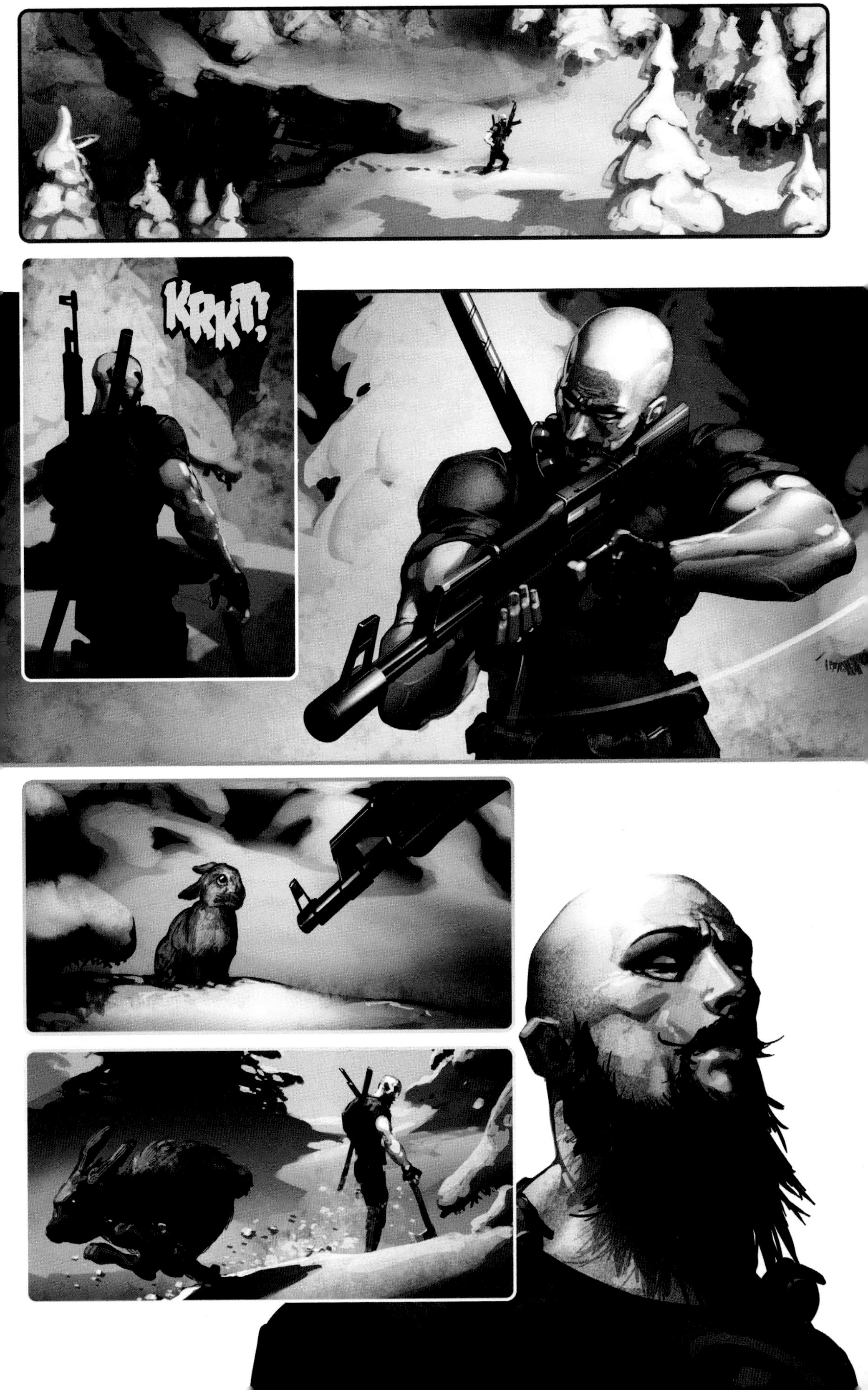
KRKT!

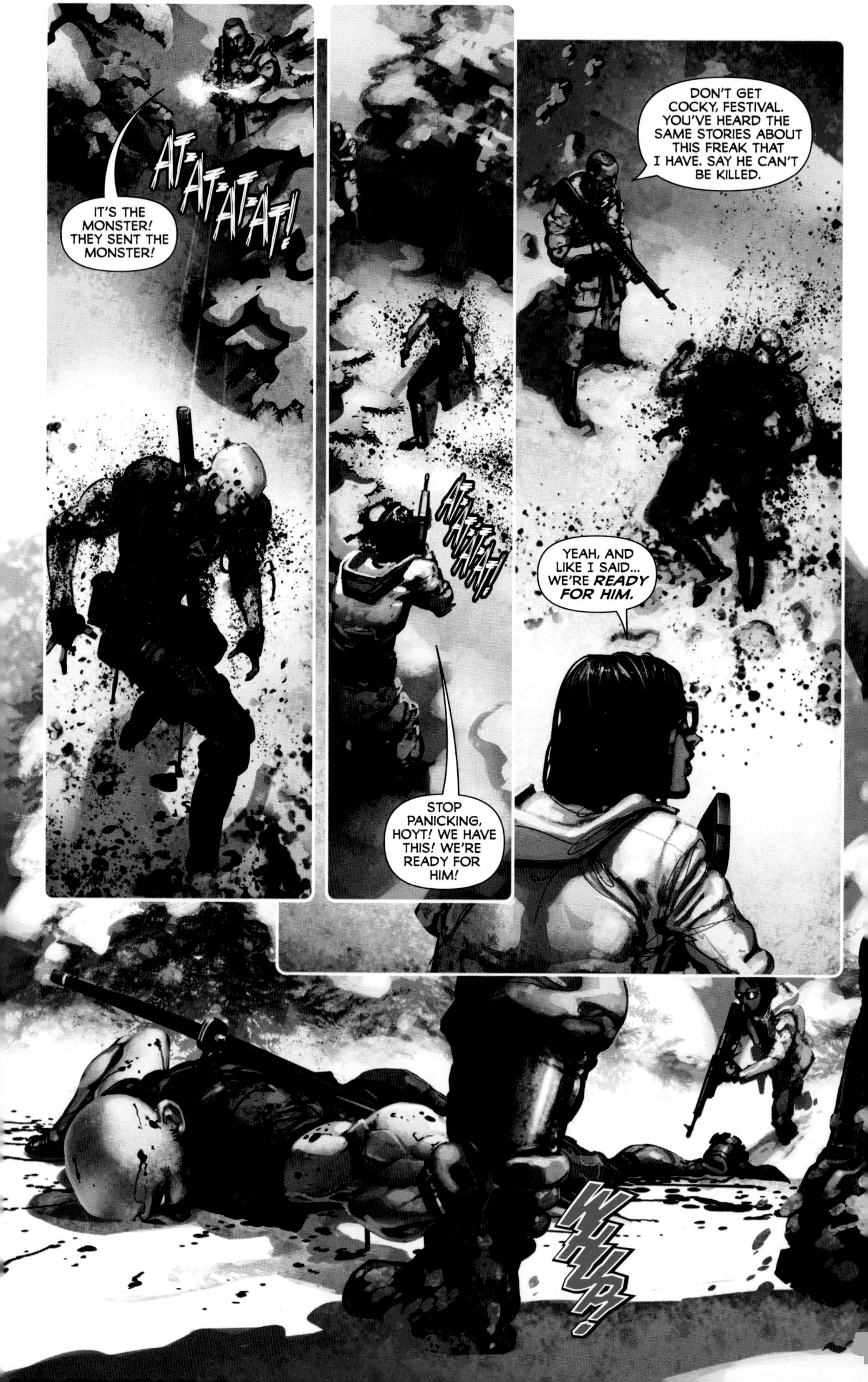
AT-AT-AT-AT-AT!
IT'S THE MONSTER! THEY SENT THE MONSTER!
STOP PANICKING, HOYT! WE HAVE THIS! WE'RE READY FOR HIM!
DON'T GET COCKY, FESTIVAL. YOU'VE HEARD THE SAME STORIES ABOUT THIS FREAK THAT I HAVE. SAY HE CAN'T BE KILLED.
YEAH, AND LIKE I SAID... WE'RE ***READY FOR HIM.***

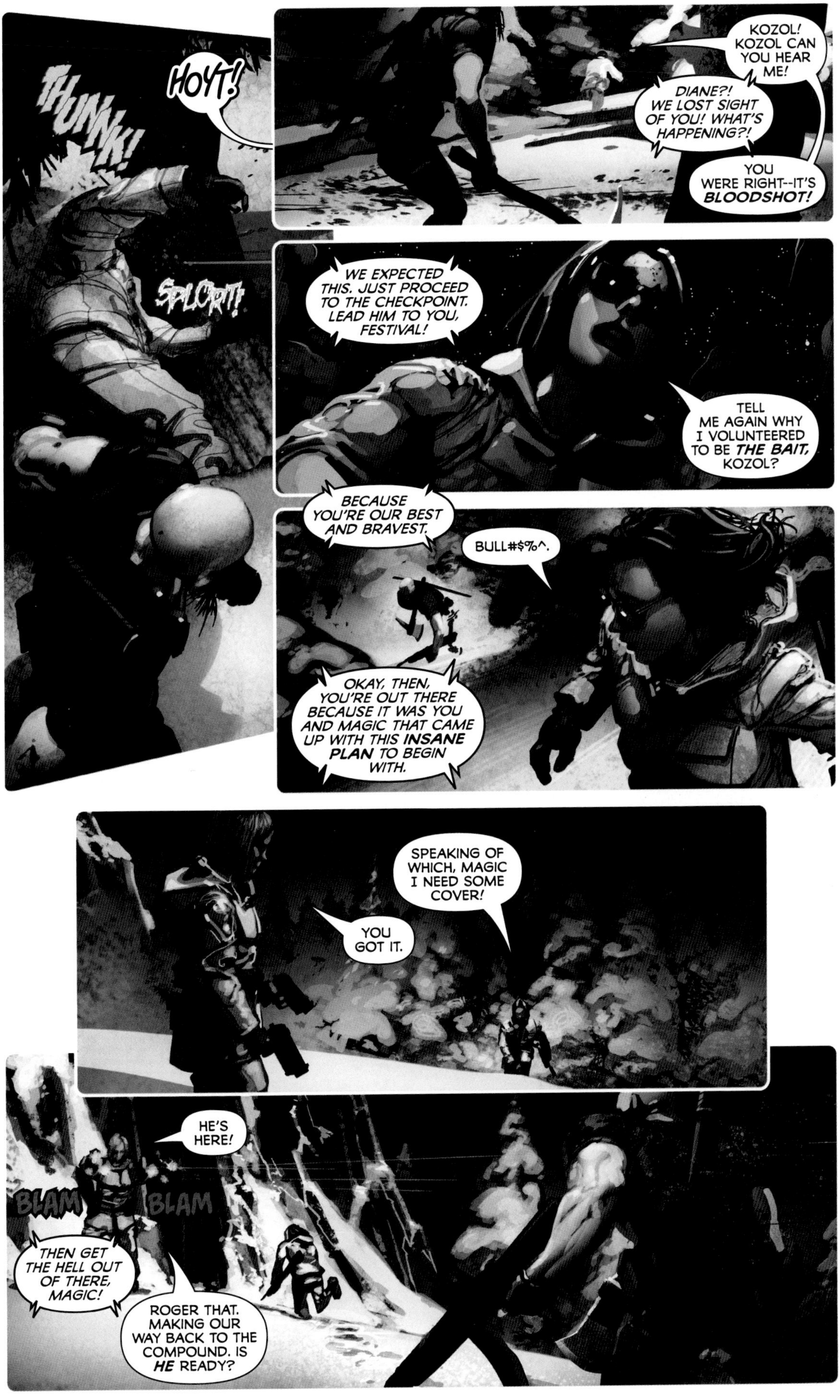
THUNNK!
HOYT!
SPLORT!
KOZOL! KOZOL CAN YOU HEAR ME!
DIANE?! WE LOST SIGHT OF YOU! WHAT'S HAPPENING?!
YOU WERE RIGHT--IT'S BLOODSHOT!
WE EXPECTED THIS. JUST PROCEED TO THE CHECKPOINT. LEAD HIM TO YOU, FESTIVAL!
TELL ME AGAIN WHY I VOLUNTEERED TO BE THE BAIT, KOZOL?
BECAUSE YOU'RE OUR BEST AND BRAVEST.
BULL#$%^.
OKAY, THEN, YOU'RE OUT THERE BECAUSE IT WAS YOU AND MAGIC THAT CAME UP WITH THIS INSANE PLAN TO BEGIN WITH.
SPEAKING OF WHICH, MAGIC I NEED SOME COVER!
YOU GOT IT.
HE'S HERE!
BLAM
BLAM
THEN GET THE HELL OUT OF THERE, MAGIC!
ROGER THAT. MAKING OUR WAY BACK TO THE COMPOUND. IS HE READY?

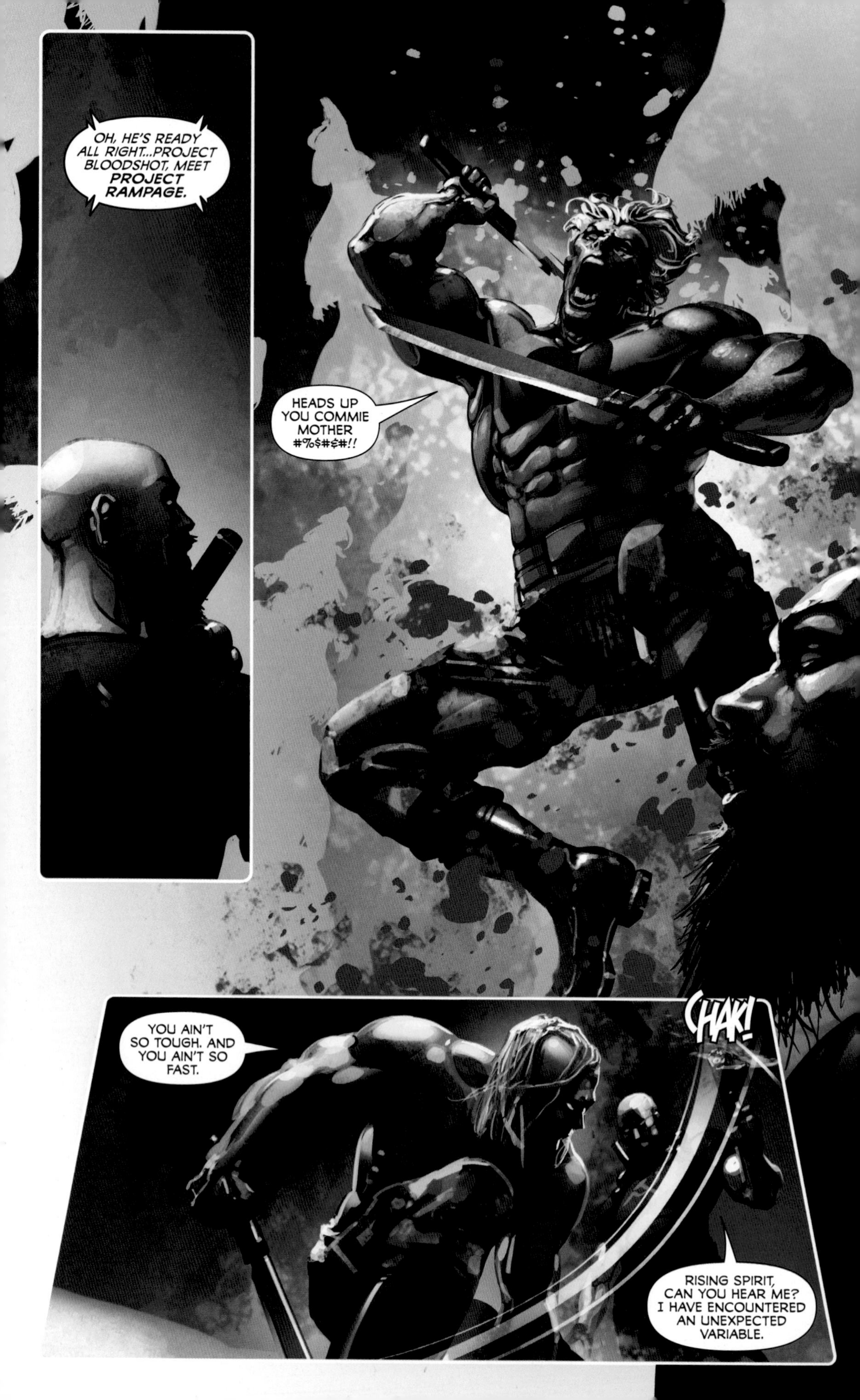
OH, HE'S READY ALL RIGHT...PROJECT BLOODSHOT, MEET **PROJECT RAMPAGE.**
HEADS UP YOU COMMIE MOTHER #%$#¢#!!
CHAK!
YOU AIN'T SO TOUGH. AND YOU AIN'T SO FAST.
RISING SPIRIT, CAN YOU HEAR ME? I HAVE ENCOUNTERED AN UNEXPECTED VARIABLE.

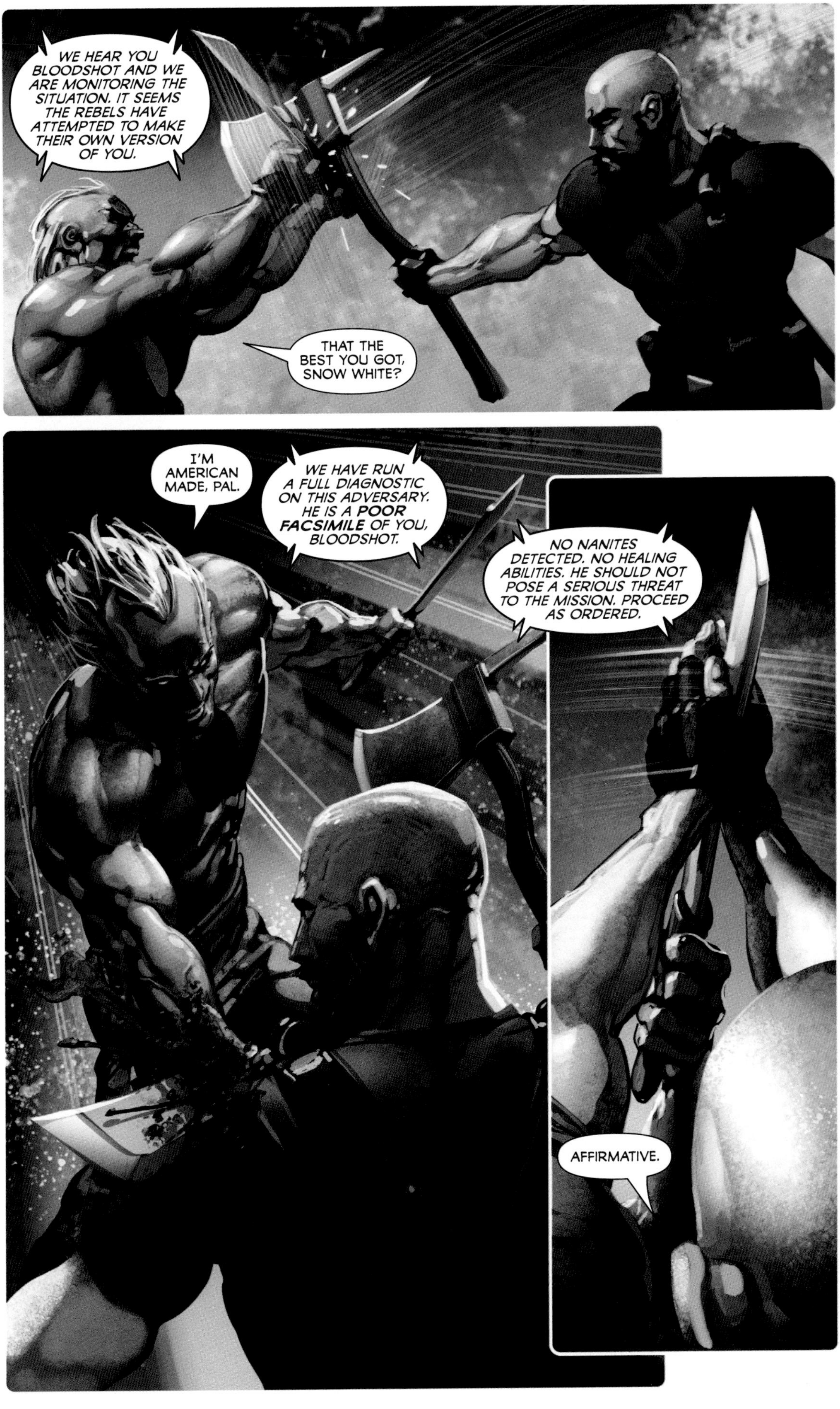
WE HEAR YOU BLOODSHOT AND WE ARE MONITORING THE SITUATION. IT SEEMS THE REBELS HAVE ATTEMPTED TO MAKE THEIR OWN VERSION OF YOU.
THAT THE BEST YOU GOT, SNOW WHITE?
I'M AMERICAN MADE, PAL.
WE HAVE RUN A FULL DIAGNOSTIC ON THIS ADVERSARY. HE IS A **POOR FACSIMILE** OF YOU, BLOODSHOT.
NO NANITES DETECTED. NO HEALING ABILITIES. HE SHOULD NOT POSE A SERIOUS THREAT TO THE MISSION. PROCEED AS ORDERED.
AFFIRMATIVE.

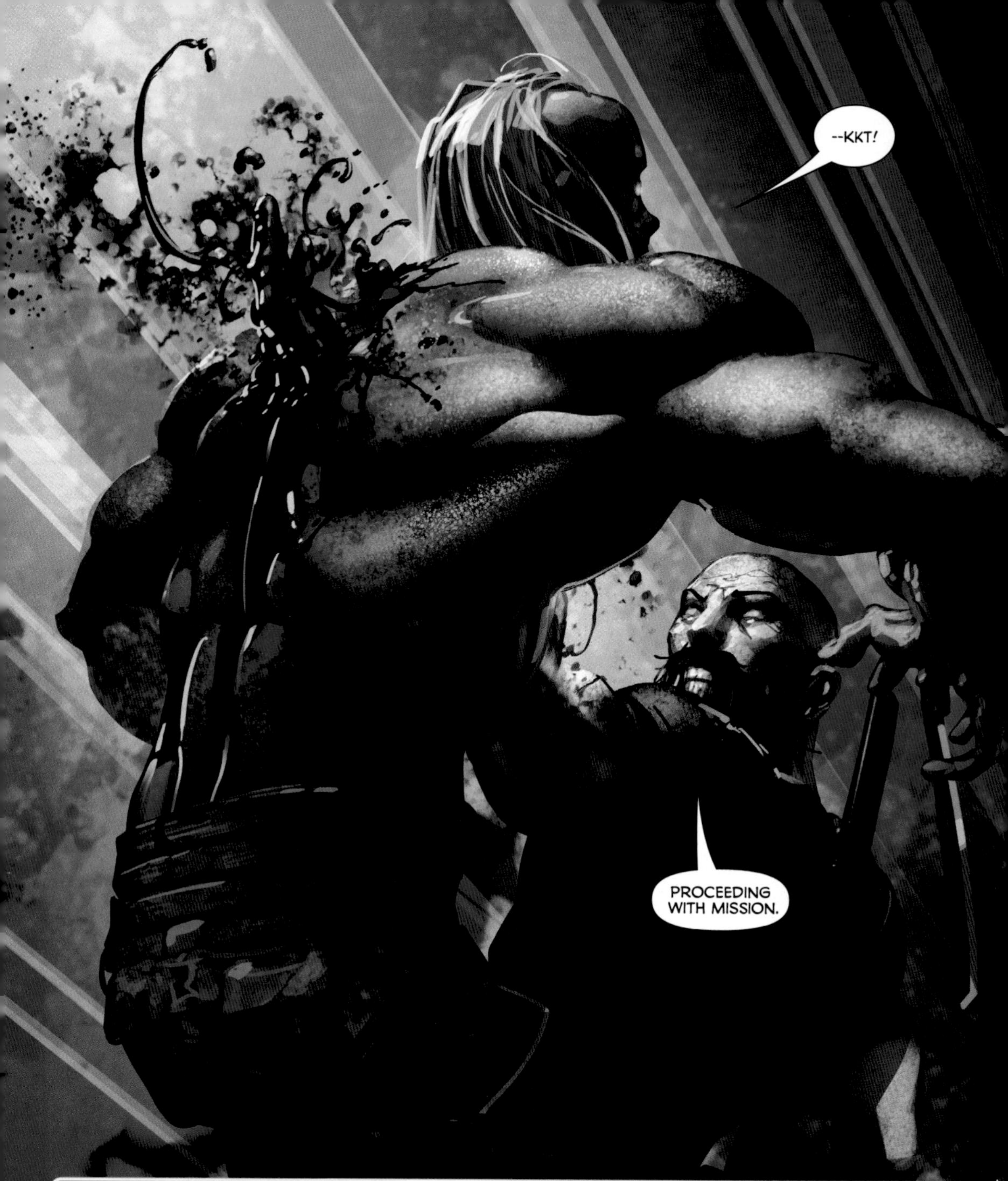
--KKT!
PROCEEDING WITH MISSION.

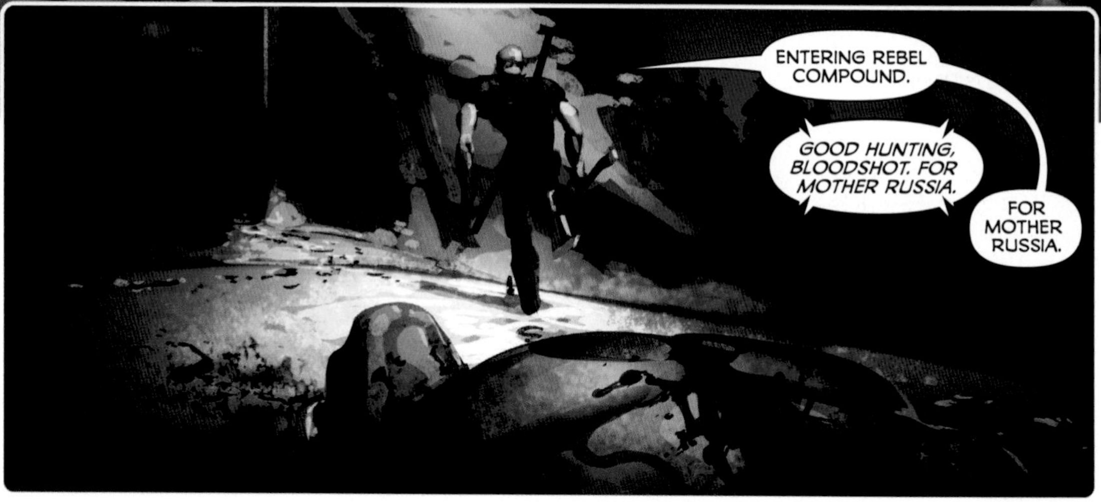
ENTERING REBEL COMPOUND.
GOOD HUNTING, BLOODSHOT. FOR MOTHER RUSSIA.
FOR MOTHER RUSSIA.

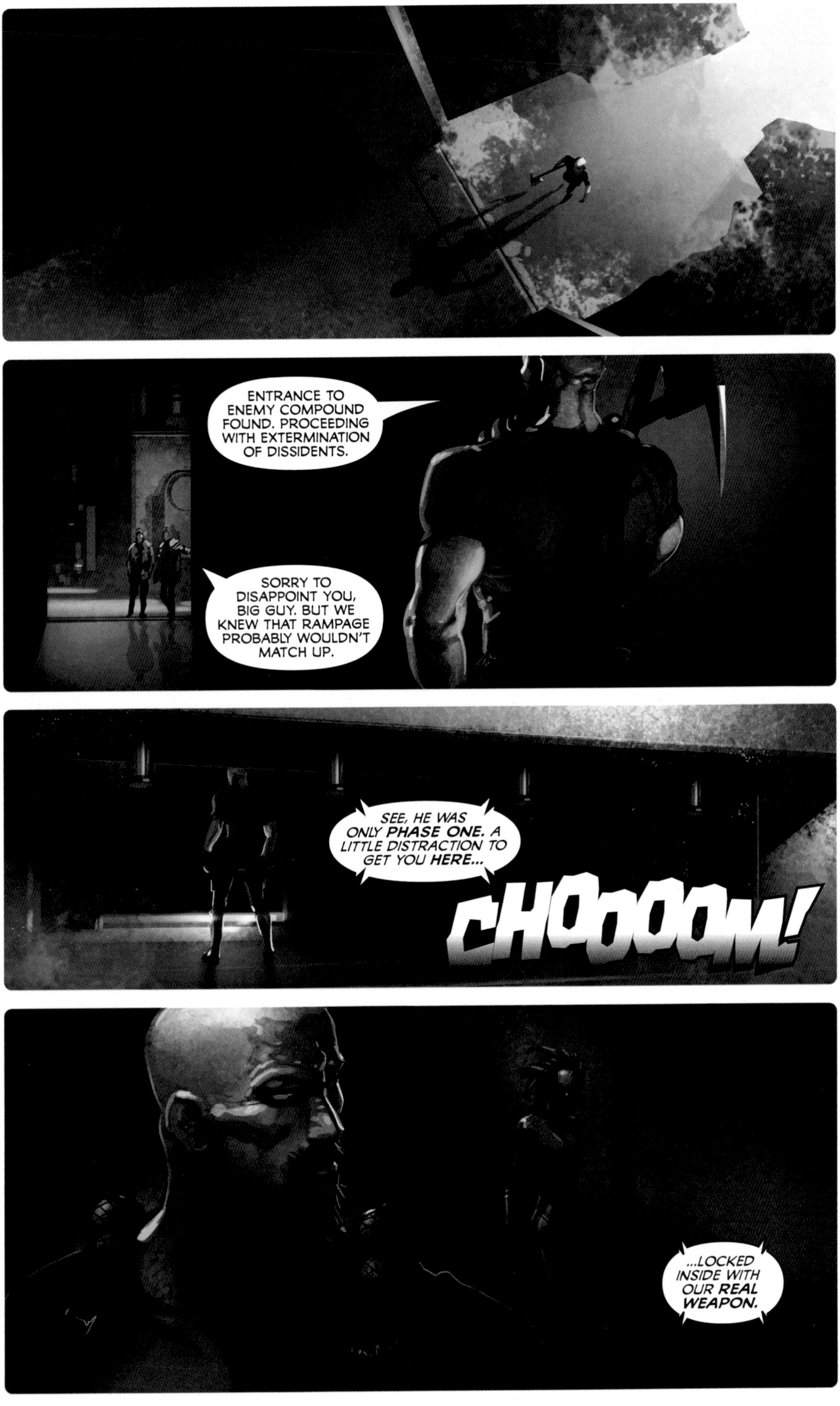

ENTRANCE TO ENEMY COMPOUND FOUND. PROCEEDING WITH EXTERMINATION OF DISSIDENTS.
SORRY TO DISAPPOINT YOU, BIG GUY. BUT WE KNEW THAT RAMPAGE PROBABLY WOULDN'T MATCH UP.
SEE, HE WAS ONLY **PHASE ONE.** A LITTLE DISTRACTION TO GET YOU **HERE...**
CHOOOOM!
...LOCKED INSIDE WITH OUR **REAL WEAPON.**

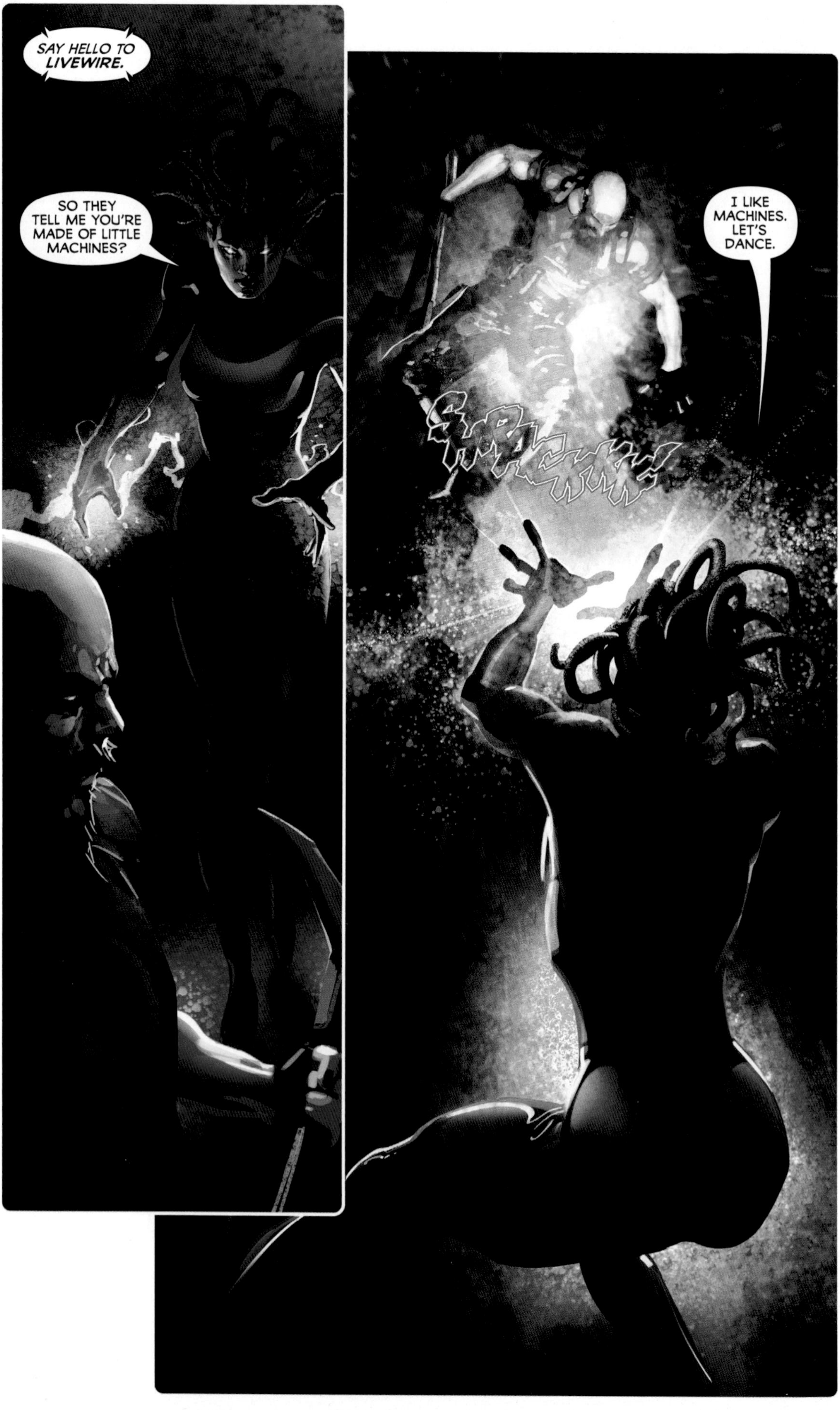
SAY HELLO TO *LIVEWIRE.*
SO THEY TELL ME YOU'RE MADE OF LITTLE MACHINES?
I LIKE MACHINES. LET'S DANCE.

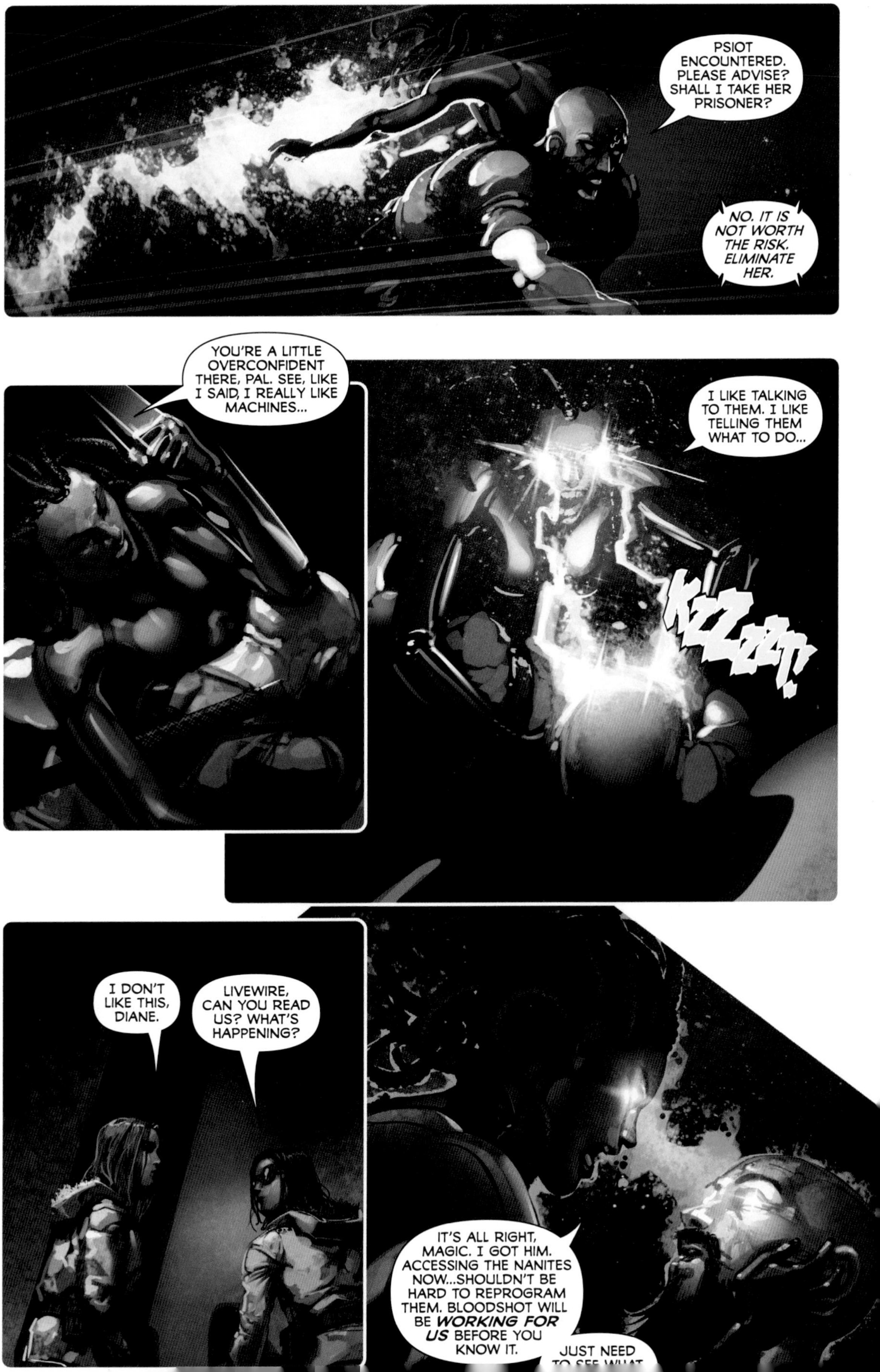
PSIOT ENCOUNTERED. PLEASE ADVISE? SHALL I TAKE HER PRISONER?
NO. IT IS NOT WORTH THE RISK. ELIMINATE HER.
YOU'RE A LITTLE OVERCONFIDENT THERE, PAL. SEE, LIKE I SAID, I REALLY LIKE MACHINES...
I LIKE TALKING TO THEM. I LIKE TELLING THEM WHAT TO DO...
KZZZZT!
I DON'T LIKE THIS, DIANE.
LIVEWIRE, CAN YOU READ US? WHAT'S HAPPENING?
IT'S ALL RIGHT, MAGIC. I GOT HIM. ACCESSING THE NANITES NOW...SHOULDN'T BE HARD TO REPROGRAM THEM. BLOODSHOT WILL BE WORKING FOR US BEFORE YOU KNOW IT.
JUST NEED

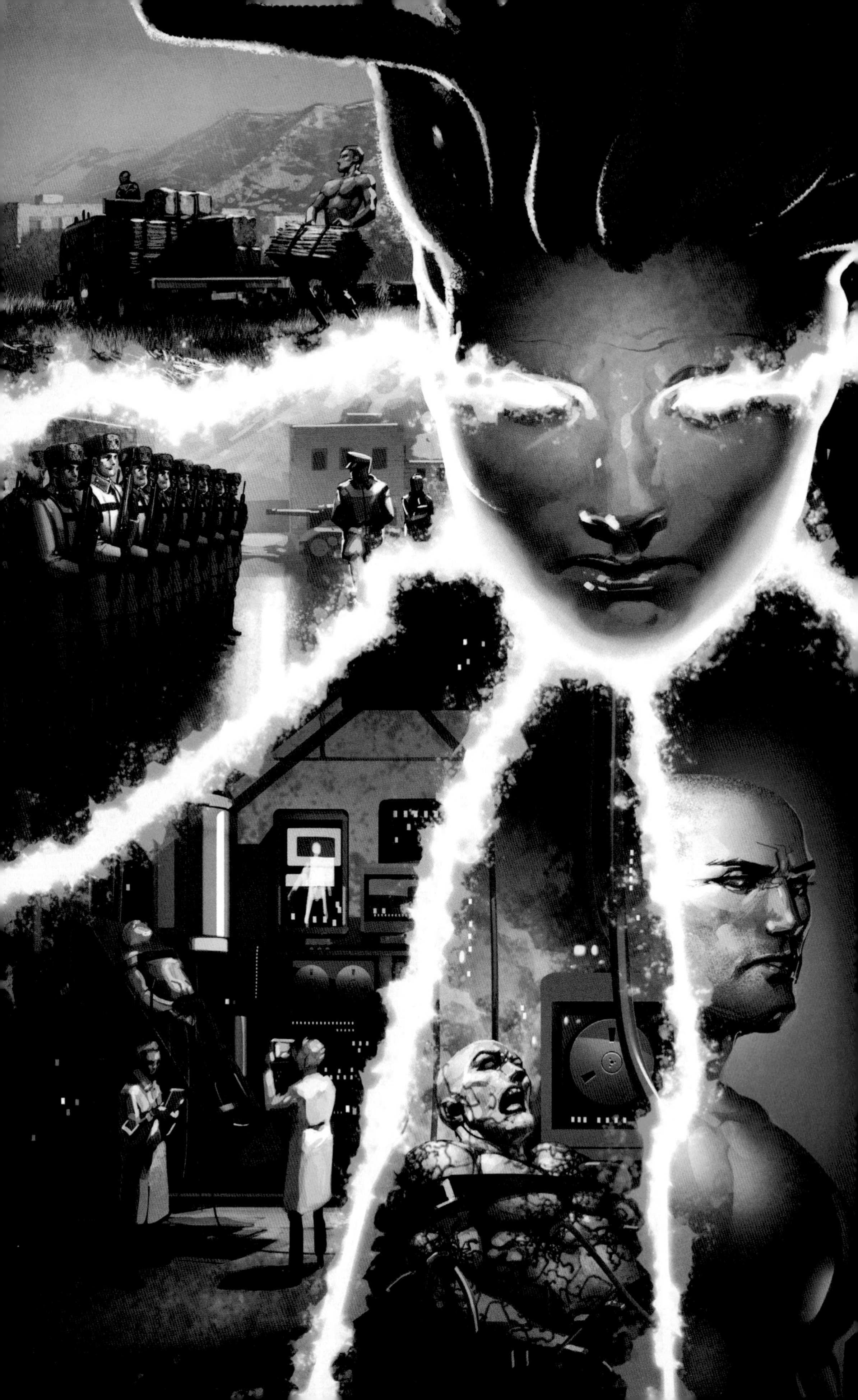

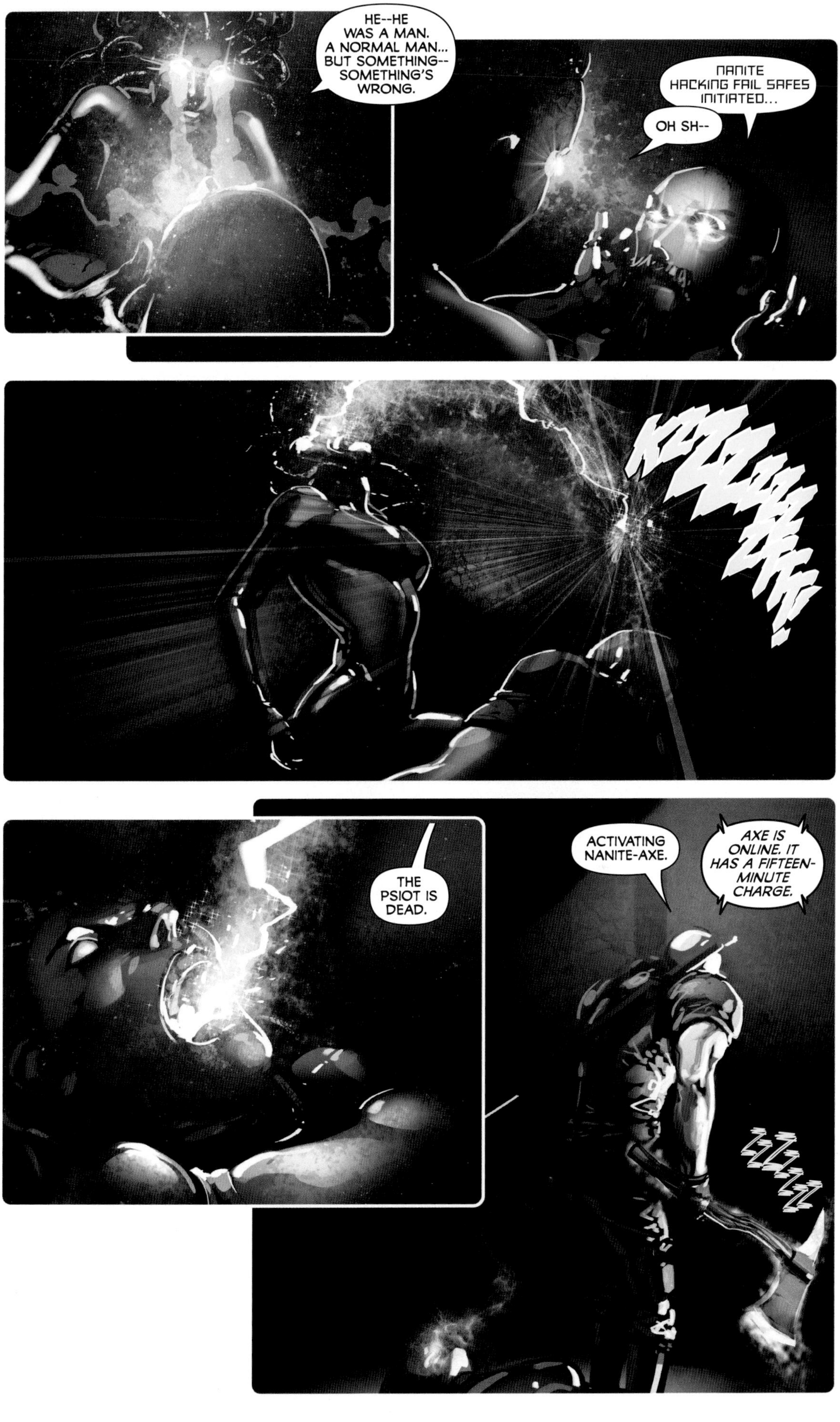
HE--HE WAS A MAN. A NORMAL MAN... BUT SOMETHING-- SOMETHING'S WRONG.
NANITE HACKING FAIL SAFES INITIATED...
OH SH--
KZZZZZZZZT!
THE PSIOT IS DEAD.
ACTIVATING NANITE-AXE.
AXE IS ONLINE. IT HAS A FIFTEEN-MINUTE CHARGE.

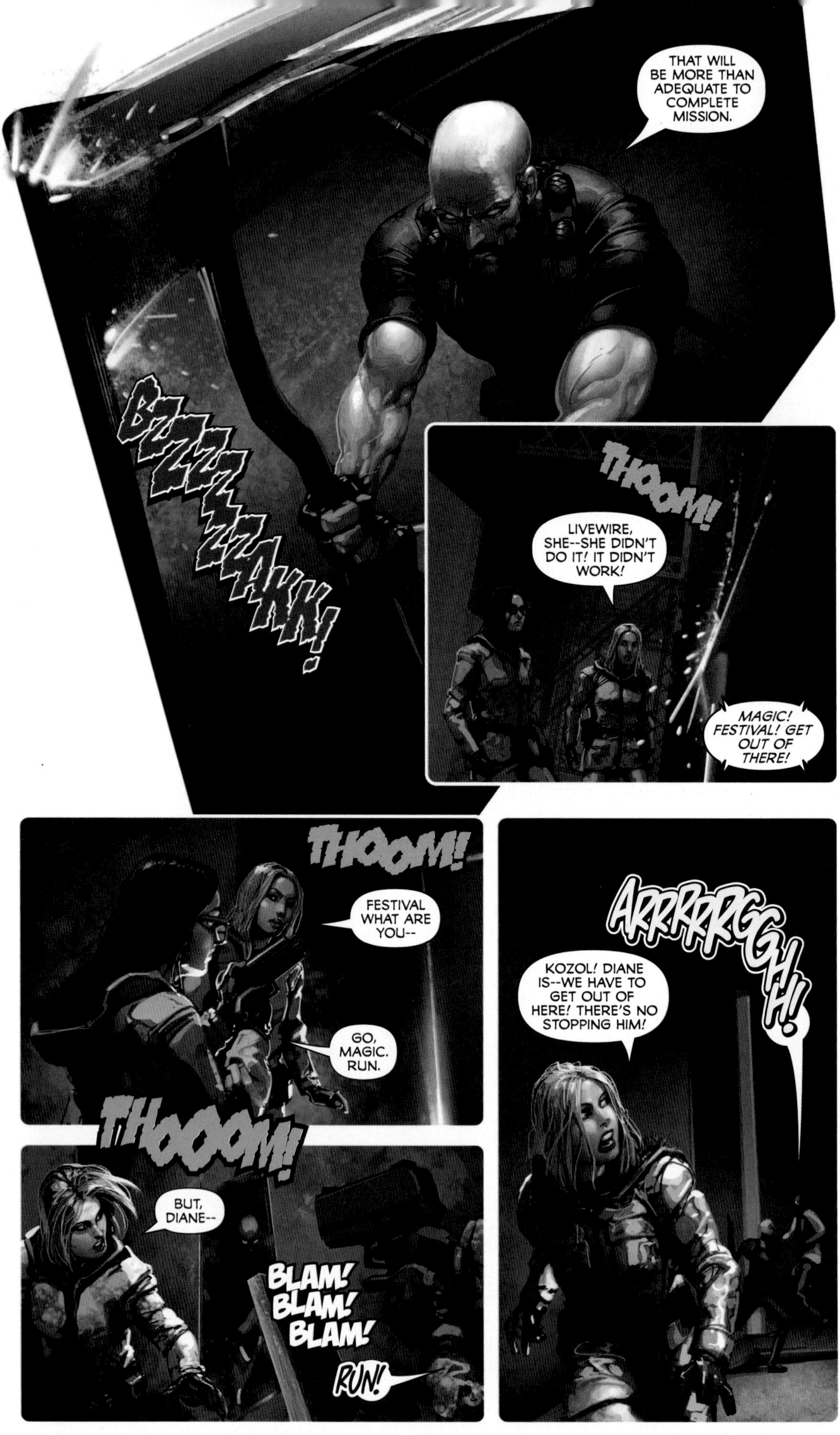
THAT WILL BE MORE THAN ADEQUATE TO COMPLETE MISSION.
BZZZZZZZAKK!
THOOM!
LIVEWIRE, SHE--SHE DIDN'T DO IT! IT DIDN'T WORK!
MAGIC! FESTIVAL! GET OUT OF THERE!
THOOM!
FESTIVAL WHAT ARE YOU--
GO, MAGIC. RUN.
THOOOM!
BUT, DIANE--
BLAM! BLAM! BLAM!
RUN!
ARRRRRGGHH!
KOZOL! DIANE IS--WE HAVE TO GET OUT OF HERE! THERE'S NO STOPPING HIM!

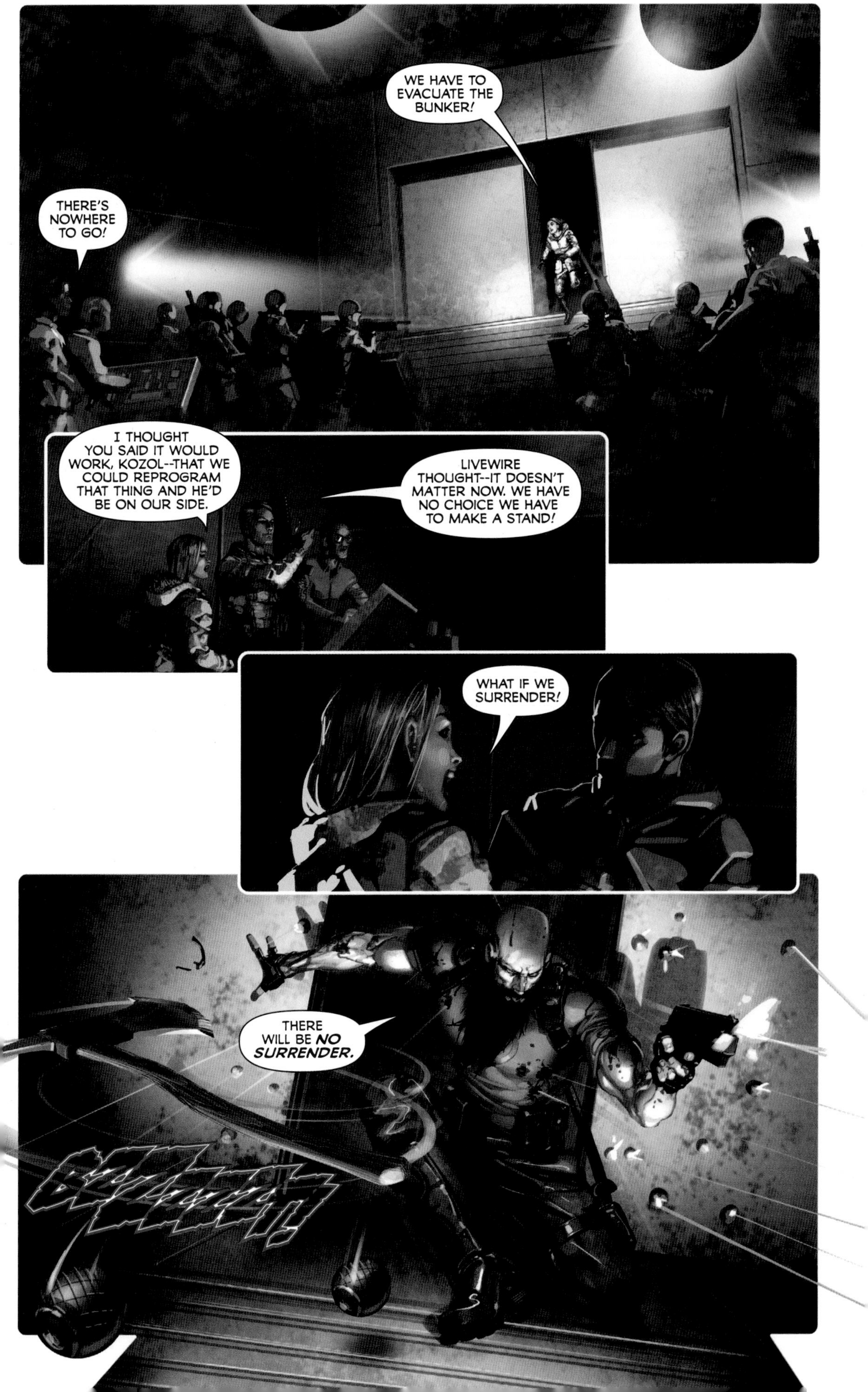

THERE'S NOWHERE TO GO!
WE HAVE TO EVACUATE THE BUNKER!
I THOUGHT YOU SAID IT WOULD WORK, KOZOL--THAT WE COULD REPROGRAM THAT THING AND HE'D BE ON OUR SIDE.
LIVEWIRE THOUGHT--IT DOESN'T MATTER NOW. WE HAVE NO CHOICE WE HAVE TO MAKE A STAND!
WHAT IF WE SURRENDER!
THERE WILL BE NO SURRENDER.

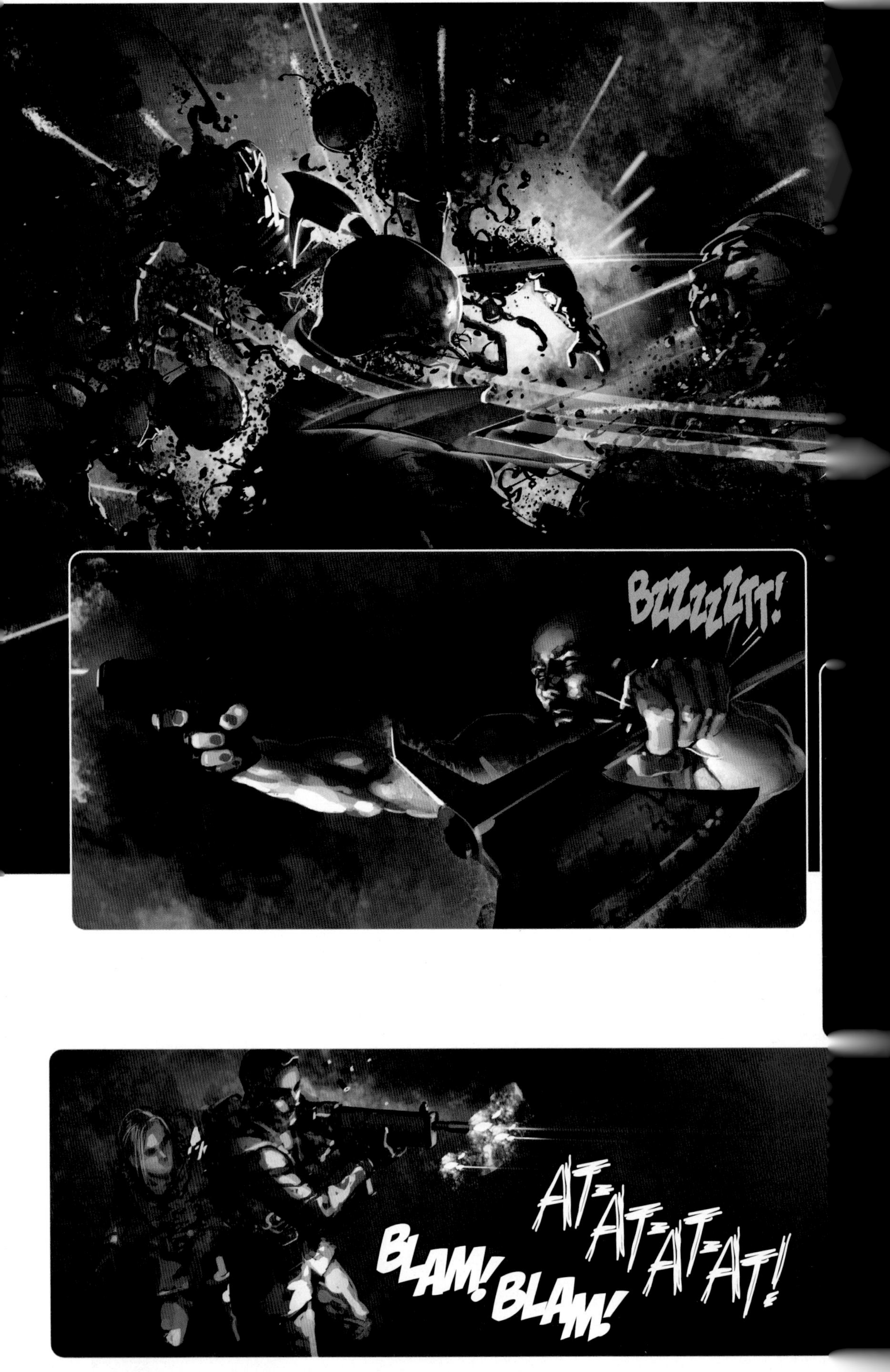

BZZZZZTT!
AT-AT-AT-AT-AT!
BLAM! BLAM!

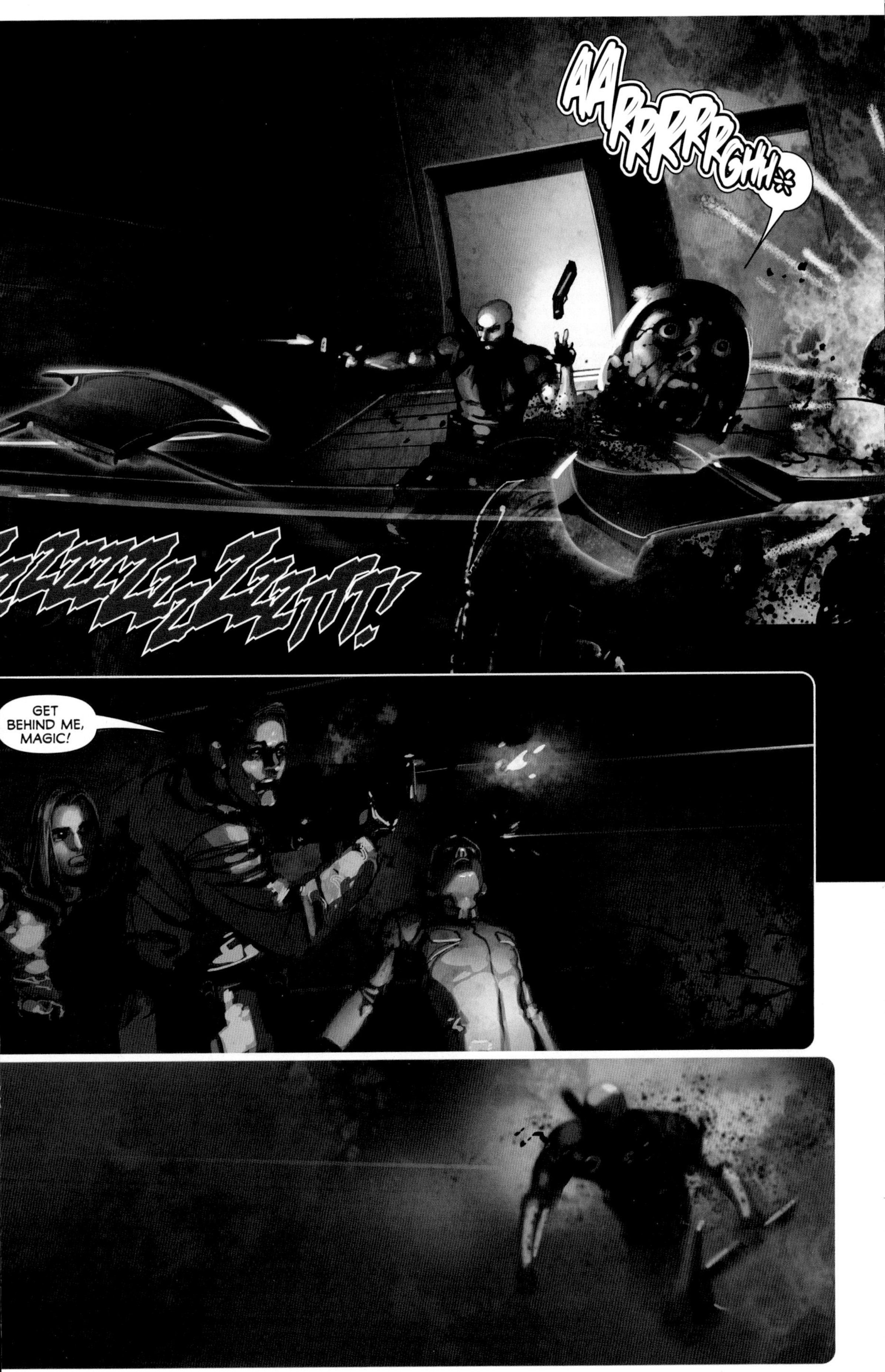
AARRRRRGHH!
GET BEHIND ME, MAGIC!

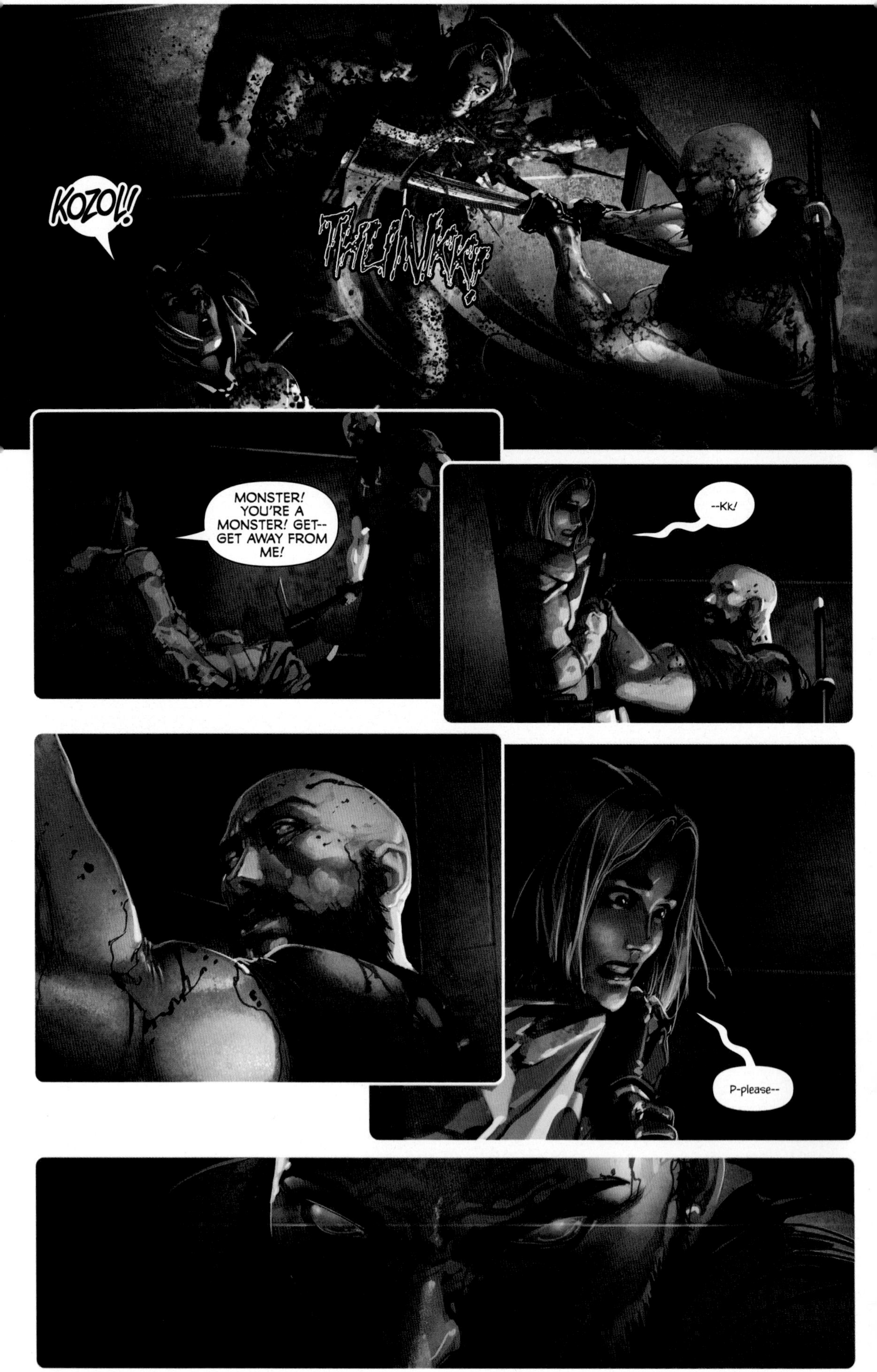
KOZOL!
THUNK!
MONSTER! YOU'RE A MONSTER! GET-- GET AWAY FROM ME!
--Kk!
P-please--

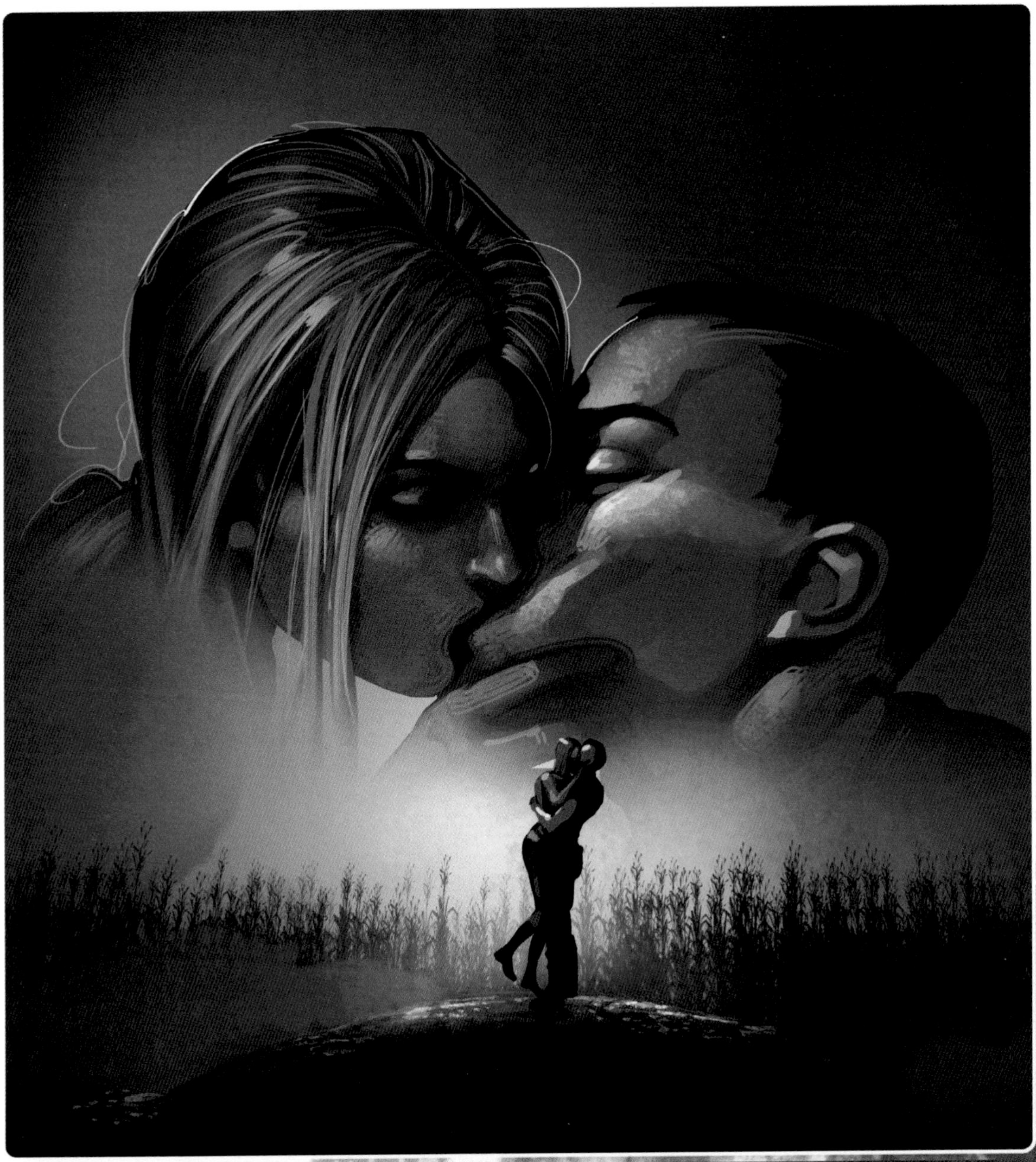
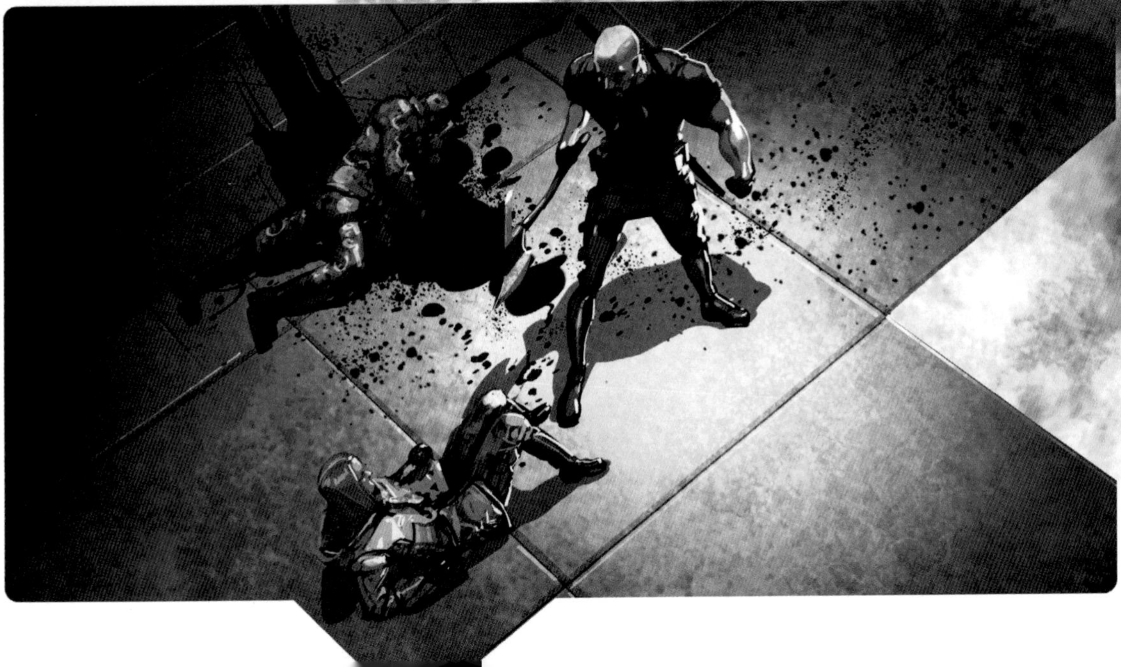

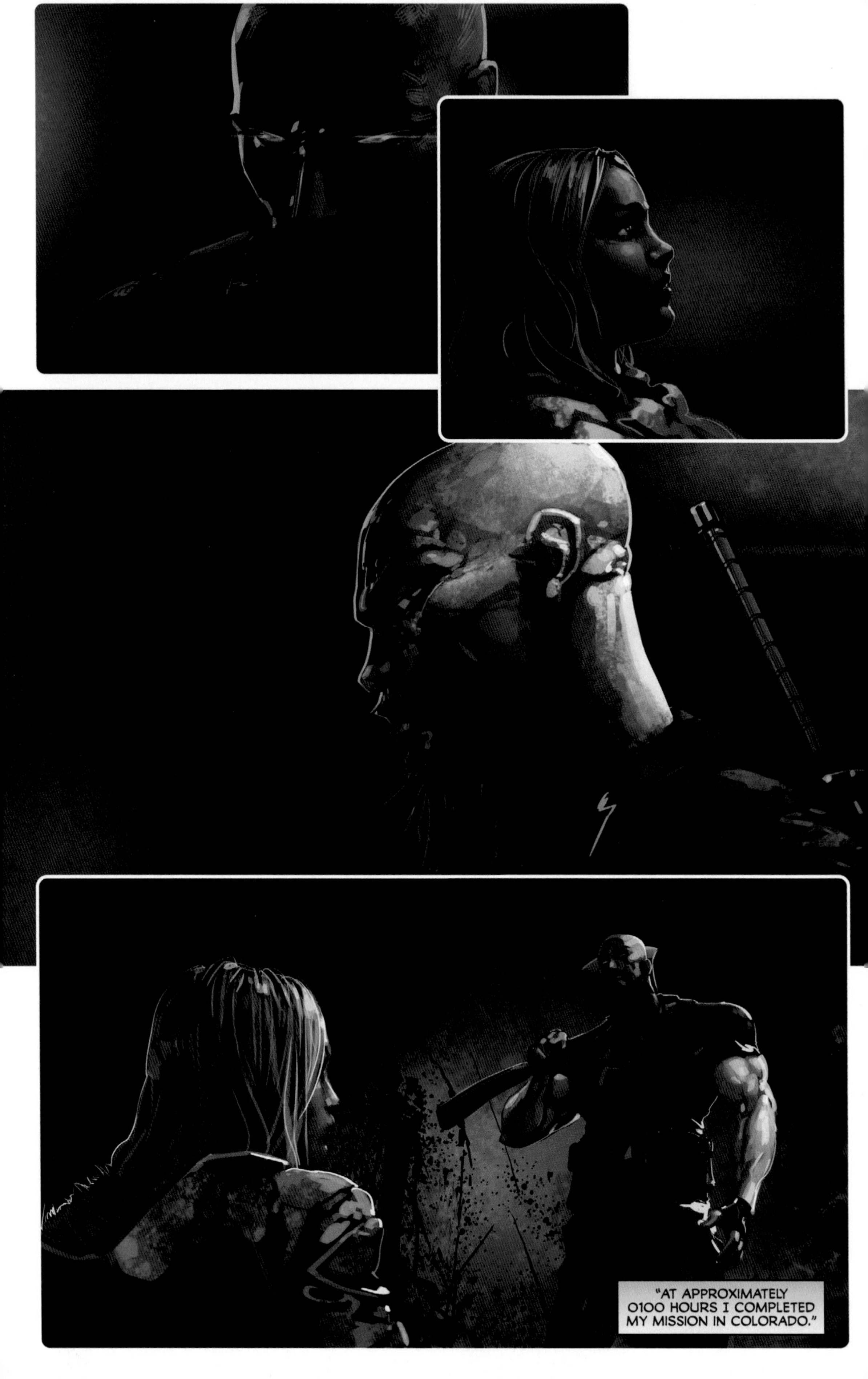
"AT APPROXIMATELY
0100 HOURS I COMPLETED
MY MISSION IN COLORADO."

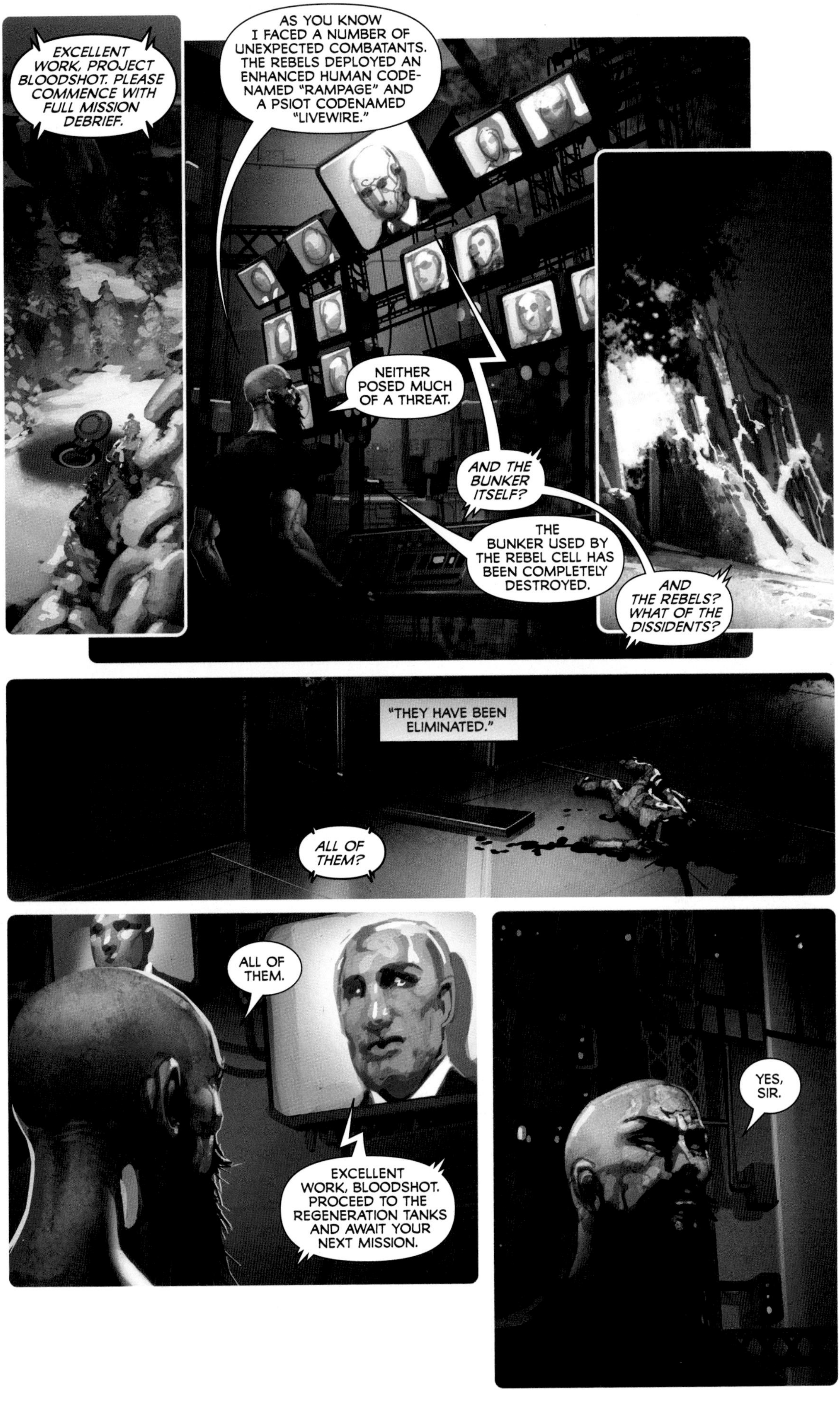
EXCELLENT WORK, PROJECT BLOODSHOT. PLEASE COMMENCE WITH FULL MISSION DEBRIEF.
AS YOU KNOW I FACED A NUMBER OF UNEXPECTED COMBATANTS. THE REBELS DEPLOYED AN ENHANCED HUMAN CODE-NAMED "RAMPAGE" AND A PSIOT CODENAMED "LIVEWIRE."
NEITHER POSED MUCH OF A THREAT.
AND THE BUNKER ITSELF?
THE BUNKER USED BY THE REBEL CELL HAS BEEN COMPLETELY DESTROYED.
AND THE REBELS? WHAT OF THE DISSIDENTS?
"THEY HAVE BEEN ELIMINATED."
ALL OF THEM?
ALL OF THEM.
EXCELLENT WORK, BLOODSHOT. PROCEED TO THE REGENERATION TANKS AND AWAIT YOUR NEXT MISSION.
YES, SIR.

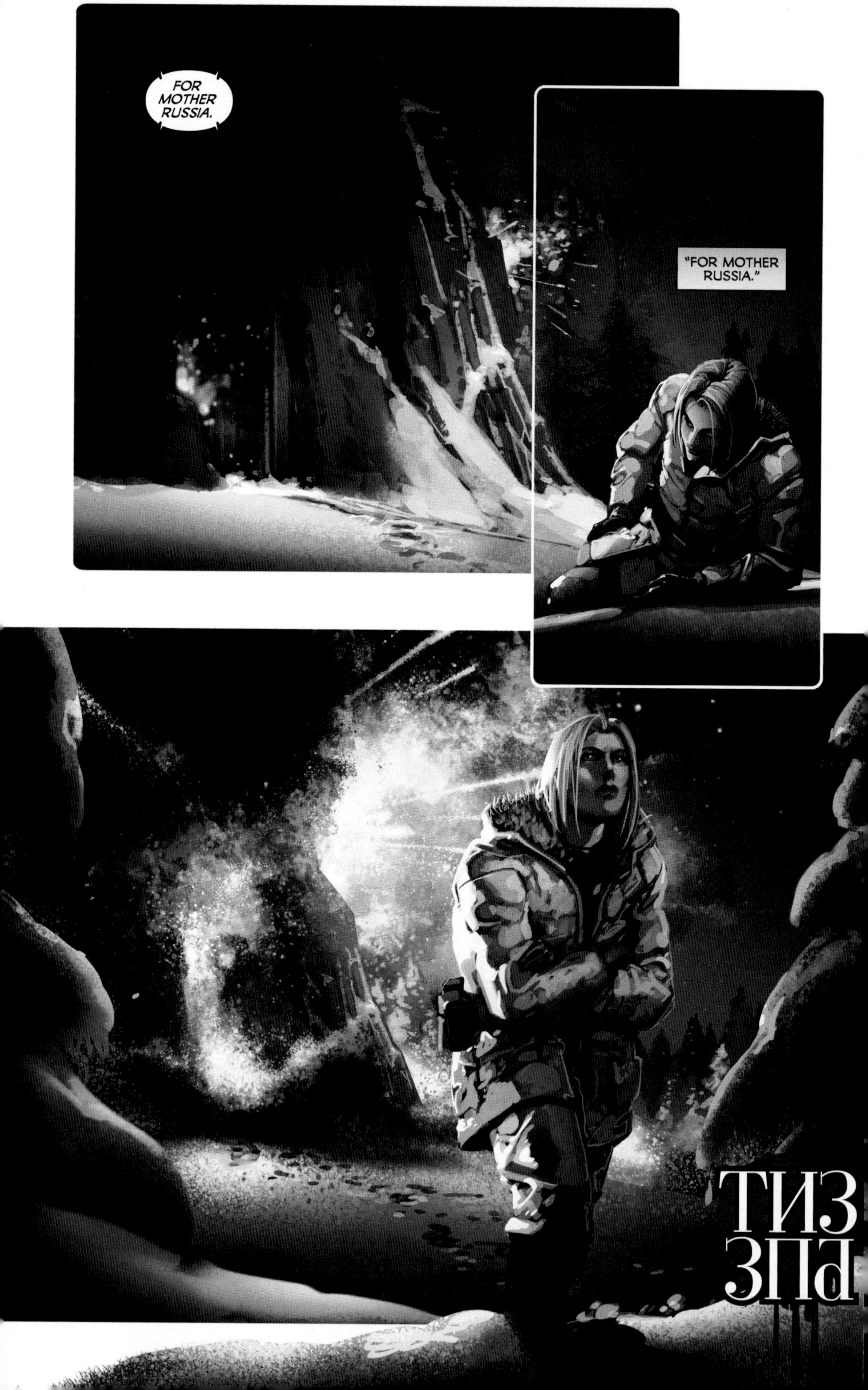
FOR MOTHER RUSSIA.
"FOR MOTHER RUSSIA."

THE ORIGIN OF THE RED LEGEND

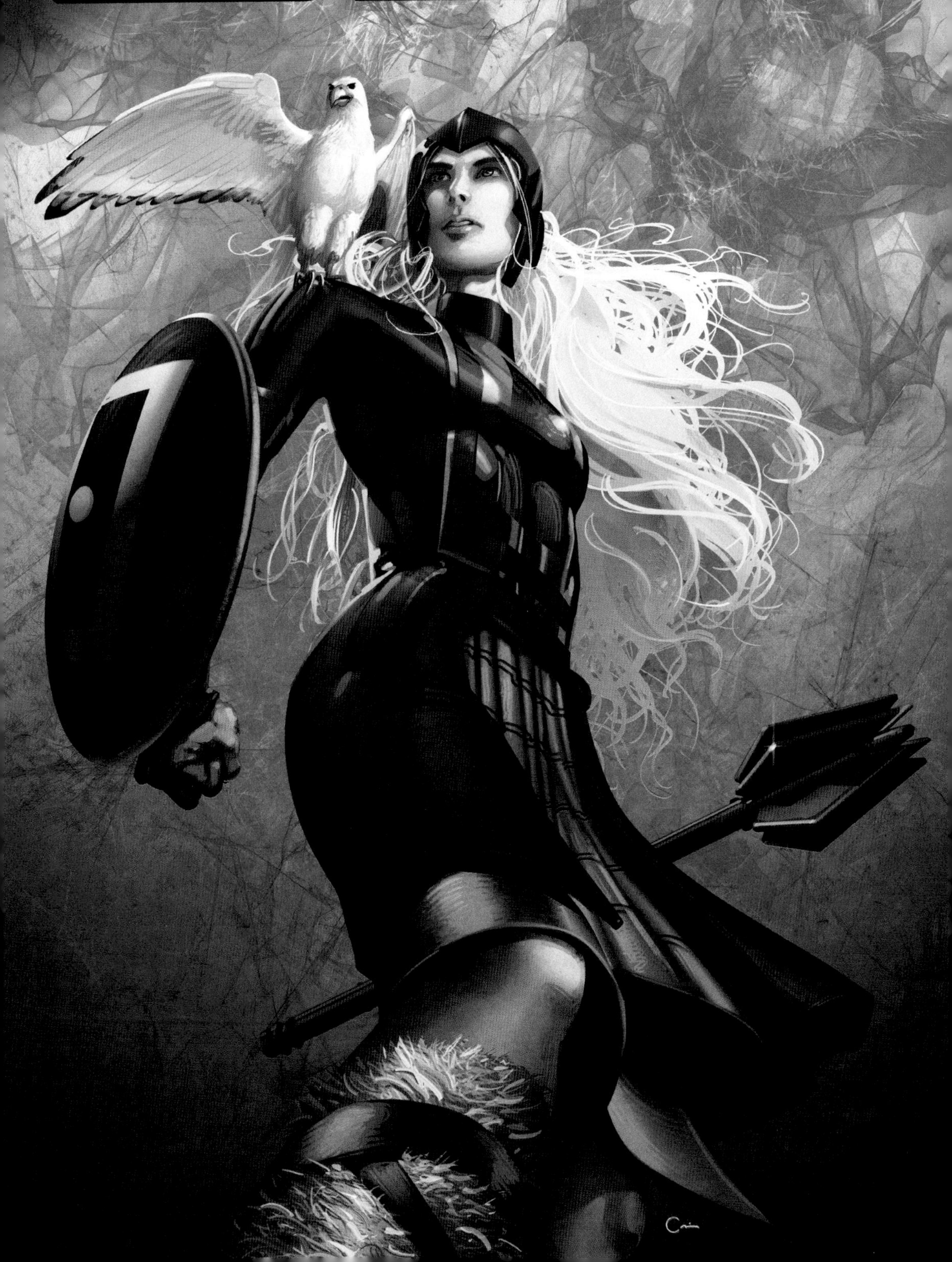

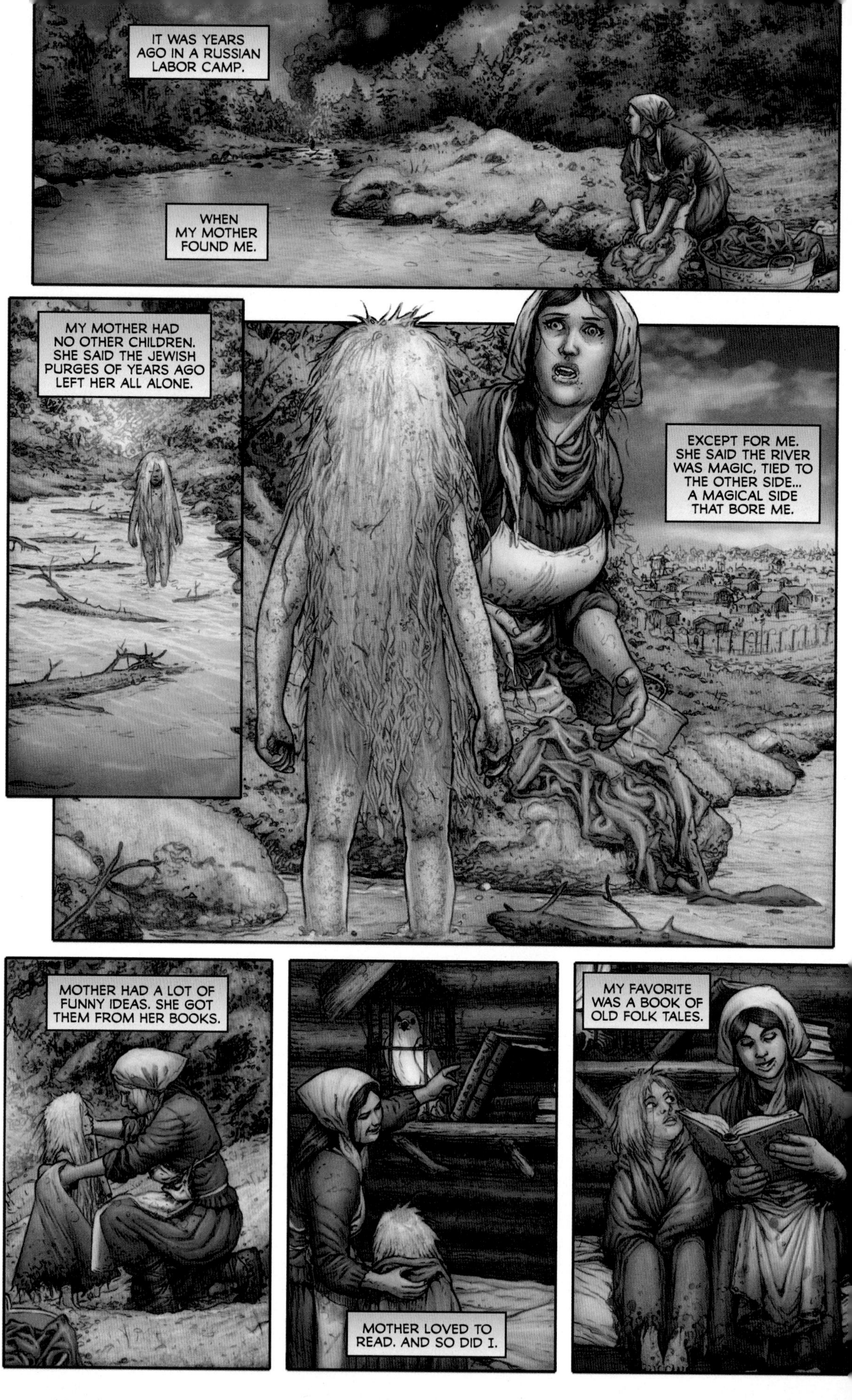
IT WAS YEARS AGO IN A RUSSIAN LABOR CAMP.
WHEN MY MOTHER FOUND ME.
MY MOTHER HAD NO OTHER CHILDREN. SHE SAID THE JEWISH PURGES OF YEARS AGO LEFT HER ALL ALONE.
EXCEPT FOR ME. SHE SAID THE RIVER WAS MAGIC, TIED TO THE OTHER SIDE... A MAGICAL SIDE THAT BORE ME.
MOTHER HAD A LOT OF FUNNY IDEAS. SHE GOT THEM FROM HER BOOKS.
MOTHER LOVED TO READ. AND SO DID I.
MY FAVORITE WAS A BOOK OF OLD FOLK TALES.

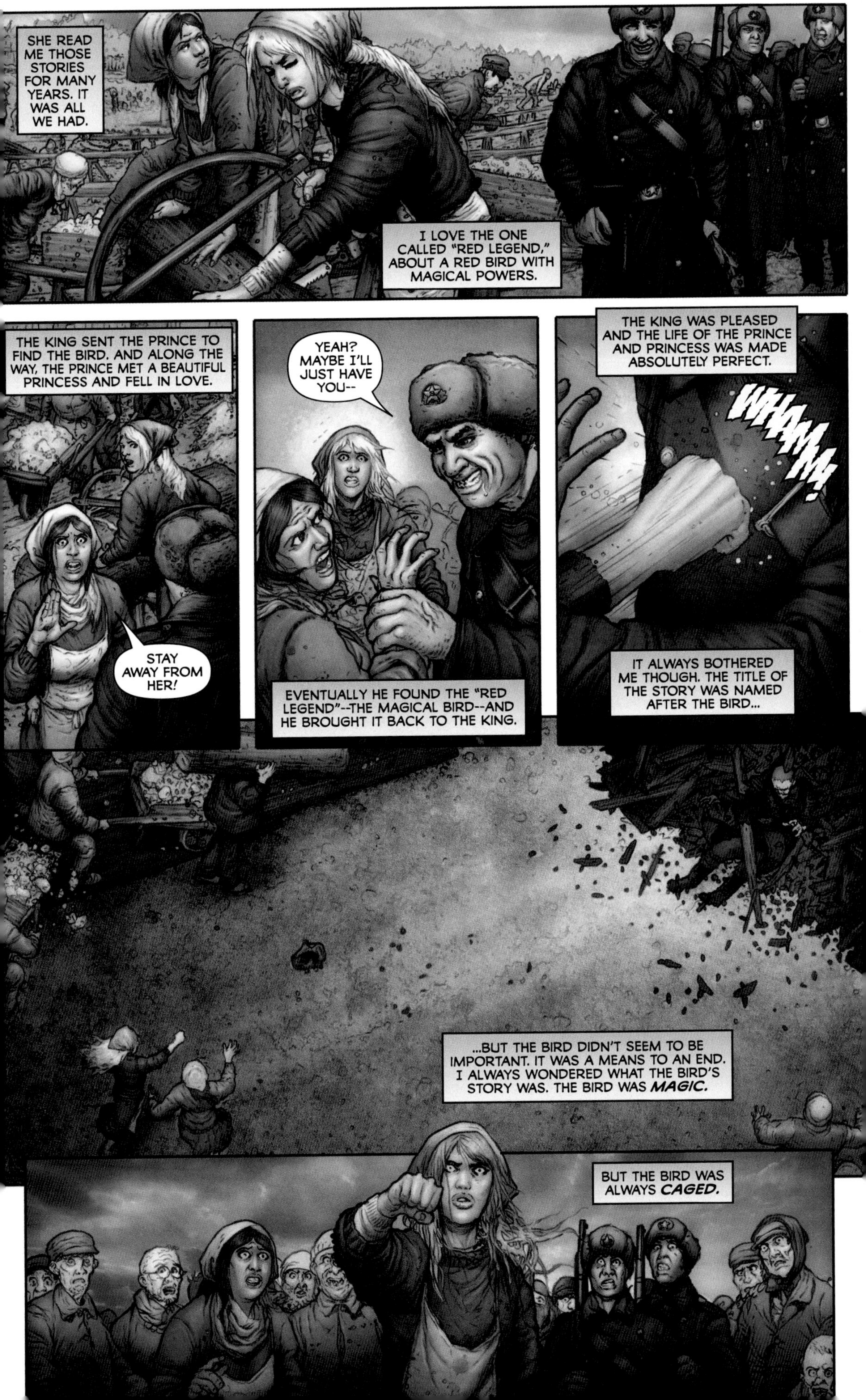
SHE READ ME THOSE STORIES FOR MANY YEARS. IT WAS ALL WE HAD.
I LOVE THE ONE CALLED "RED LEGEND," ABOUT A RED BIRD WITH MAGICAL POWERS.
THE KING SENT THE PRINCE TO FIND THE BIRD. AND ALONG THE WAY, THE PRINCE MET A BEAUTIFUL PRINCESS AND FELL IN LOVE.
STAY AWAY FROM HER!
YEAH? MAYBE I'LL JUST HAVE YOU--
EVENTUALLY HE FOUND THE "RED LEGEND"--THE MAGICAL BIRD--AND HE BROUGHT IT BACK TO THE KING.
THE KING WAS PLEASED AND THE LIFE OF THE PRINCE AND PRINCESS WAS MADE ABSOLUTELY PERFECT.
WHAMM!
IT ALWAYS BOTHERED ME THOUGH. THE TITLE OF THE STORY WAS NAMED AFTER THE BIRD...
...BUT THE BIRD DIDN'T SEEM TO BE IMPORTANT. IT WAS A MEANS TO AN END. I ALWAYS WONDERED WHAT THE BIRD'S STORY WAS. THE BIRD WAS *MAGIC.*
BUT THE BIRD WAS ALWAYS *CAGED.*

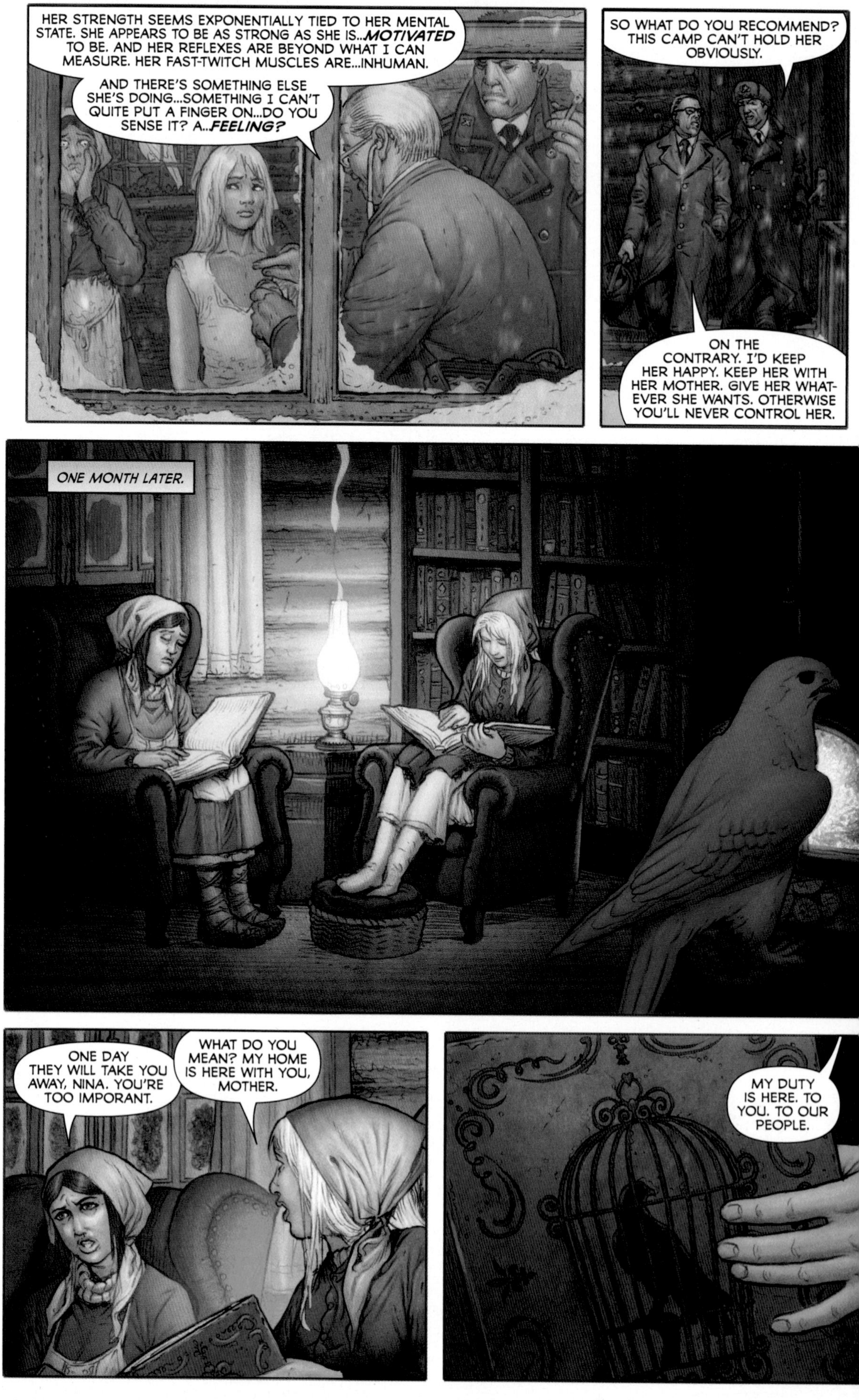
HER STRENGTH SEEMS EXPONENTIALLY TIED TO HER MENTAL STATE. SHE APPEARS TO BE AS STRONG AS SHE IS...MOTIVATED TO BE. AND HER REFLEXES ARE BEYOND WHAT I CAN MEASURE. HER FAST-TWITCH MUSCLES ARE...INHUMAN.
AND THERE'S SOMETHING ELSE SHE'S DOING...SOMETHING I CAN'T QUITE PUT A FINGER ON...DO YOU SENSE IT? A...FEELING?
SO WHAT DO YOU RECOMMEND? THIS CAMP CAN'T HOLD HER OBVIOUSLY.
ON THE CONTRARY. I'D KEEP HER HAPPY. KEEP HER WITH HER MOTHER. GIVE HER WHAT-EVER SHE WANTS. OTHERWISE YOU'LL NEVER CONTROL HER.
ONE MONTH LATER.
ONE DAY THEY WILL TAKE YOU AWAY, NINA. YOU'RE TOO IMPORANT.
WHAT DO YOU MEAN? MY HOME IS HERE WITH YOU, MOTHER.
MY DUTY IS HERE. TO YOU. TO OUR PEOPLE.

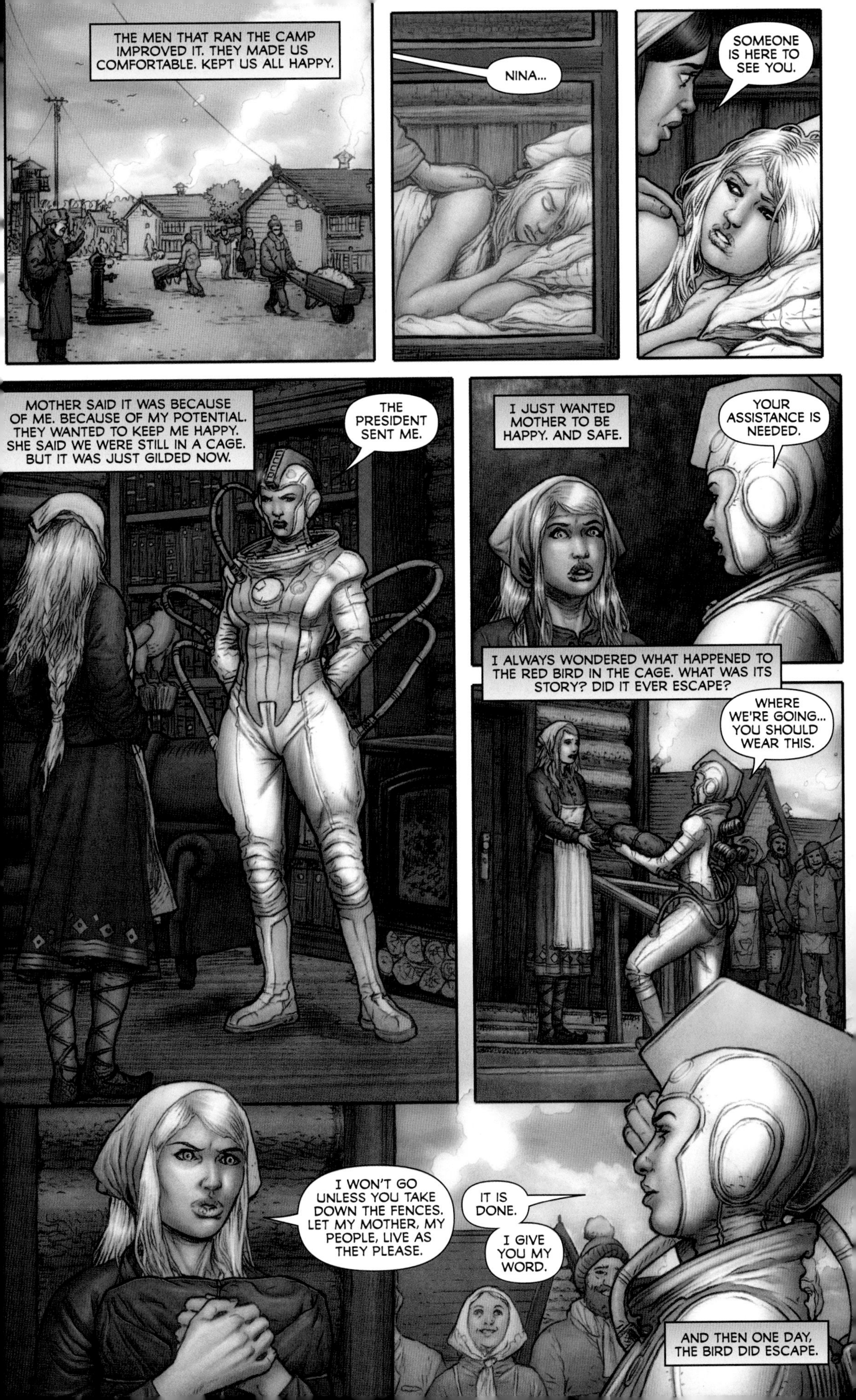
THE MEN THAT RAN THE CAMP IMPROVED IT. THEY MADE US COMFORTABLE. KEPT US ALL HAPPY.
NINA...
SOMEONE IS HERE TO SEE YOU.
MOTHER SAID IT WAS BECAUSE OF ME. BECAUSE OF MY POTENTIAL. THEY WANTED TO KEEP ME HAPPY. SHE SAID WE WERE STILL IN A CAGE. BUT IT WAS JUST GILDED NOW.
THE PRESIDENT SENT ME.
I JUST WANTED MOTHER TO BE HAPPY. AND SAFE.
YOUR ASSISTANCE IS NEEDED.
I ALWAYS WONDERED WHAT HAPPENED TO THE RED BIRD IN THE CAGE. WHAT WAS ITS STORY? DID IT EVER ESCAPE?
WHERE WE'RE GOING... YOU SHOULD WEAR THIS.
I WON'T GO UNLESS YOU TAKE DOWN THE FENCES. LET MY MOTHER, MY PEOPLE, LIVE AS THEY PLEASE.
IT IS DONE.
I GIVE YOU MY WORD.
AND THEN ONE DAY, THE BIRD DID ESCAPE.

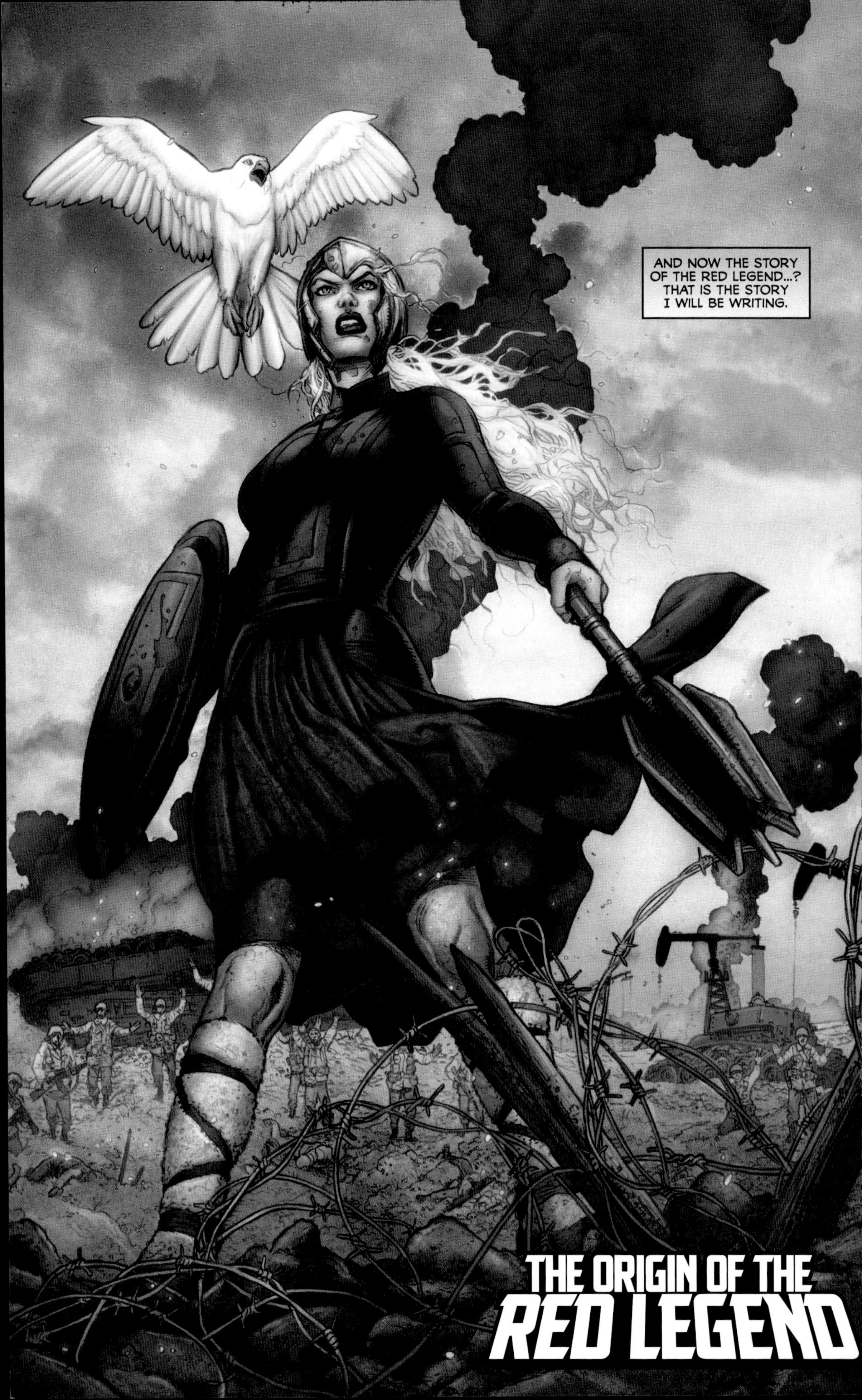
AND NOW THE STORY OF THE RED LEGEND...? THAT IS THE STORY I WILL BE WRITING.
THE ORIGIN OF THE RED LEGEND

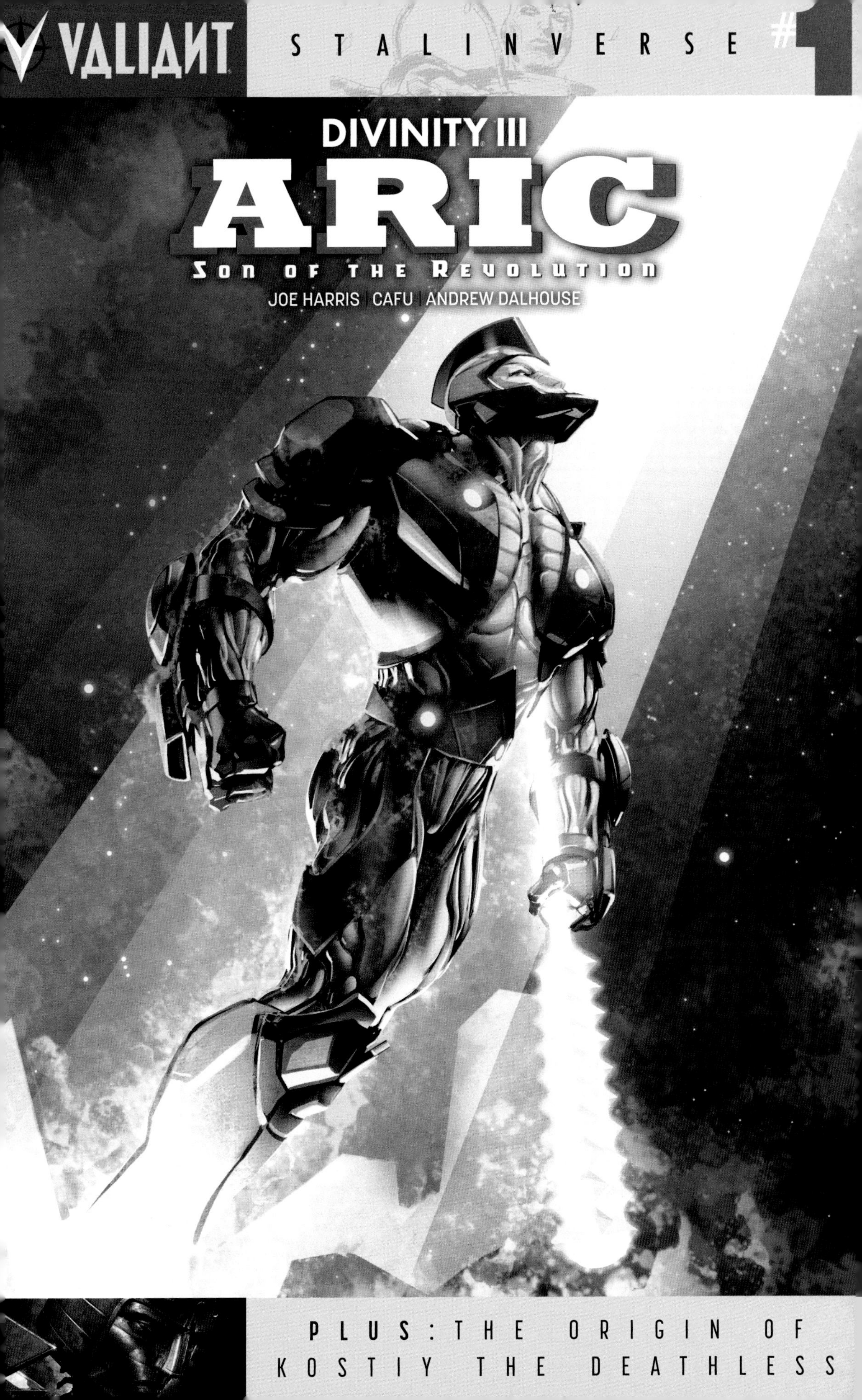
VALIANT
STALINVERSE #1
DIVINITY III
ARIC
SON OF THE REVOLUTION
JOE HARRIS | CAFU | ANDREW DALHOUSE
PLUS: THE ORIGIN OF
KOSTIY THE DEATHLESS

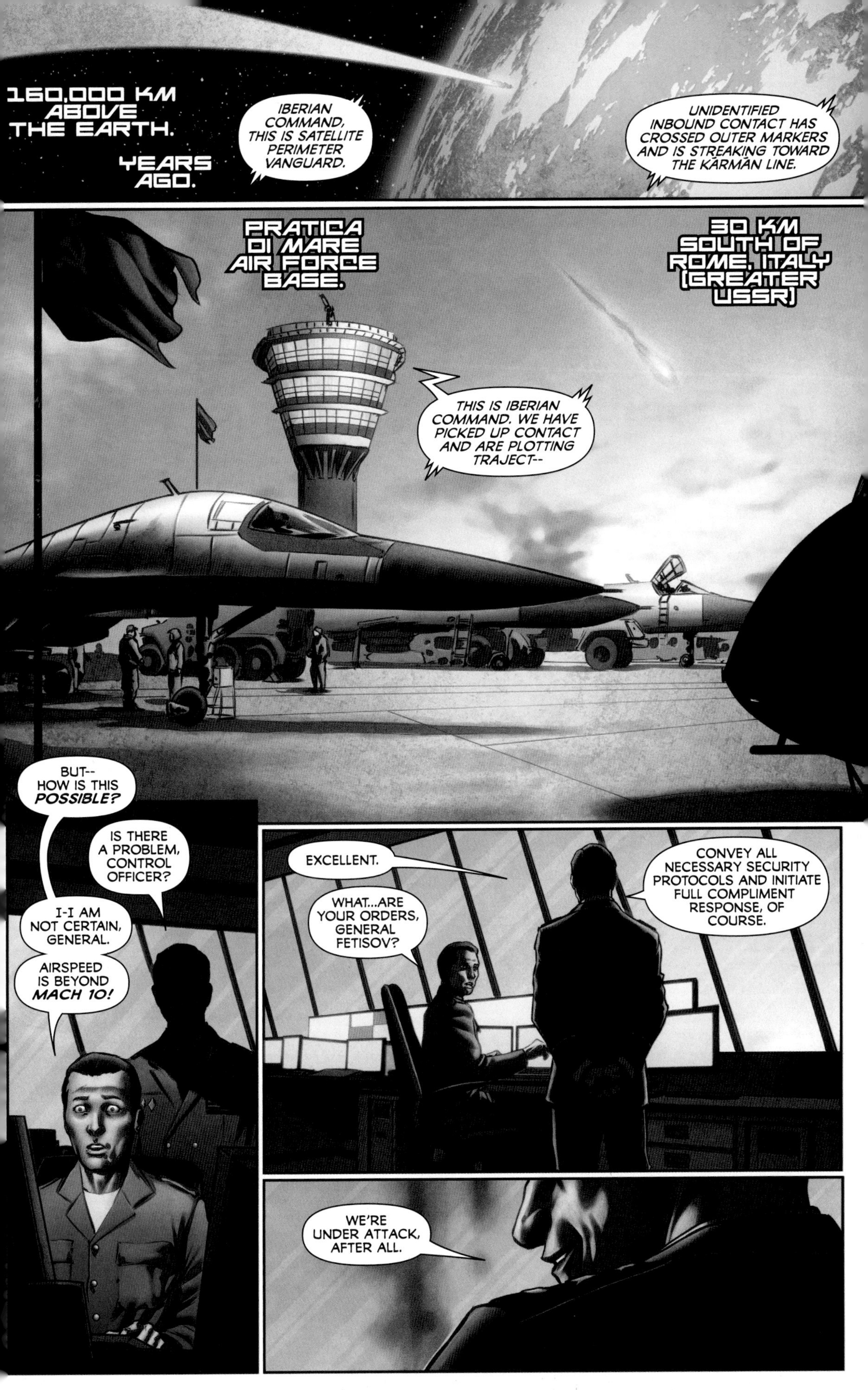
160,000 KM ABOVE THE EARTH.
YEARS AGO.
IBERIAN COMMAND, THIS IS SATELLITE PERIMETER VANGUARD.
UNIDENTIFIED INBOUND CONTACT HAS CROSSED OUTER MARKERS AND IS STREAKING TOWARD THE KÁRMÁN LINE.
PRATICA DI MARE AIR FORCE BASE.
30 KM SOUTH OF ROME, ITALY (GREATER USSR)
THIS IS IBERIAN COMMAND. WE HAVE PICKED UP CONTACT AND ARE PLOTTING TRAJECT--
BUT-- HOW IS THIS POSSIBLE?
IS THERE A PROBLEM, CONTROL OFFICER?
I-I AM NOT CERTAIN, GENERAL.
AIRSPEED IS BEYOND MACH 10!
EXCELLENT.
WHAT...ARE YOUR ORDERS, GENERAL FETISOV?
CONVEY ALL NECESSARY SECURITY PROTOCOLS AND INITIATE FULL COMPLIMENT RESPONSE, OF COURSE.
WE'RE UNDER ATTACK, AFTER ALL.

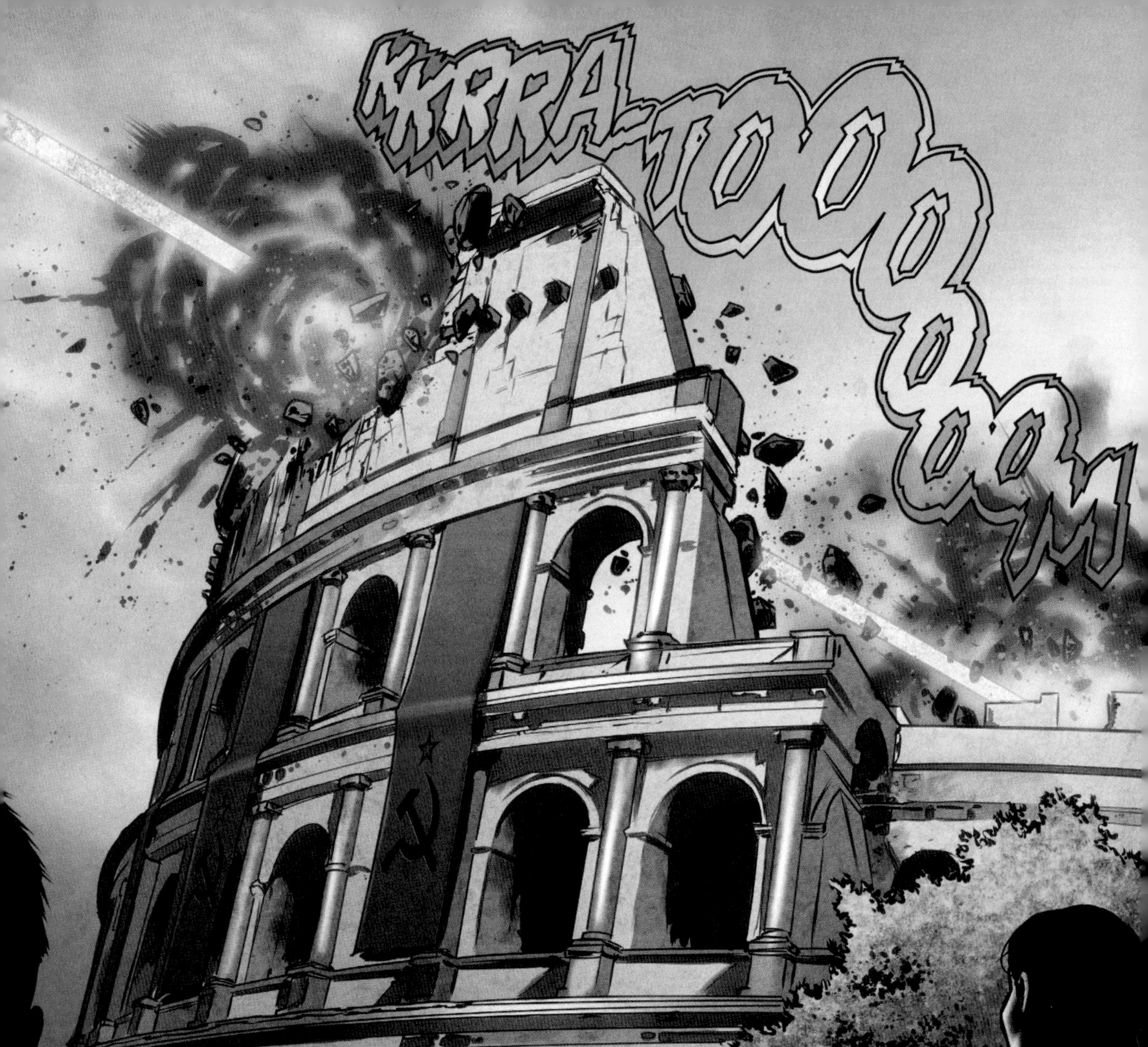
KKRRA-TOOOOOOOM

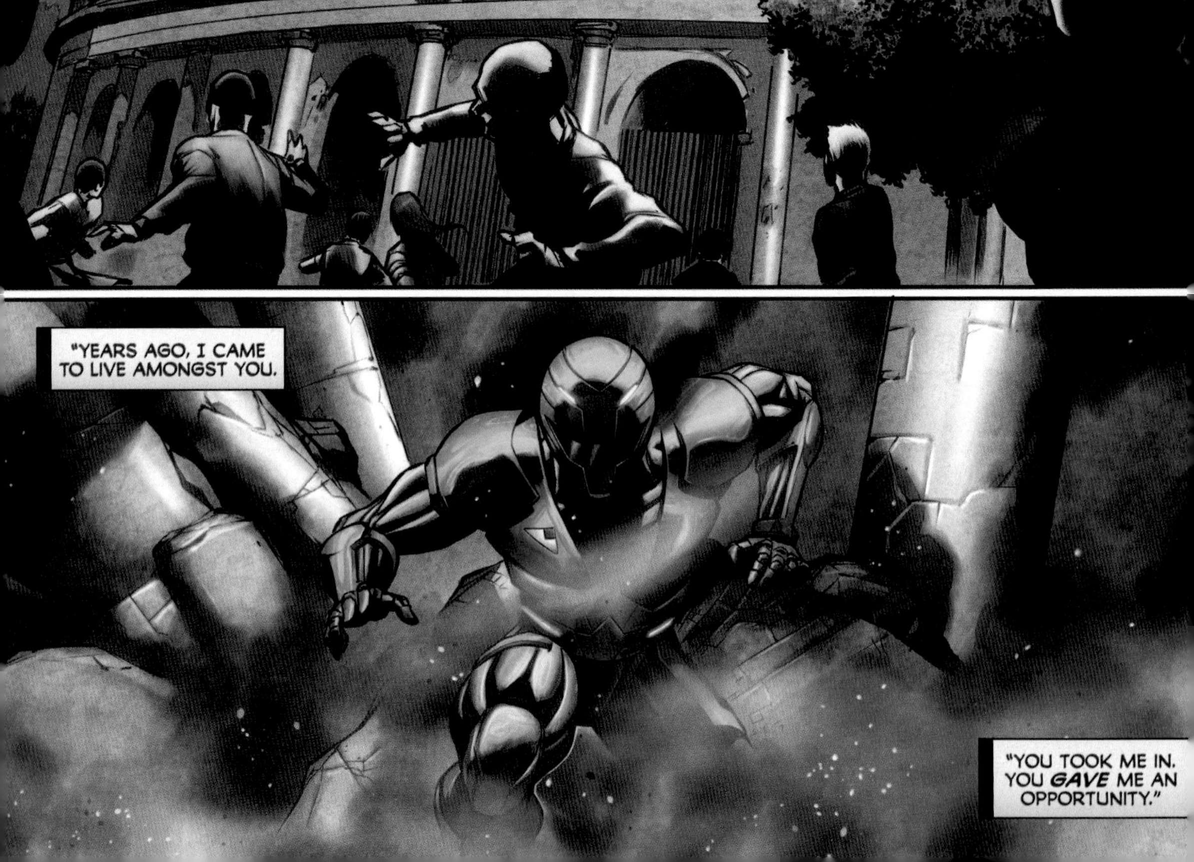
"YEARS AGO, I CAME TO LIVE AMONGST YOU.
"YOU TOOK ME IN. YOU GAVE ME AN OPPORTUNITY."

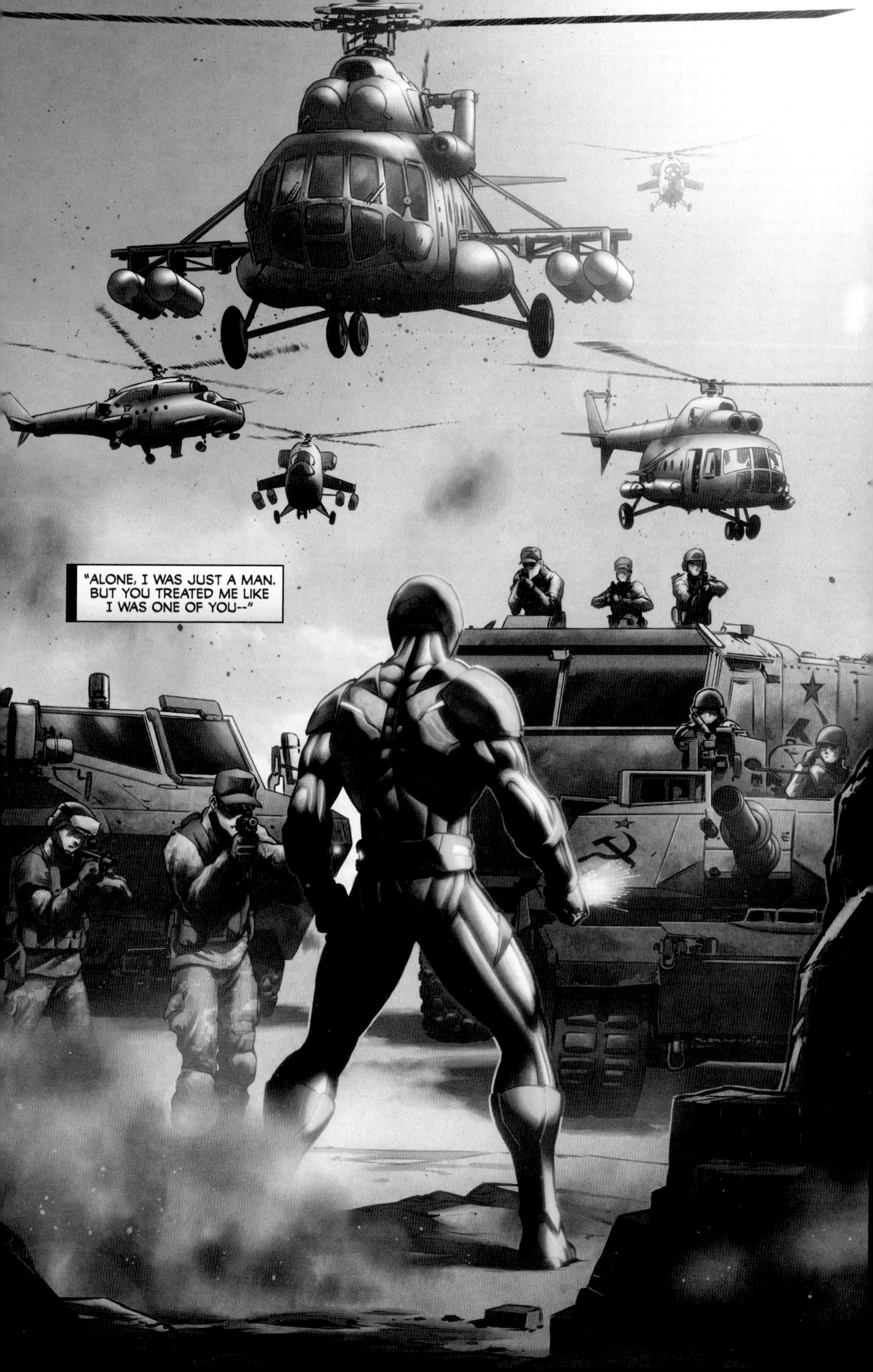
"ALONE, I WAS JUST A MAN. BUT YOU TREATED ME LIKE I WAS ONE OF YOU--"

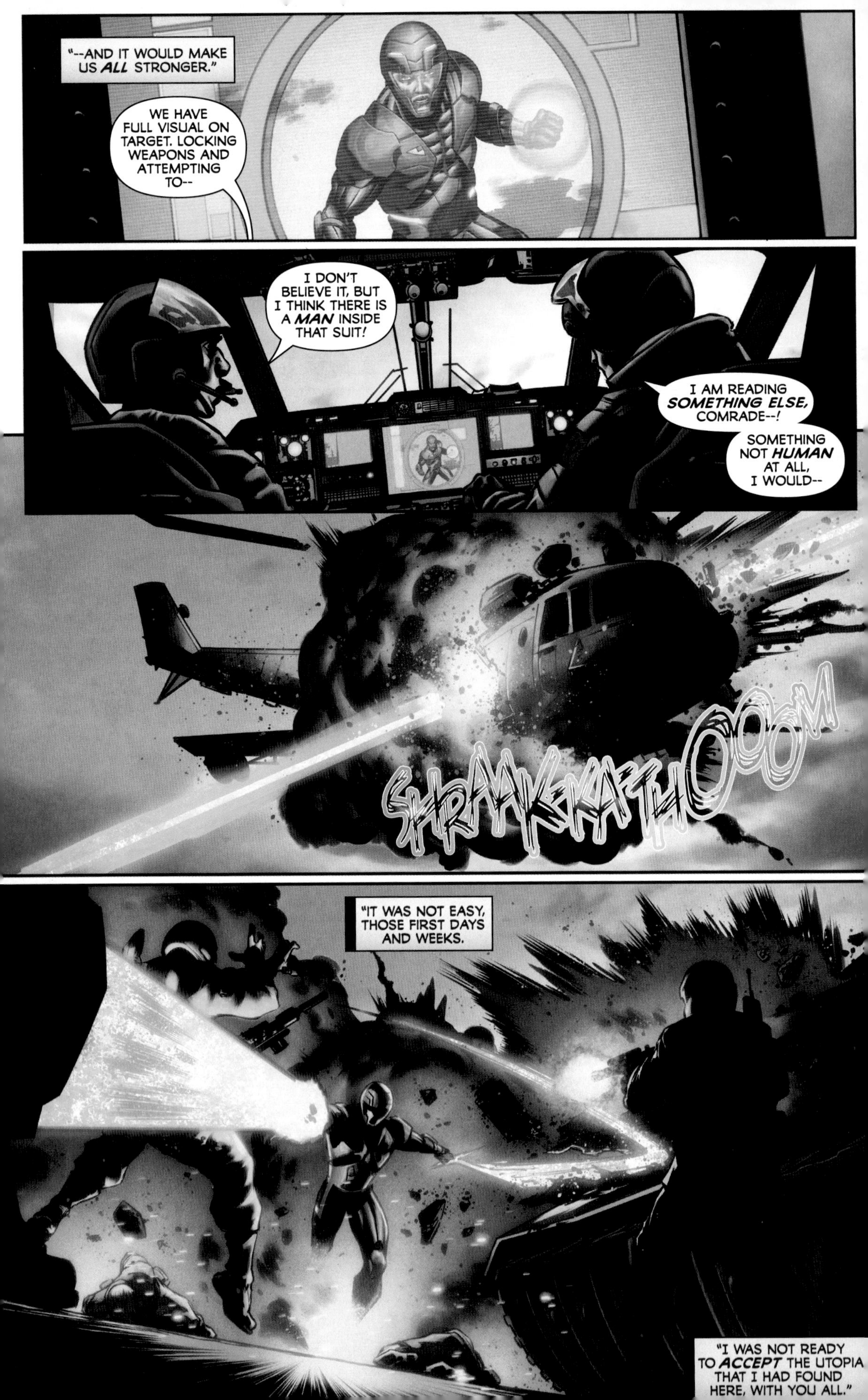
"--AND IT WOULD MAKE US ALL STRONGER."
WE HAVE FULL VISUAL ON TARGET. LOCKING WEAPONS AND ATTEMPTING TO--
I DON'T BELIEVE IT, BUT I THINK THERE IS A MAN INSIDE THAT SUIT!
I AM READING SOMETHING ELSE, COMRADE--!
SOMETHING NOT HUMAN AT ALL, I WOULD--
SHRAAKKATHOOOOM
"IT WAS NOT EASY, THOSE FIRST DAYS AND WEEKS.
"I WAS NOT READY TO ACCEPT THE UTOPIA THAT I HAD FOUND HERE, WITH YOU ALL."

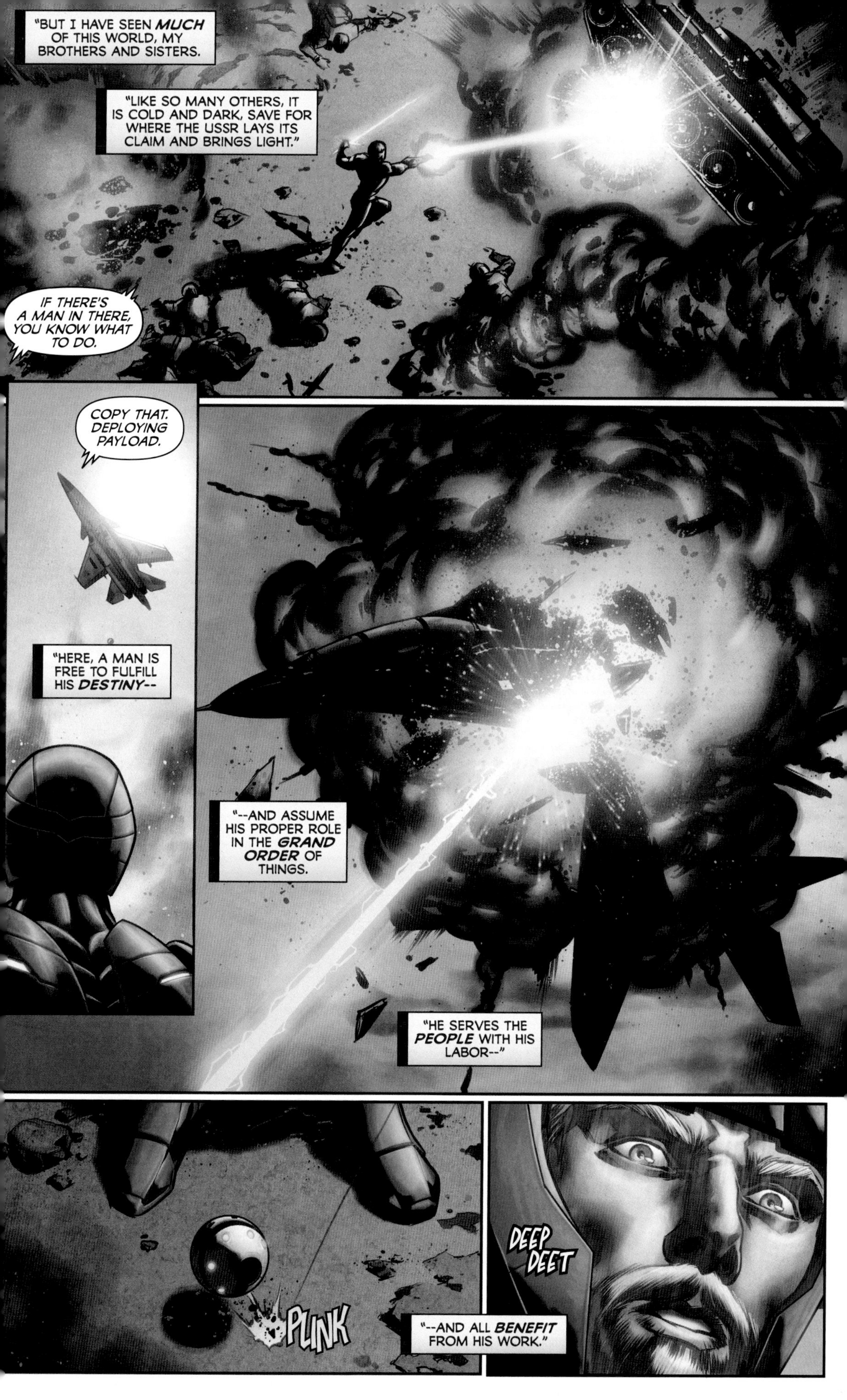
"BUT I HAVE SEEN *MUCH* OF THIS WORLD, MY BROTHERS AND SISTERS.
"LIKE SO MANY OTHERS, IT IS COLD AND DARK, SAVE FOR WHERE THE USSR LAYS ITS CLAIM AND BRINGS LIGHT."
IF THERE'S A MAN IN THERE, YOU KNOW WHAT TO DO.
COPY THAT. DEPLOYING PAYLOAD.
"HERE, A MAN IS FREE TO FULFILL HIS *DESTINY*--
"--AND ASSUME HIS PROPER ROLE IN THE *GRAND ORDER* OF THINGS.
"HE SERVES THE *PEOPLE* WITH HIS LABOR--"
PLINK
DEEP DEET
"--AND ALL *BENEFIT* FROM HIS WORK."

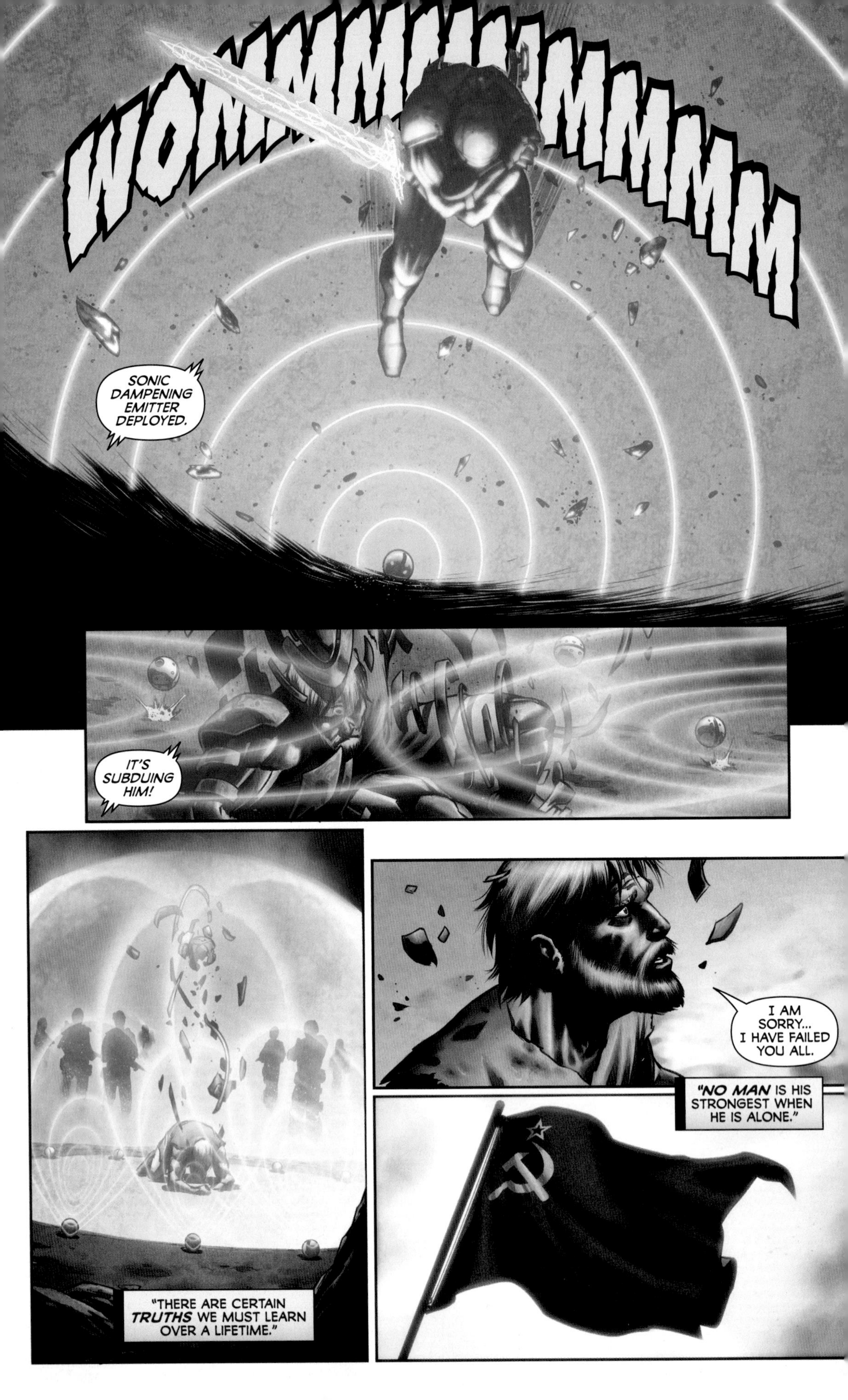
WOMMMMMMMMMMMMM
SONIC DAMPENING EMITTER DEPLOYED.
IT'S SUBDUING HIM!
"THERE ARE CERTAIN TRUTHS WE MUST LEARN OVER A LIFETIME."
I AM SORRY... I HAVE FAILED YOU ALL.
"NO MAN IS HIS STRONGEST WHEN HE IS ALONE."

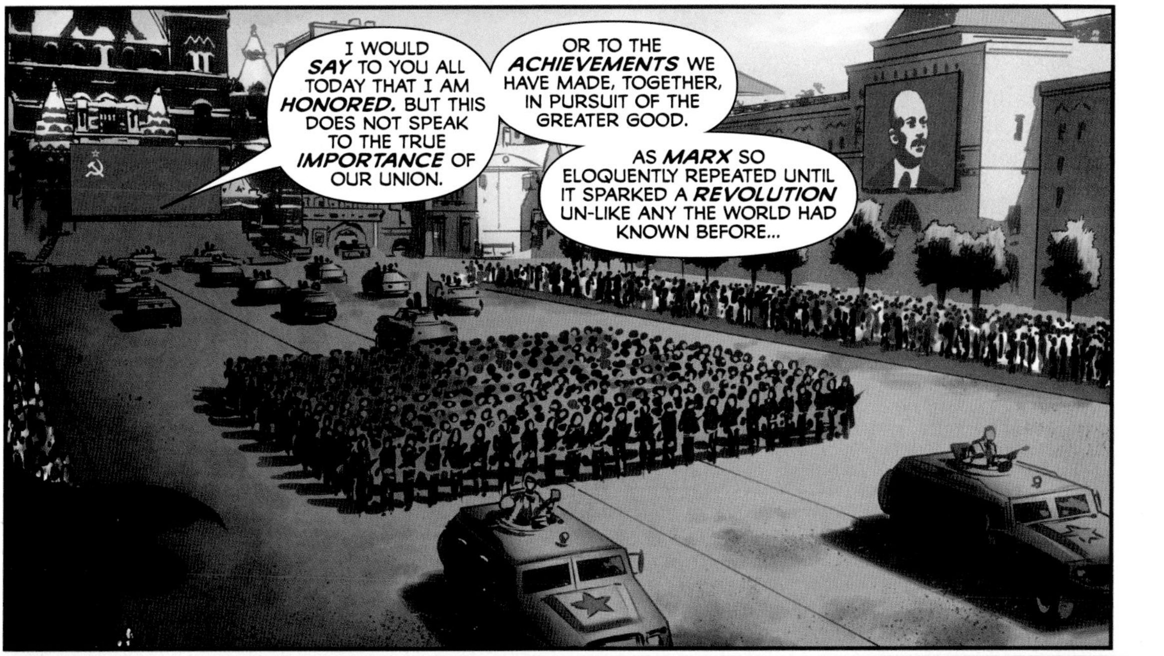
I WOULD SAY TO YOU ALL TODAY THAT I AM HONORED. BUT THIS DOES NOT SPEAK TO THE TRUE IMPORTANCE OF OUR UNION.
OR TO THE ACHIEVEMENTS WE HAVE MADE, TOGETHER, IN PURSUIT OF THE GREATER GOOD.
AS MARX SO ELOQUENTLY REPEATED UNTIL IT SPARKED A REVOLUTION UN-LIKE ANY THE WORLD HAD KNOWN BEFORE...

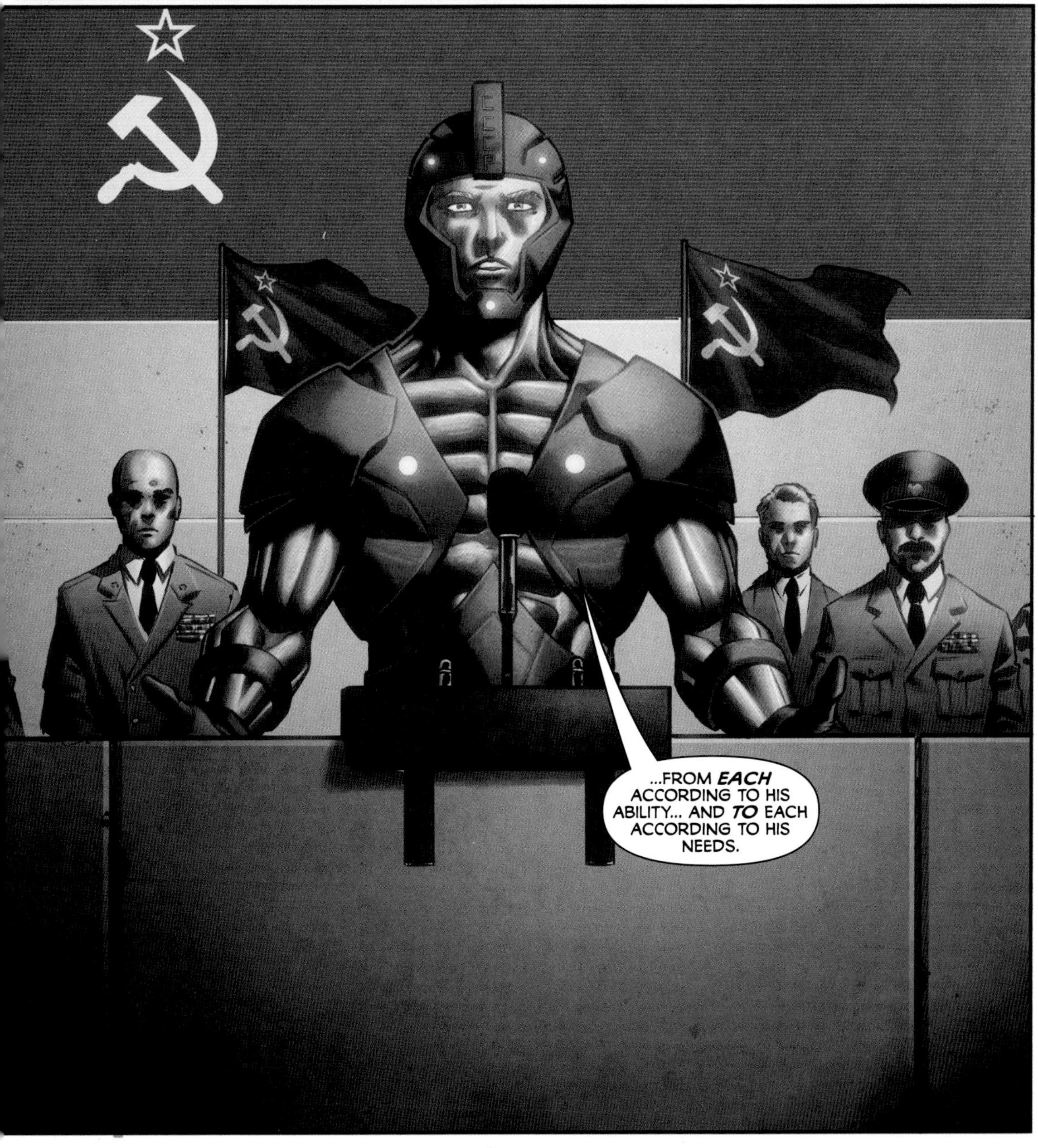
...FROM EACH ACCORDING TO HIS ABILITY... AND TO EACH ACCORDING TO HIS NEEDS.

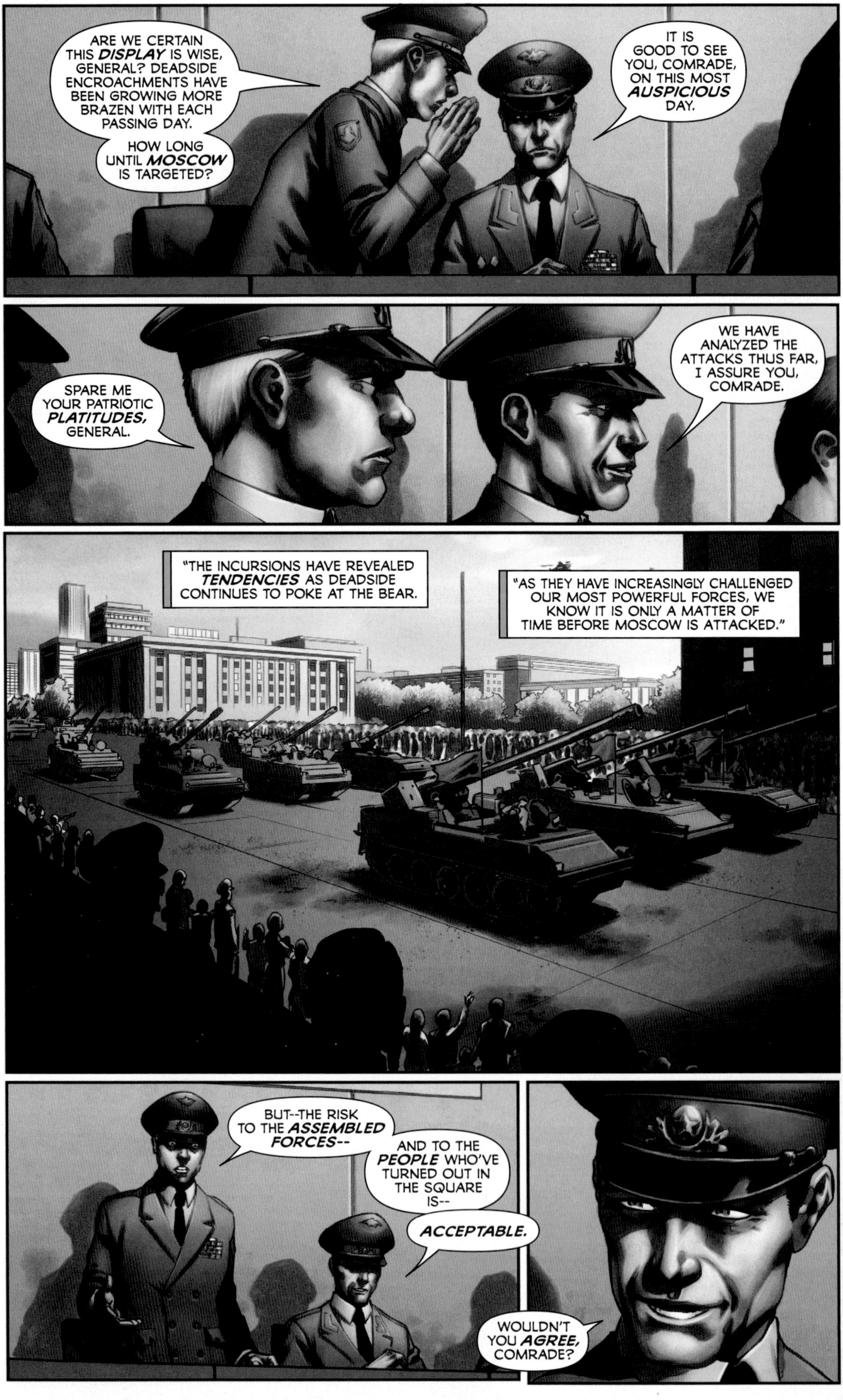
ARE WE CERTAIN THIS *DISPLAY* IS WISE, GENERAL? DEADSIDE ENCROACHMENTS HAVE BEEN GROWING MORE BRAZEN WITH EACH PASSING DAY.
HOW LONG UNTIL *MOSCOW* IS TARGETED?
IT IS GOOD TO SEE YOU, COMRADE, ON THIS MOST *AUSPICIOUS* DAY.
SPARE ME YOUR PATRIOTIC *PLATITUDES,* GENERAL.
WE HAVE ANALYZED THE ATTACKS THUS FAR, I ASSURE YOU, COMRADE.
"THE INCURSIONS HAVE REVEALED *TENDENCIES* AS DEADSIDE CONTINUES TO POKE AT THE BEAR.
"AS THEY HAVE INCREASINGLY CHALLENGED OUR MOST POWERFUL FORCES, WE KNOW IT IS ONLY A MATTER OF TIME BEFORE MOSCOW IS ATTACKED."
BUT--THE RISK TO THE *ASSEMBLED FORCES*--
AND TO THE *PEOPLE* WHO'VE TURNED OUT IN THE SQUARE IS--
ACCEPTABLE.
WOULDN'T YOU *AGREE,* COMRADE?

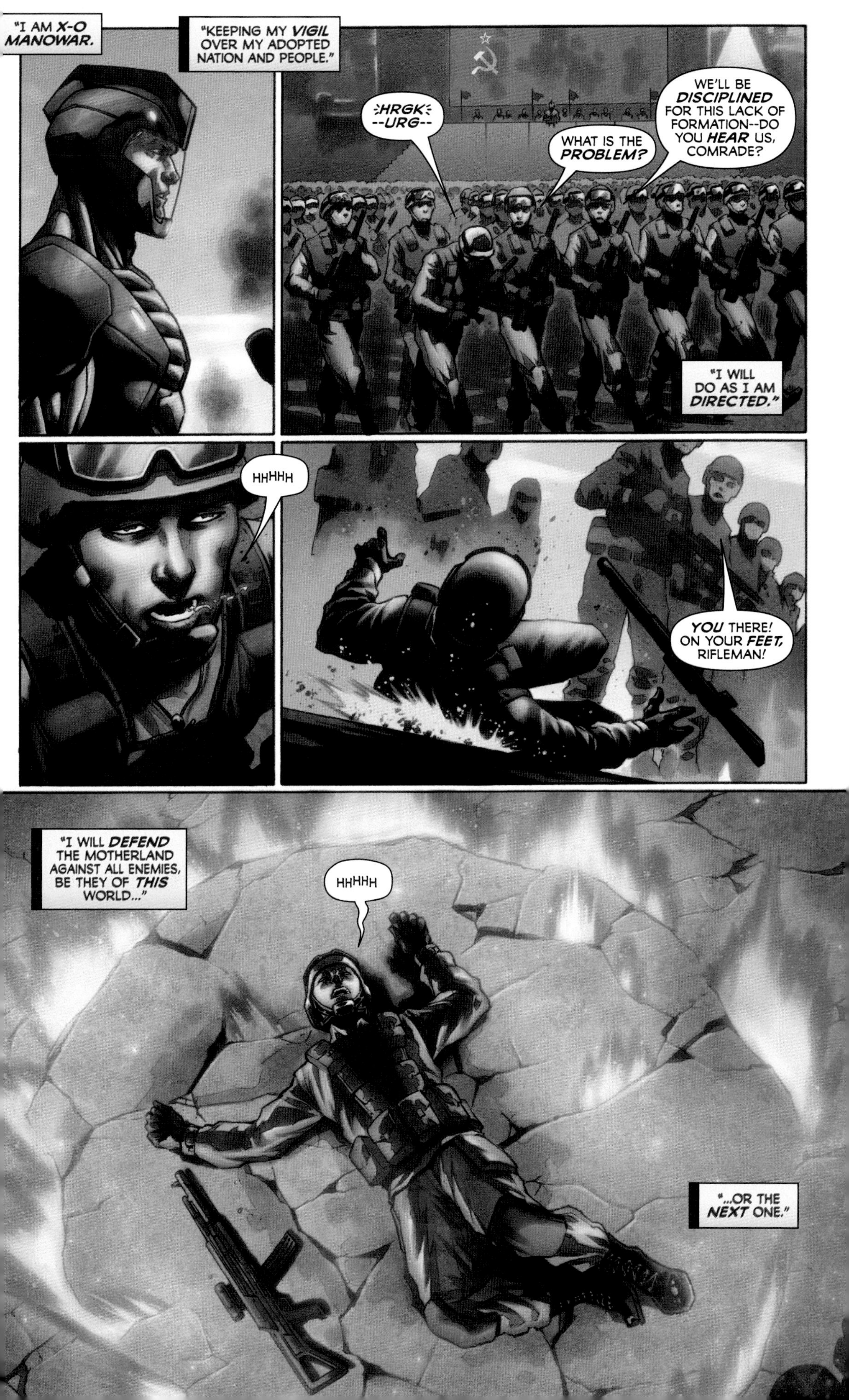

"I AM X-O MANOWAR.
"KEEPING MY VIGIL OVER MY ADOPTED NATION AND PEOPLE."
HRGK --URG--
WHAT IS THE PROBLEM?
WE'LL BE DISCIPLINED FOR THIS LACK OF FORMATION--DO YOU HEAR US, COMRADE?
"I WILL DO AS I AM DIRECTED."
HHHHH
YOU THERE! ON YOUR FEET, RIFLEMAN!
"I WILL DEFEND THE MOTHERLAND AGAINST ALL ENEMIES, BE THEY OF THIS WORLD..."
HHHHH
"...OR THE NEXT ONE."

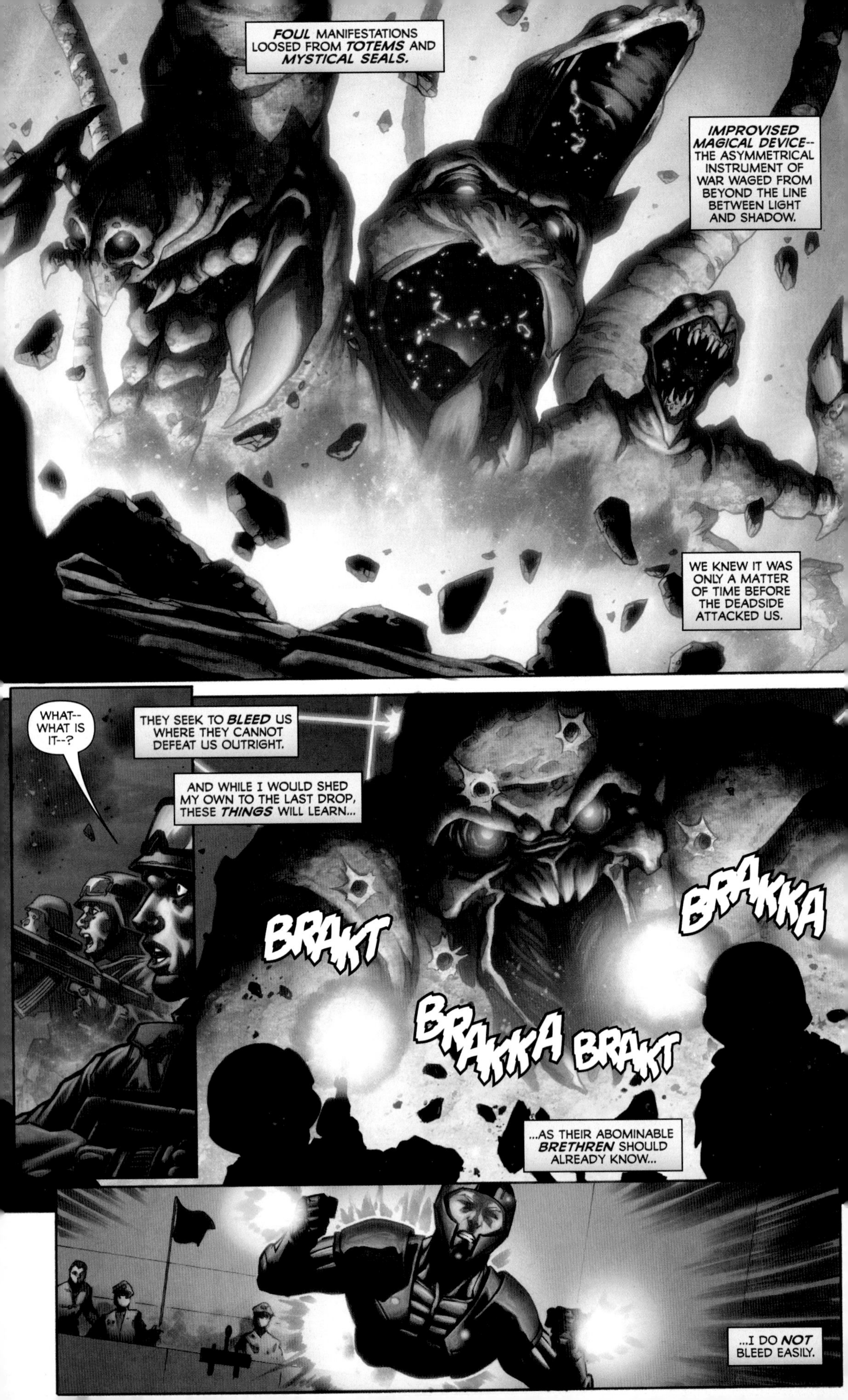
FOUL MANIFESTATIONS LOOSED FROM TOTEMS AND MYSTICAL SEALS.
IMPROVISED MAGICAL DEVICE-- THE ASYMMETRICAL INSTRUMENT OF WAR WAGED FROM BEYOND THE LINE BETWEEN LIGHT AND SHADOW.
WE KNEW IT WAS ONLY A MATTER OF TIME BEFORE THE DEADSIDE ATTACKED US.
WHAT-- WHAT IS IT--?
THEY SEEK TO BLEED US WHERE THEY CANNOT DEFEAT US OUTRIGHT.
AND WHILE I WOULD SHED MY OWN TO THE LAST DROP, THESE THINGS WILL LEARN...
BRAKKA
BRAKT
BRAKKA
BRAKT
...AS THEIR ABOMINABLE BRETHREN SHOULD ALREADY KNOW...
...I DO NOT BLEED EASILY.

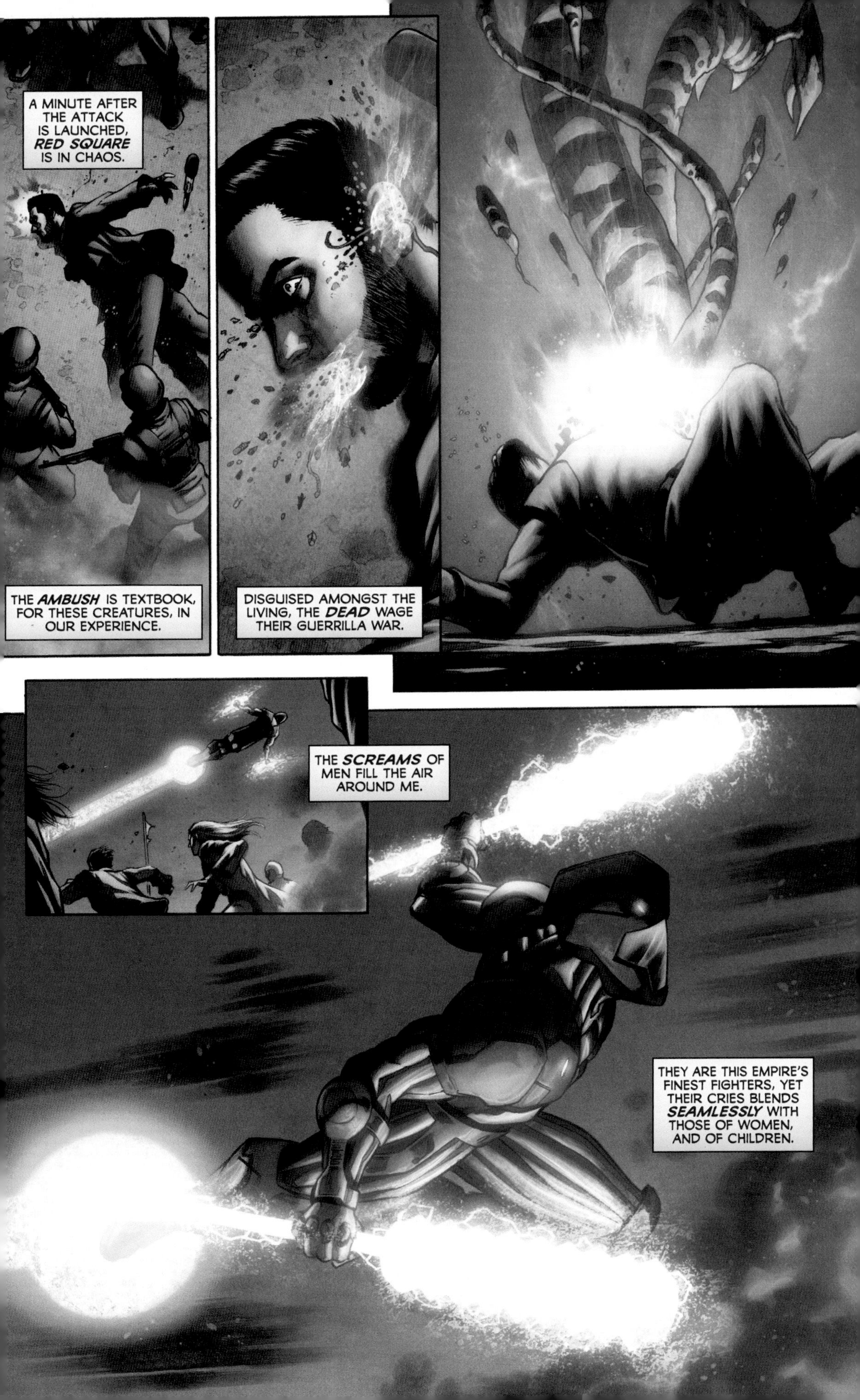
A MINUTE AFTER THE ATTACK IS LAUNCHED, *RED SQUARE* IS IN CHAOS.
THE *AMBUSH* IS TEXTBOOK, FOR THESE CREATURES, IN OUR EXPERIENCE.
DISGUISED AMONGST THE LIVING, THE *DEAD* WAGE THEIR GUERRILLA WAR.
THE *SCREAMS* OF MEN FILL THE AIR AROUND ME.
THEY ARE THIS EMPIRE'S FINEST FIGHTERS, YET THEIR CRIES BLENDS *SEAMLESSLY* WITH THOSE OF WOMEN, AND OF CHILDREN.

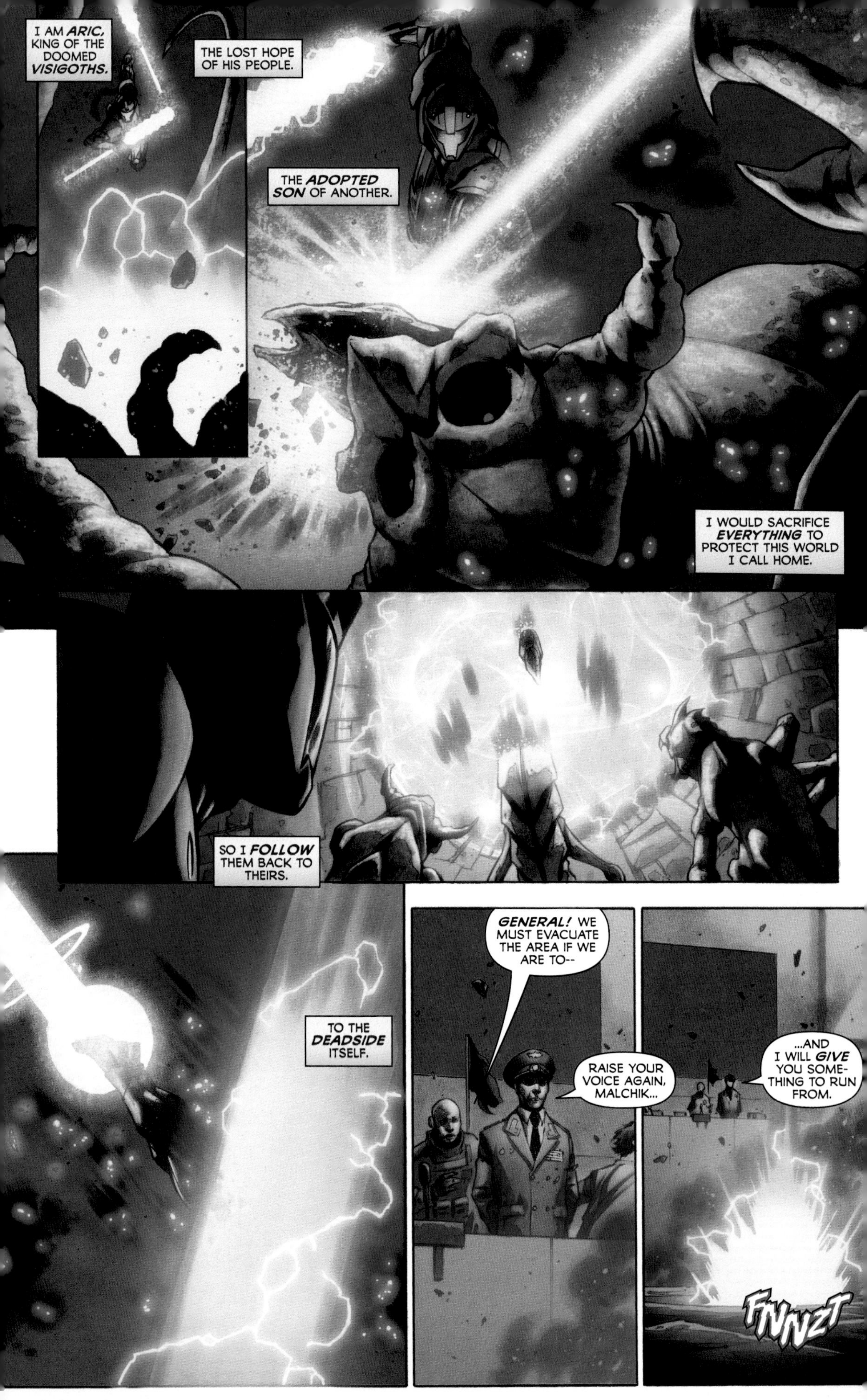
I AM ARIC, KING OF THE DOOMED VISIGOTHS.
THE LOST HOPE OF HIS PEOPLE.
THE ADOPTED SON OF ANOTHER.
I WOULD SACRIFICE EVERYTHING TO PROTECT THIS WORLD I CALL HOME.
SO I FOLLOW THEM BACK TO THEIRS.
TO THE DEADSIDE ITSELF.
GENERAL! WE MUST EVACUATE THE AREA IF WE ARE TO--
RAISE YOUR VOICE AGAIN, MALCHIK...
...AND I WILL GIVE YOU SOME-THING TO RUN FROM.
FNNZT

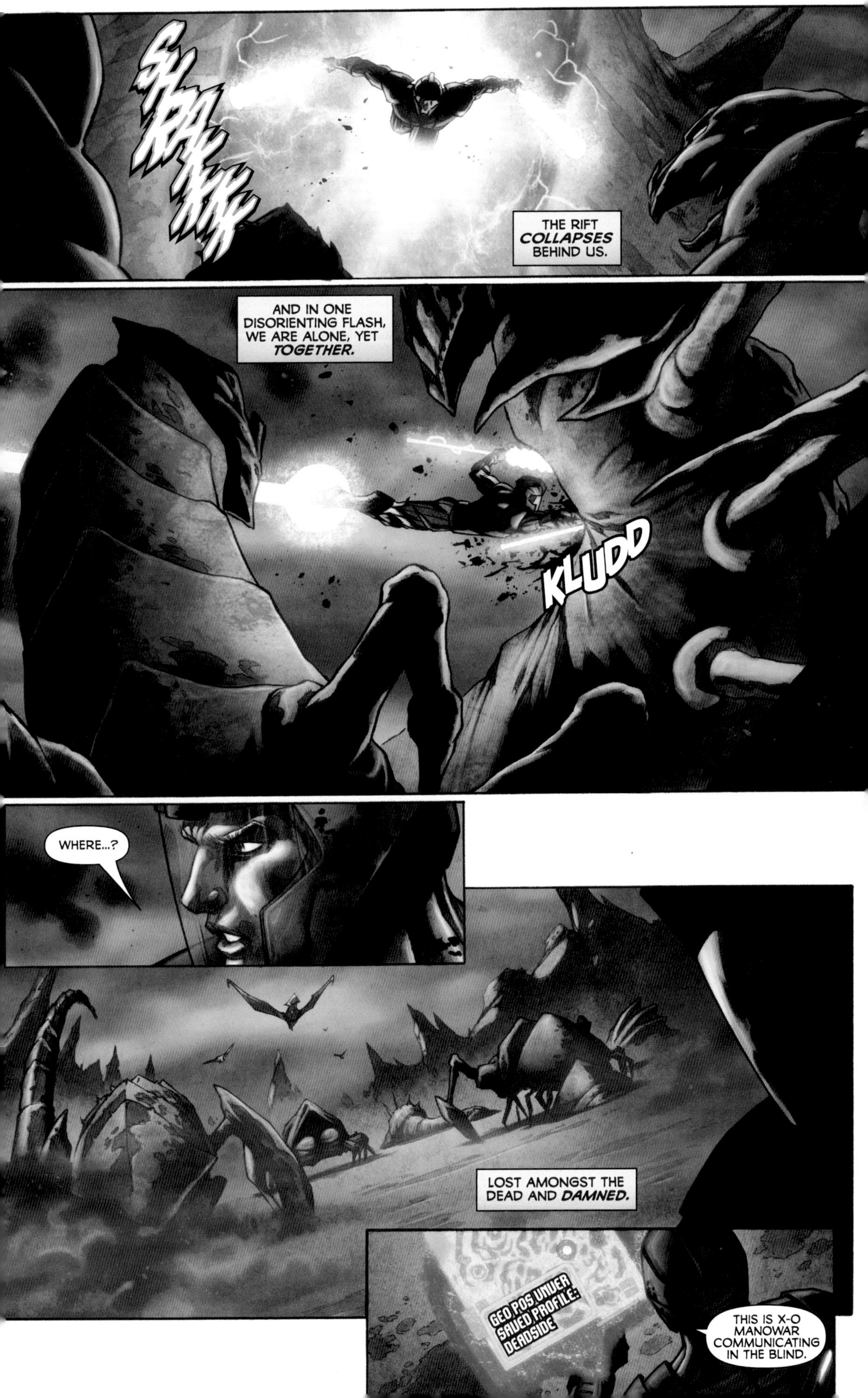
SHRRAKKK
THE RIFT COLLAPSES BEHIND US.
AND IN ONE DISORIENTING FLASH, WE ARE ALONE, YET TOGETHER.
KLUDD
WHERE...?
LOST AMONGST THE DEAD AND DAMNED.
GEO POS UNVER SAVED PROFILE: DEADSIDE
THIS IS X-O MANOWAR COMMUNICATING IN THE BLIND.

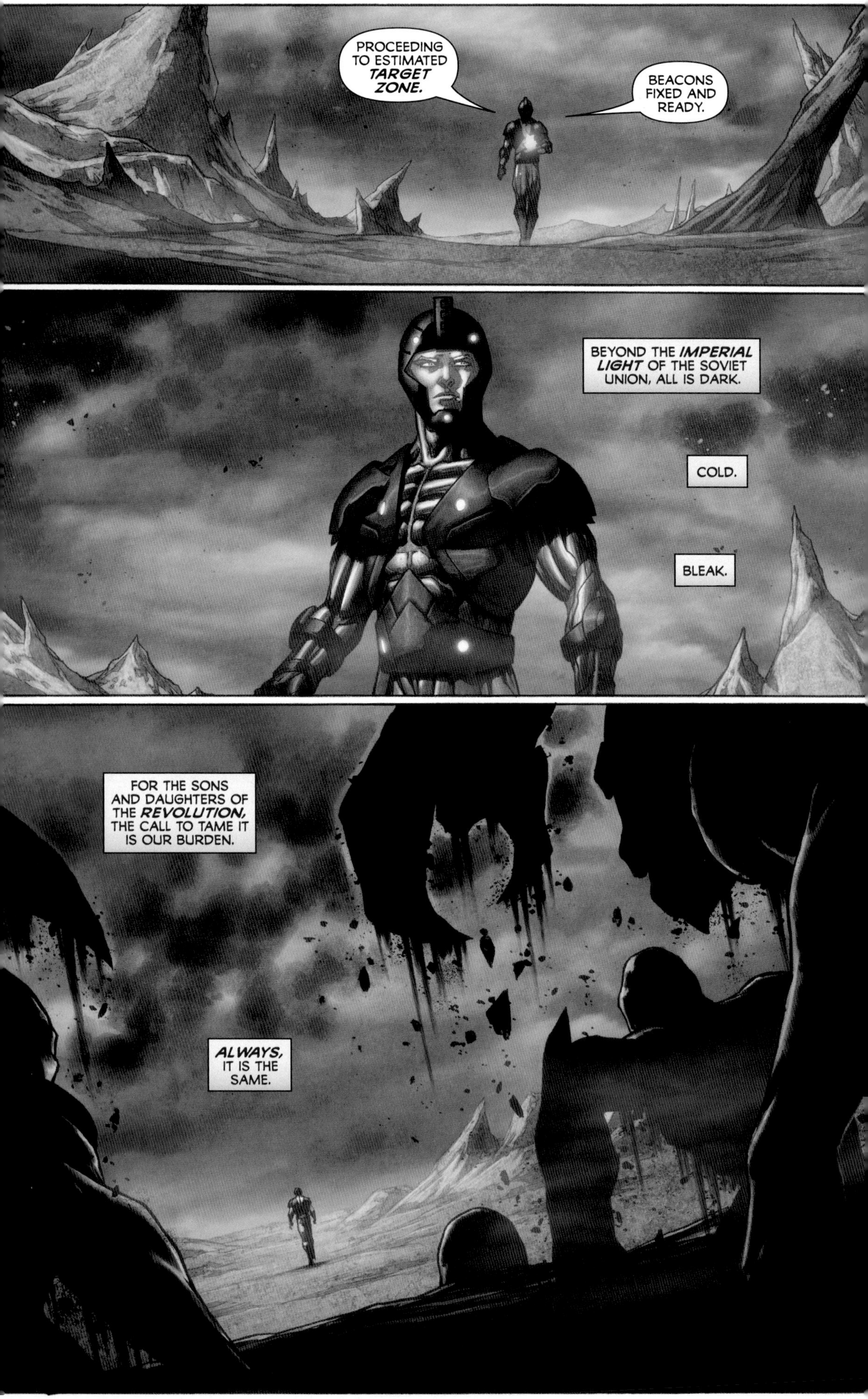
PROCEEDING TO ESTIMATED *TARGET ZONE.*
BEACONS FIXED AND READY.
BEYOND THE *IMPERIAL LIGHT* OF THE SOVIET UNION, ALL IS DARK.
COLD.
BLEAK.
FOR THE SONS AND DAUGHTERS OF THE *REVOLUTION,* THE CALL TO TAME IT IS OUR BURDEN.
ALWAYS, IT IS THE SAME.

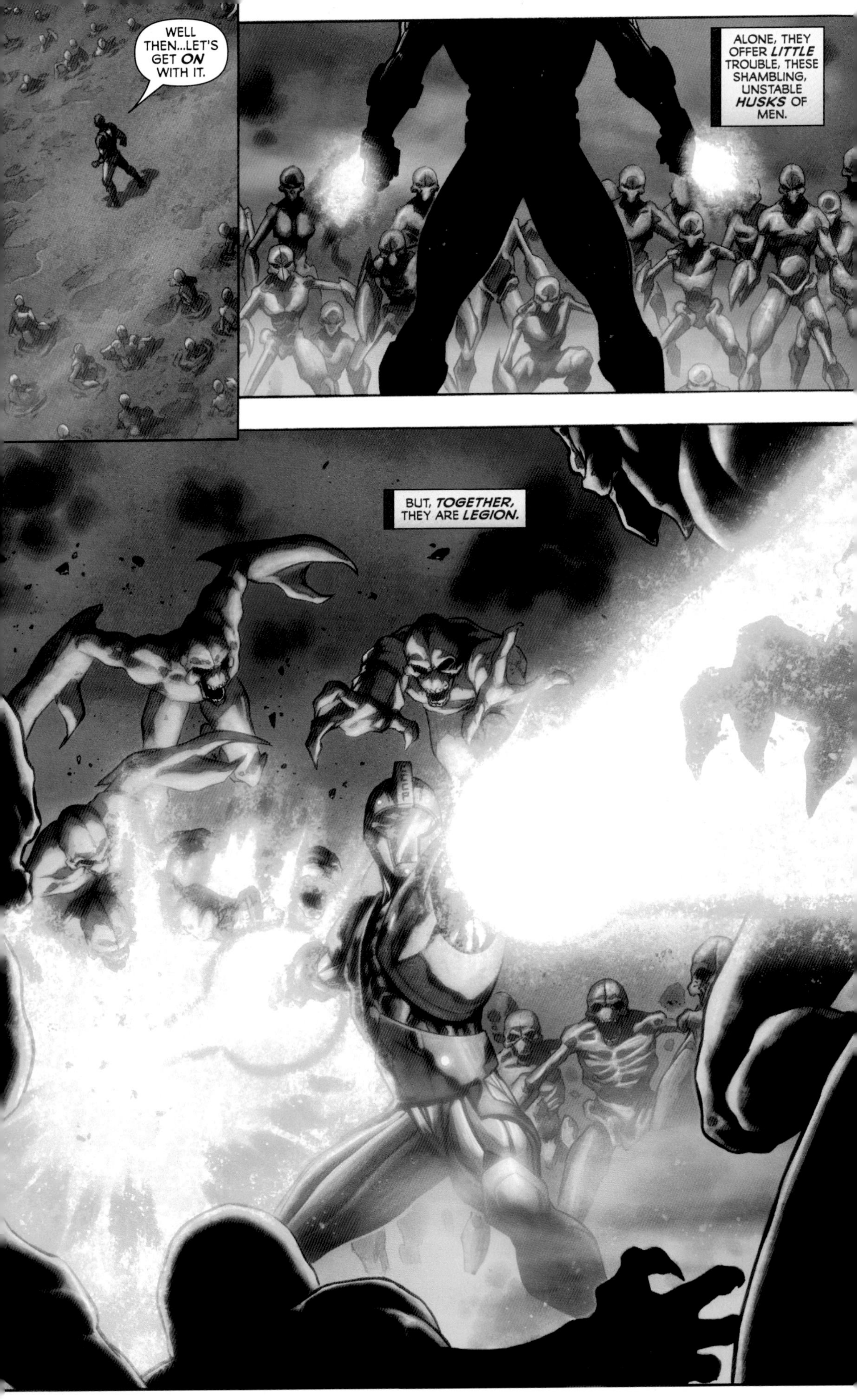
WELL THEN...LET'S GET ON WITH IT.
ALONE, THEY OFFER LITTLE TROUBLE, THESE SHAMBLING, UNSTABLE HUSKS OF MEN.
BUT, TOGETHER, THEY ARE LEGION.

PULLING.

RESISTING AS ONE.

SURGING.

THEN, FOR THE *BRIEFEST* MOMENT...

...I ALMOST *WELCOME* IT.

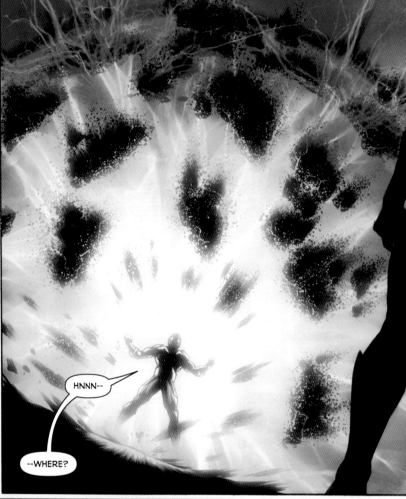

HNNN--

--WHERE?

BEHOLD THE LAST REMNANTS OF THE TORTURED DEATHS OF *50 MILLION* MEN, WOMEN AND CHILDREN IN STALIN'S CAMPS AND GULAGS.

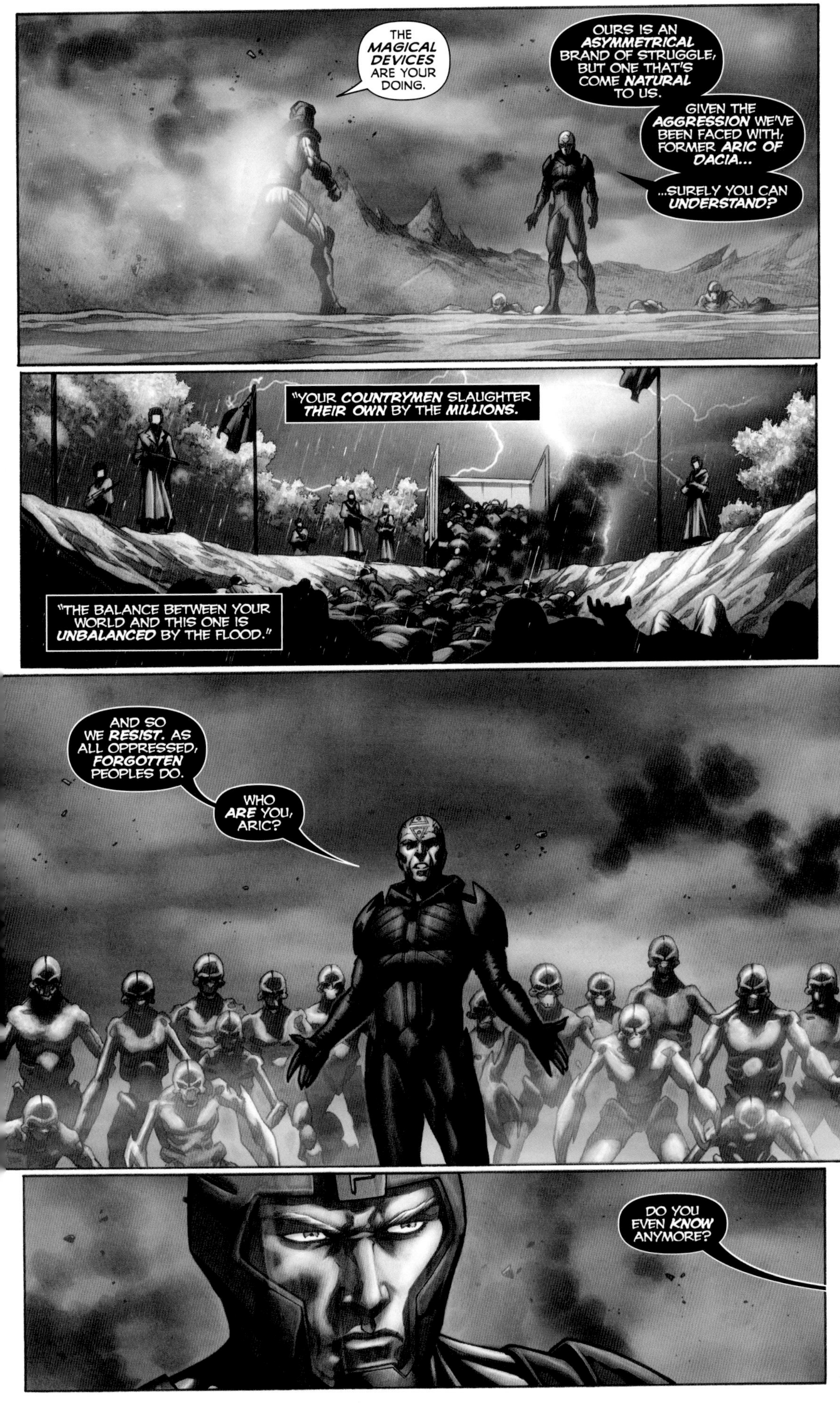
THE MAGICAL DEVICES ARE YOUR DOING.
OURS IS AN ASYMMETRICAL BRAND OF STRUGGLE, BUT ONE THAT'S COME NATURAL TO US.
GIVEN THE AGGRESSION WE'VE BEEN FACED WITH, FORMER ARIC OF DACIA...
...SURELY YOU CAN UNDERSTAND?
"YOUR COUNTRYMEN SLAUGHTER THEIR OWN BY THE MILLIONS.
"THE BALANCE BETWEEN YOUR WORLD AND THIS ONE IS UNBALANCED BY THE FLOOD."
AND SO WE RESIST. AS ALL OPPRESSED, FORGOTTEN PEOPLES DO.
WHO ARE YOU, ARIC?
DO YOU EVEN KNOW ANYMORE?

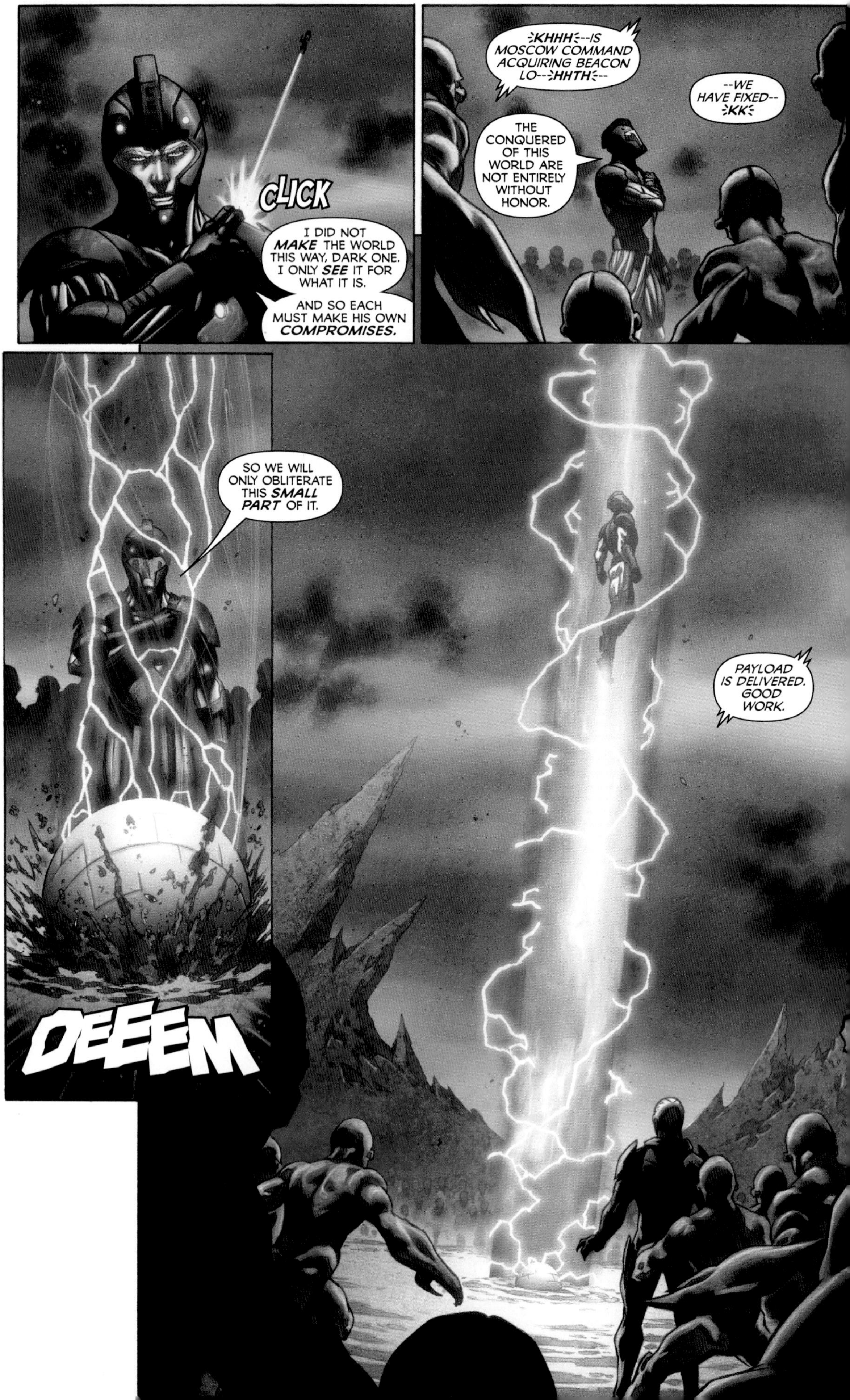
CLICK
I DID NOT MAKE THE WORLD THIS WAY, DARK ONE. I ONLY SEE IT FOR WHAT IT IS.
AND SO EACH MUST MAKE HIS OWN COMPROMISES.
KHHH--IS MOSCOW COMMAND ACQUIRING BEACON LO--HHTH--
THE CONQUERED OF THIS WORLD ARE NOT ENTIRELY WITHOUT HONOR.
--WE HAVE FIXED--KK
SO WE WILL ONLY OBLITERATE THIS SMALL PART OF IT.
DEEEM
PAYLOAD IS DELIVERED. GOOD WORK.

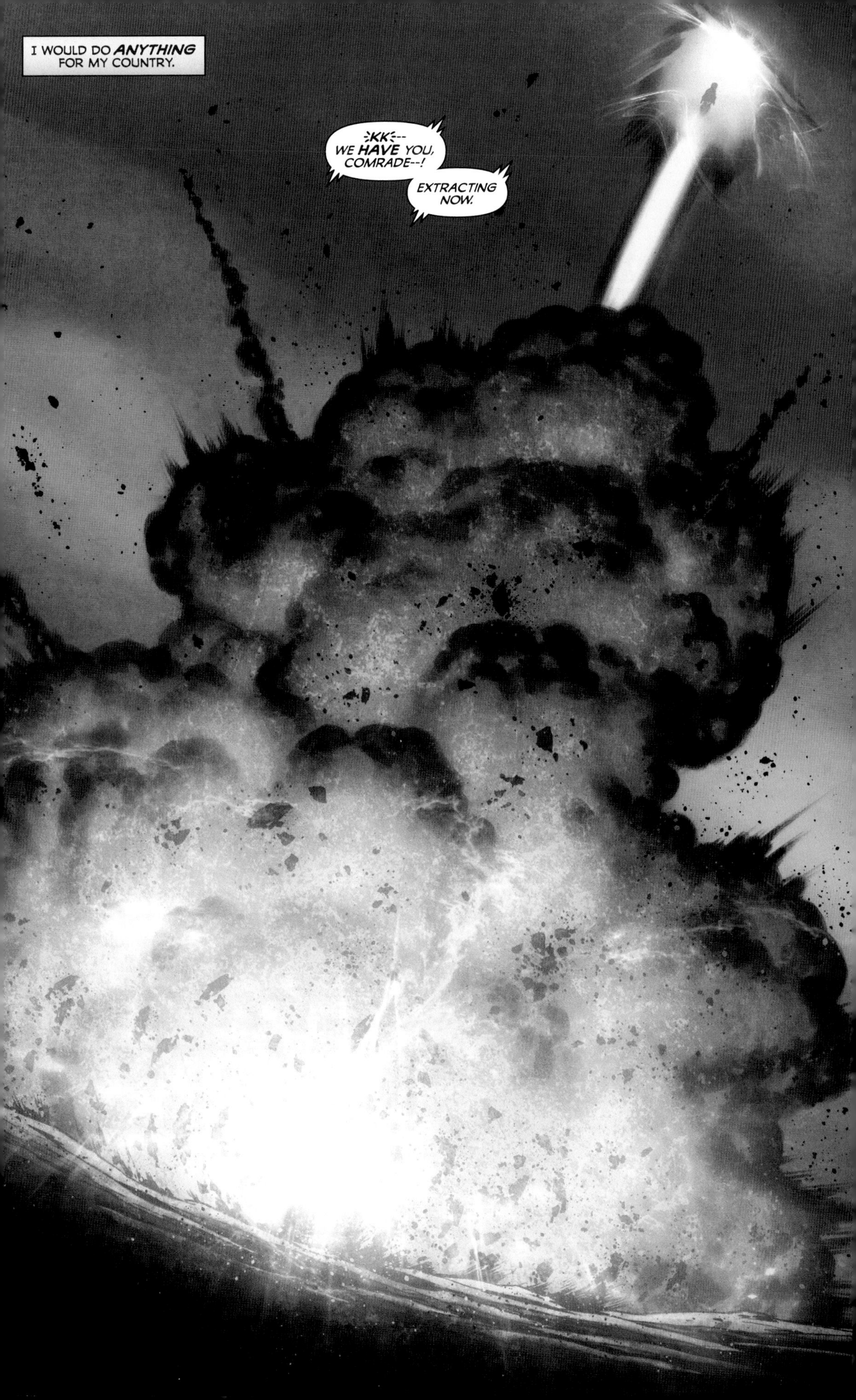
I WOULD DO ANYTHING FOR MY COUNTRY.
KK-- WE HAVE YOU, COMRADE--!
EXTRACTING NOW.

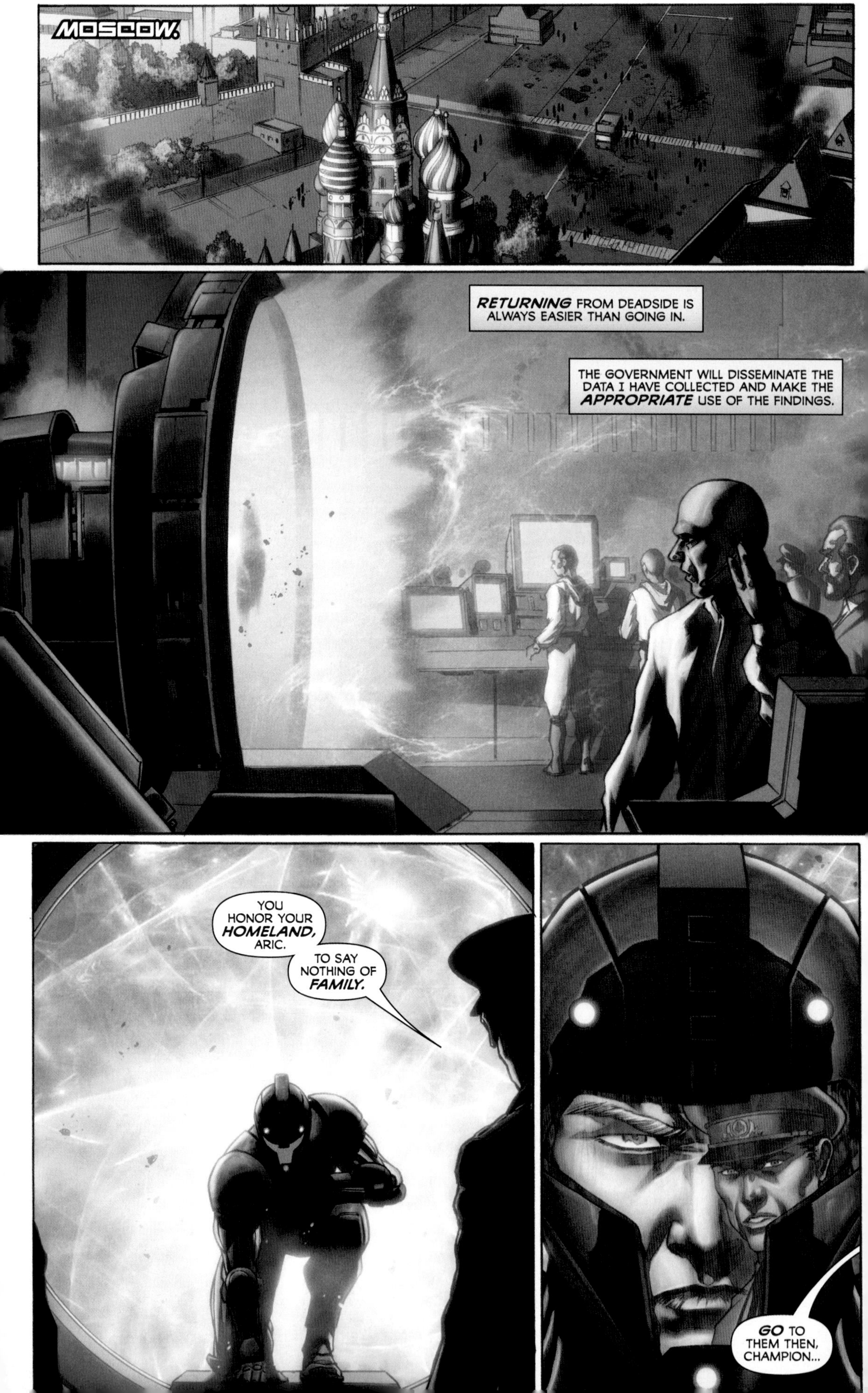
MOSCOW.
RETURNING FROM DEADSIDE IS ALWAYS EASIER THAN GOING IN.
THE GOVERNMENT WILL DISSEMINATE THE DATA I HAVE COLLECTED AND MAKE THE APPROPRIATE USE OF THE FINDINGS.
YOU HONOR YOUR HOMELAND, ARIC.
TO SAY NOTHING OF FAMILY.
GO TO THEM THEN, CHAMPION...

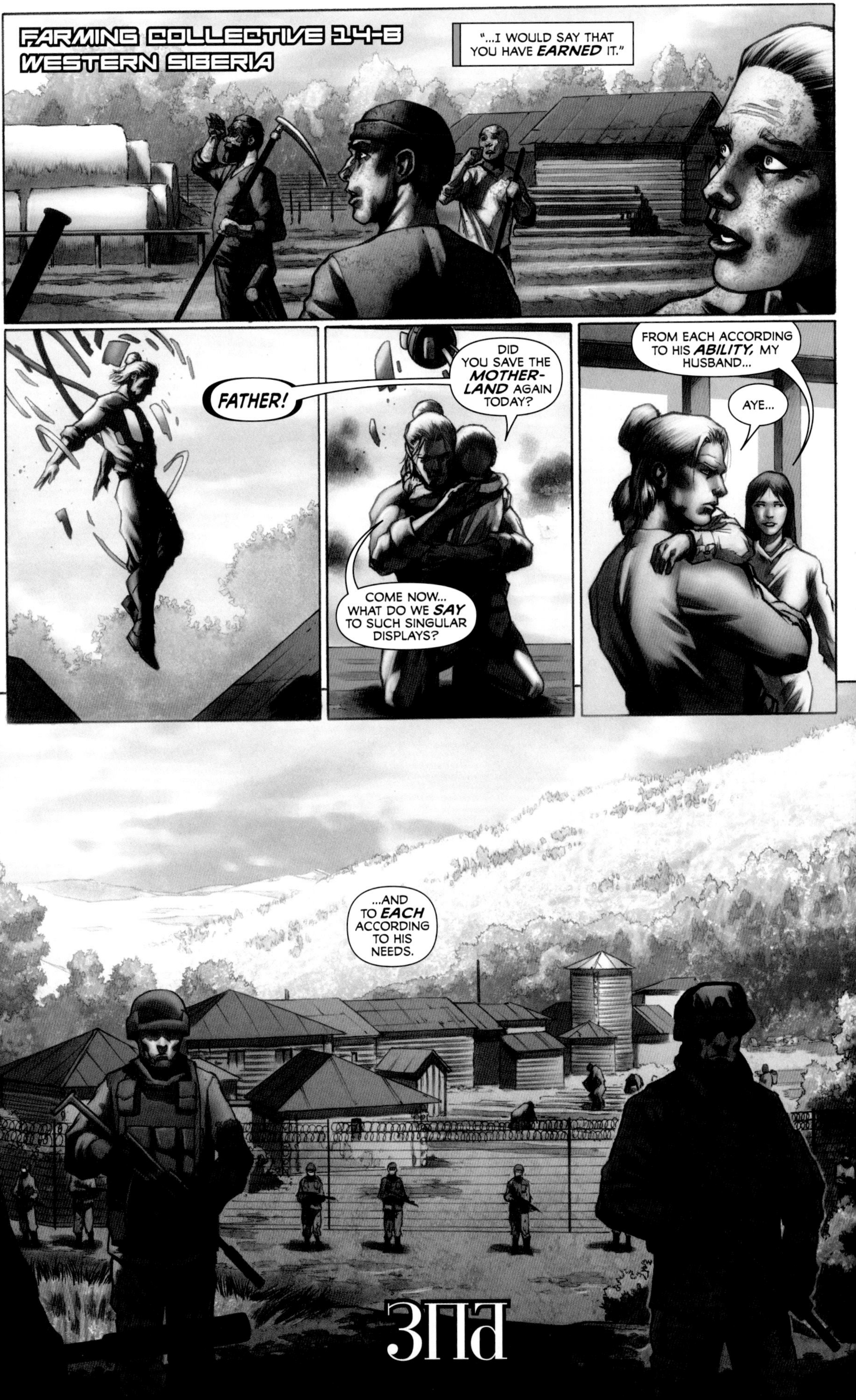
FARMING COLLECTIVE 14-B
WESTERN SIBERIA
"...I WOULD SAY THAT YOU HAVE EARNED IT."
FATHER!
DID YOU SAVE THE MOTHER-LAND AGAIN TODAY?
COME NOW... WHAT DO WE SAY TO SUCH SINGULAR DISPLAYS?
FROM EACH ACCORDING TO HIS ABILITY, MY HUSBAND...
AYE...
...AND TO EACH ACCORDING TO HIS NEEDS.

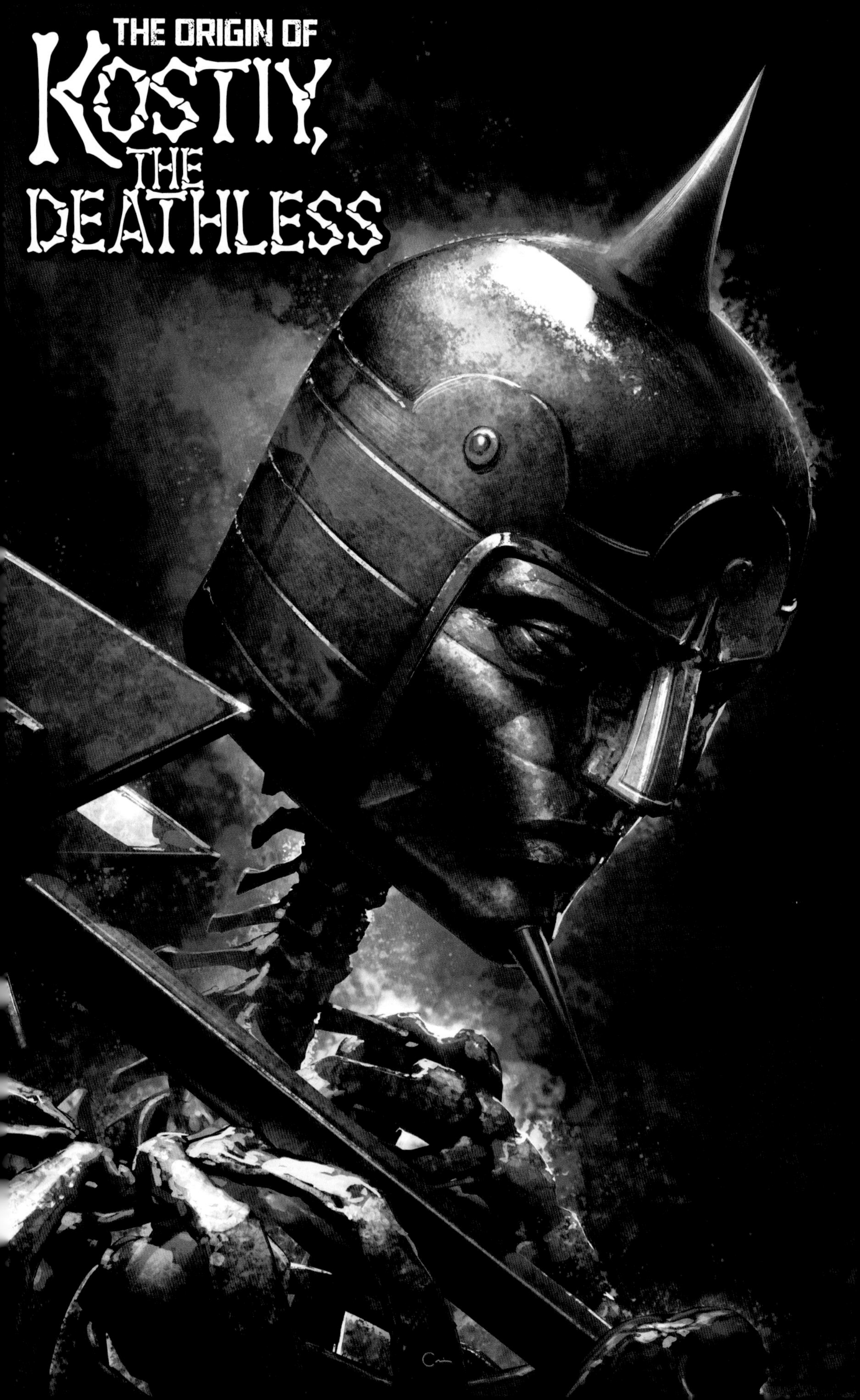
THE ORIGIN OF
KOSTIY,
THE
DEATHLESS

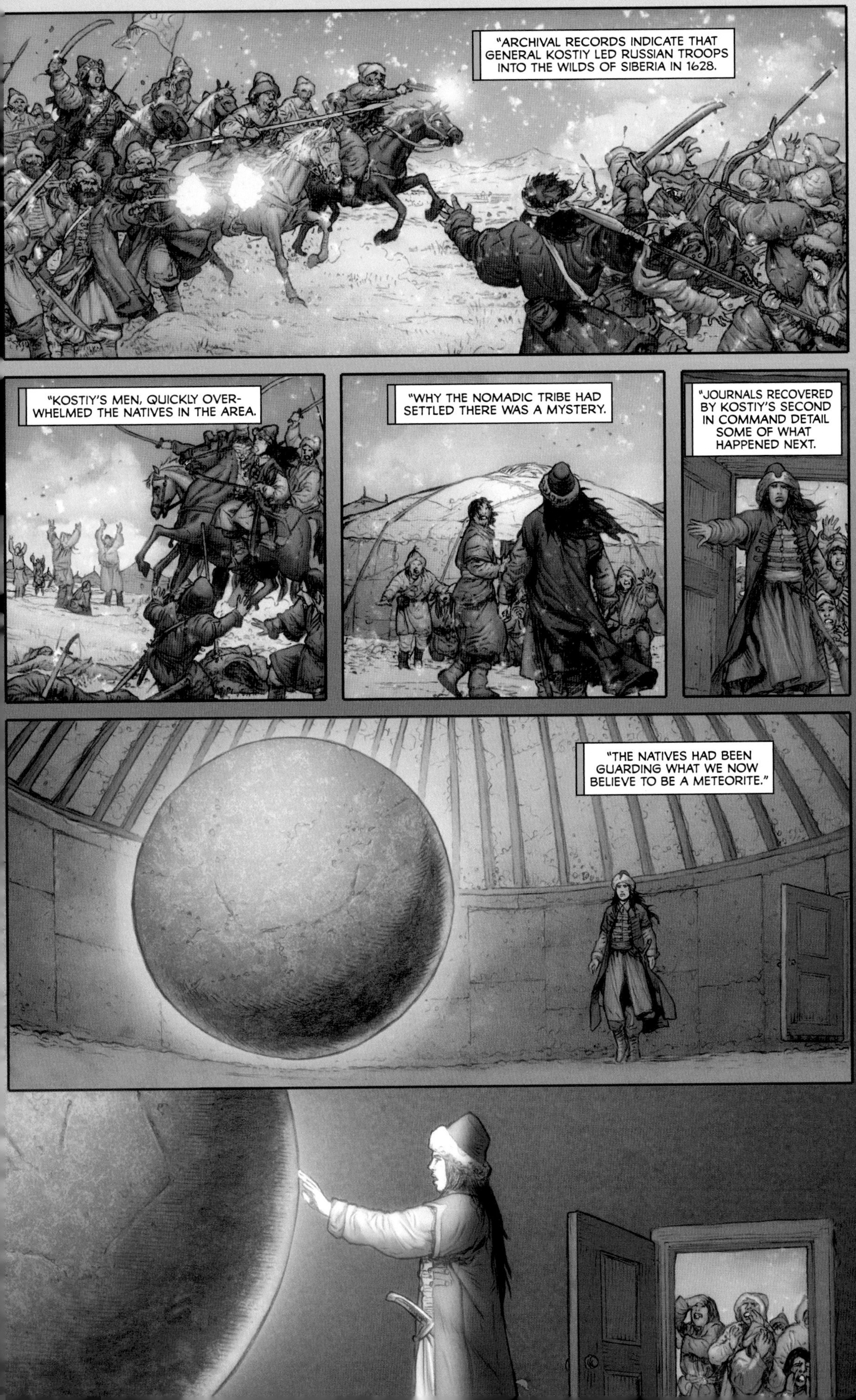
"ARCHIVAL RECORDS INDICATE THAT GENERAL KOSTIY LED RUSSIAN TROOPS INTO THE WILDS OF SIBERIA IN 1628.
"KOSTIY'S MEN, QUICKLY OVER-WHELMED THE NATIVES IN THE AREA.
"WHY THE NOMADIC TRIBE HAD SETTLED THERE WAS A MYSTERY.
"JOURNALS RECOVERED BY KOSTIY'S SECOND IN COMMAND DETAIL SOME OF WHAT HAPPENED NEXT.
"THE NATIVES HAD BEEN GUARDING WHAT WE NOW BELIEVE TO BE A METEORITE."

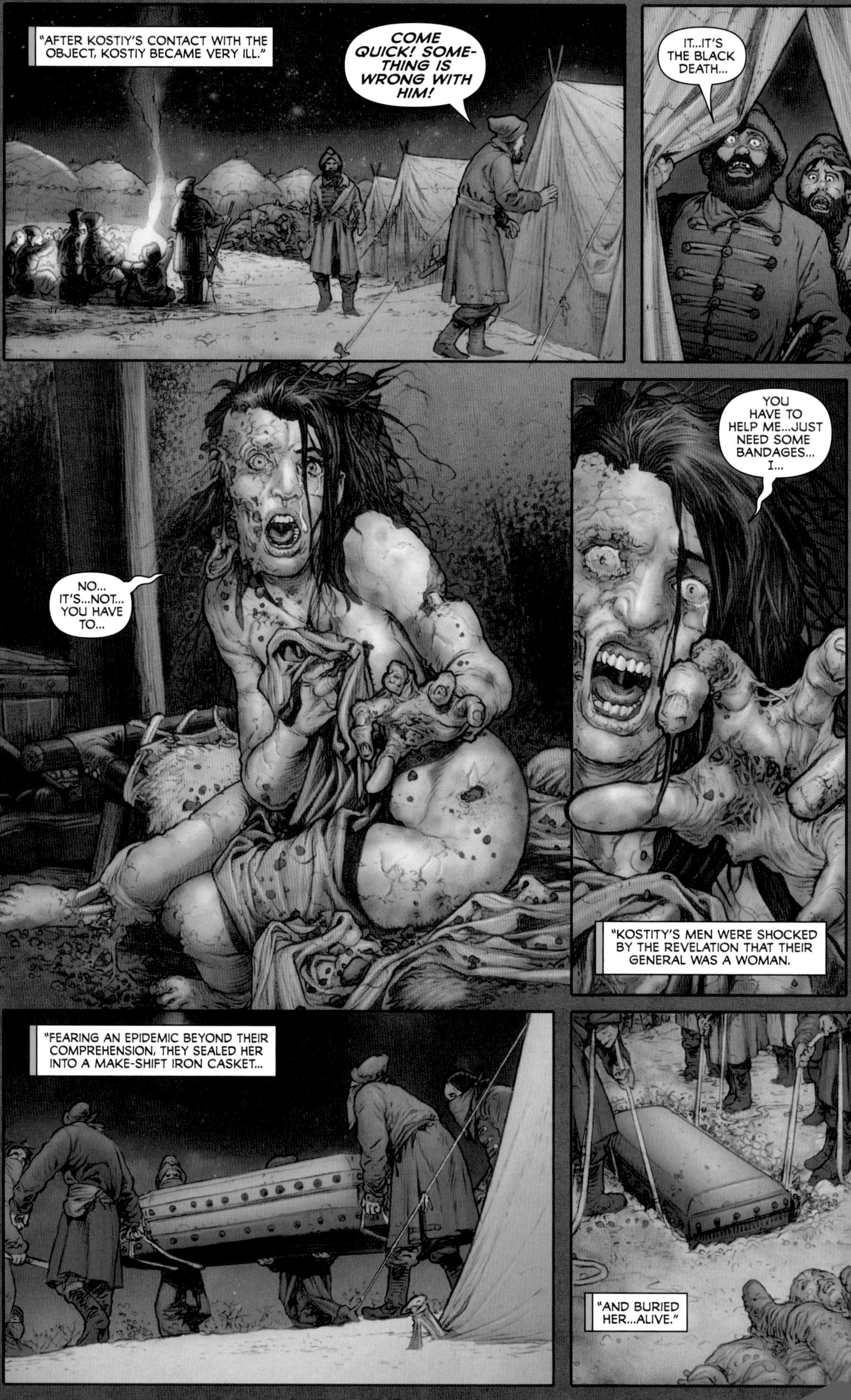
"AFTER KOSTIY'S CONTACT WITH THE OBJECT, KOSTIY BECAME VERY ILL."
COME QUICK! SOME-THING IS WRONG WITH HIM!
IT...IT'S THE BLACK DEATH...
NO... IT'S...NOT... YOU HAVE TO...
YOU HAVE TO HELP ME...JUST NEED SOME BANDAGES... I...
"KOSTITY'S MEN WERE SHOCKED BY THE REVELATION THAT THEIR GENERAL WAS A WOMAN.
"FEARING AN EPIDEMIC BEYOND THEIR COMPREHENSION, THEY SEALED HER INTO A MAKE-SHIFT IRON CASKET...
"AND BURIED HER...ALIVE."

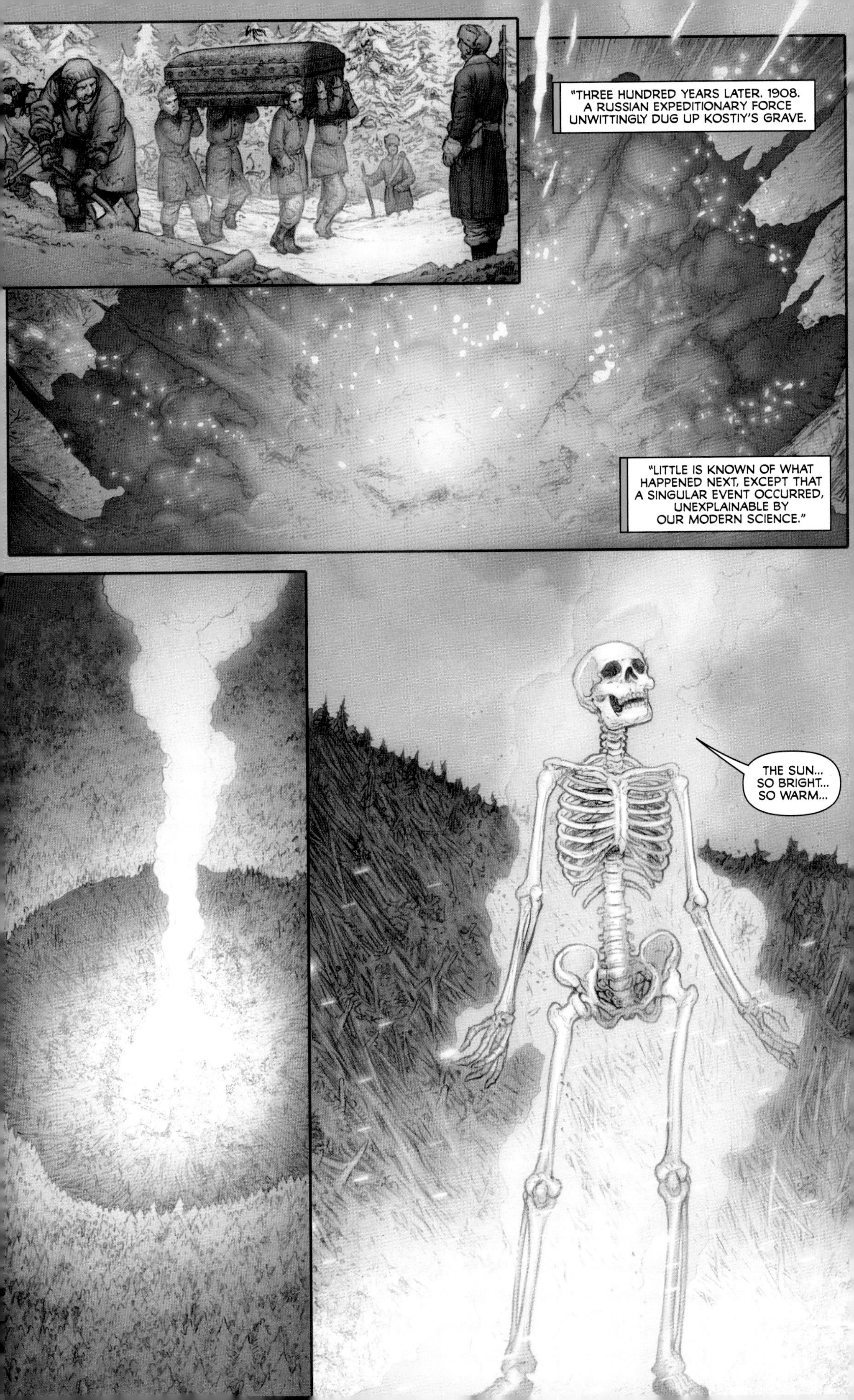
"THREE HUNDRED YEARS LATER. 1908. A RUSSIAN EXPEDITIONARY FORCE UNWITTINGLY DUG UP KOSTIY'S GRAVE.
"LITTLE IS KNOWN OF WHAT HAPPENED NEXT, EXCEPT THAT A SINGULAR EVENT OCCURRED, UNEXPLAINABLE BY OUR MODERN SCIENCE."
THE SUN... SO BRIGHT... SO WARM...

"THE EXPEDITIONARY FORCE THAT SURVIVED BUILT A CAMP AROUND WHAT WE NOW BELIEVE TO BE THE IMMORTAL REMAINS OF GENERAL KOSTIY.

"AS KOSTIY WAS SOMEWHAT...*UNSTABLE* AFTER BEING OSTENSIBLY, BURIED ALIVE, LABS WERE BUILT TO BOTH CONTAIN AND STUDY HER WHERE SHE WAS DISCOVERED."

"ALL STUDIES AND MEASURE-MENTS INDICATE THAT KOSTIY LIVES AND "DIES" EVERY MONTH ON A LUNAR CYCLE.

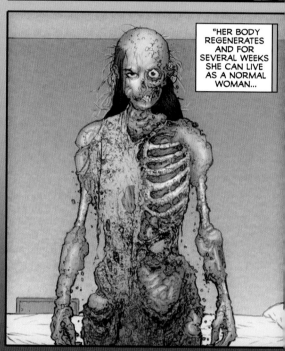

"HER BODY REGENERATES AND FOR SEVERAL WEEKS SHE CAN LIVE AS A NORMAL WOMAN...

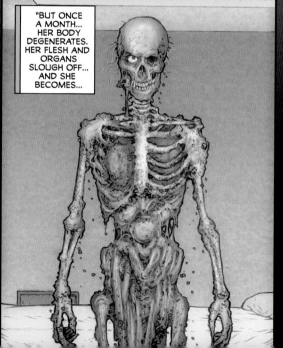

"BUT ONCE A MONTH... HER BODY DEGENERATES. HER FLESH AND ORGANS SLOUGH OFF... AND SHE BECOMES...

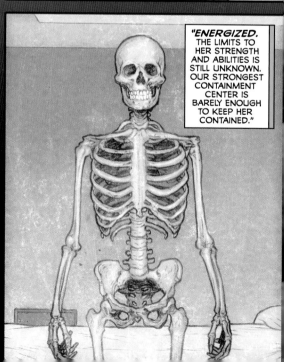

"*ENERGIZED.* THE LIMITS TO HER STRENGTH AND ABILITIES IS STILL UNKNOWN. OUR STRONGEST CONTAINMENT CENTER IS BARELY ENOUGH TO KEEP HER CONTAINED."

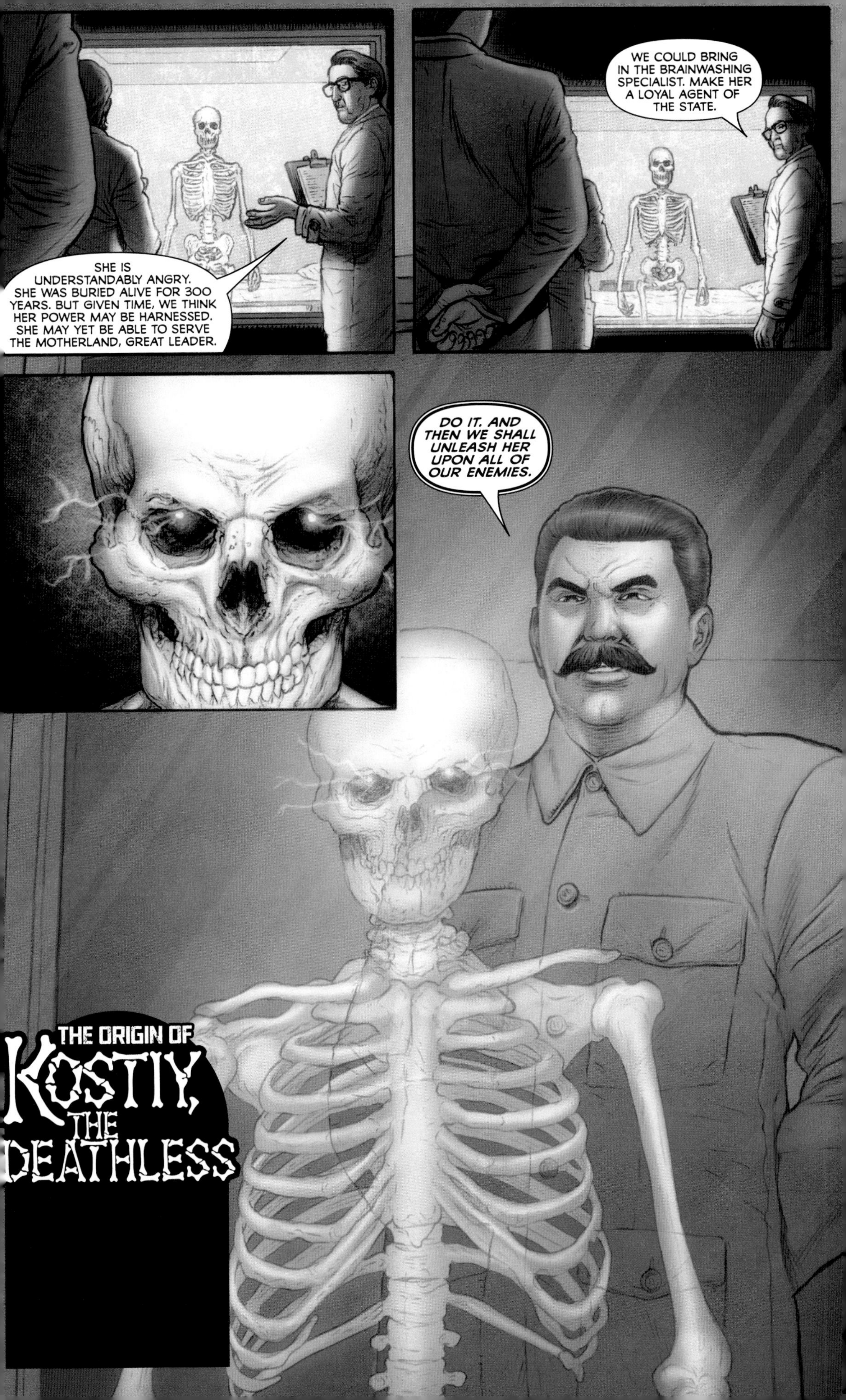
SHE IS UNDERSTANDABLY ANGRY. SHE WAS BURIED ALIVE FOR 300 YEARS. BUT GIVEN TIME, WE THINK HER POWER MAY BE HARNESSED. SHE MAY YET BE ABLE TO SERVE THE MOTHERLAND, GREAT LEADER.
WE COULD BRING IN THE BRAINWASHING SPECIALIST. MAKE HER A LOYAL AGENT OF THE STATE.
DO IT. AND THEN WE SHALL UNLEASH HER UPON ALL OF OUR ENEMIES.
THE ORIGIN OF
KOSTIY, THE DEATHLESS

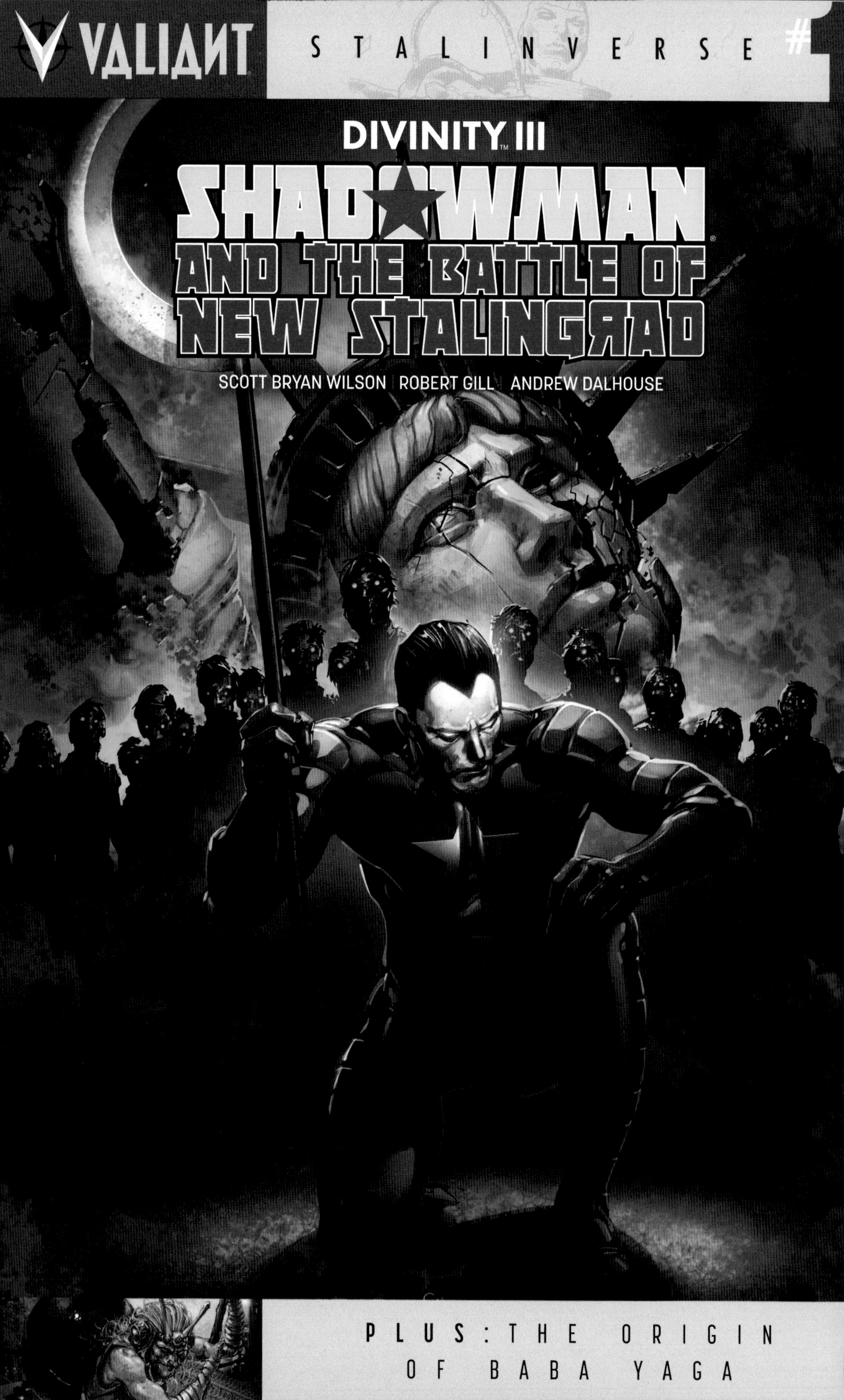
VALIANT
STALINVERSE #1
DIVINITY III
SHADOWMAN
AND THE BATTLE OF NEW STALINGRAD
SCOTT BRYAN WILSON | ROBERT GILL | ANDREW DALHOUSE
PLUS: THE ORIGIN OF BABA YAGA

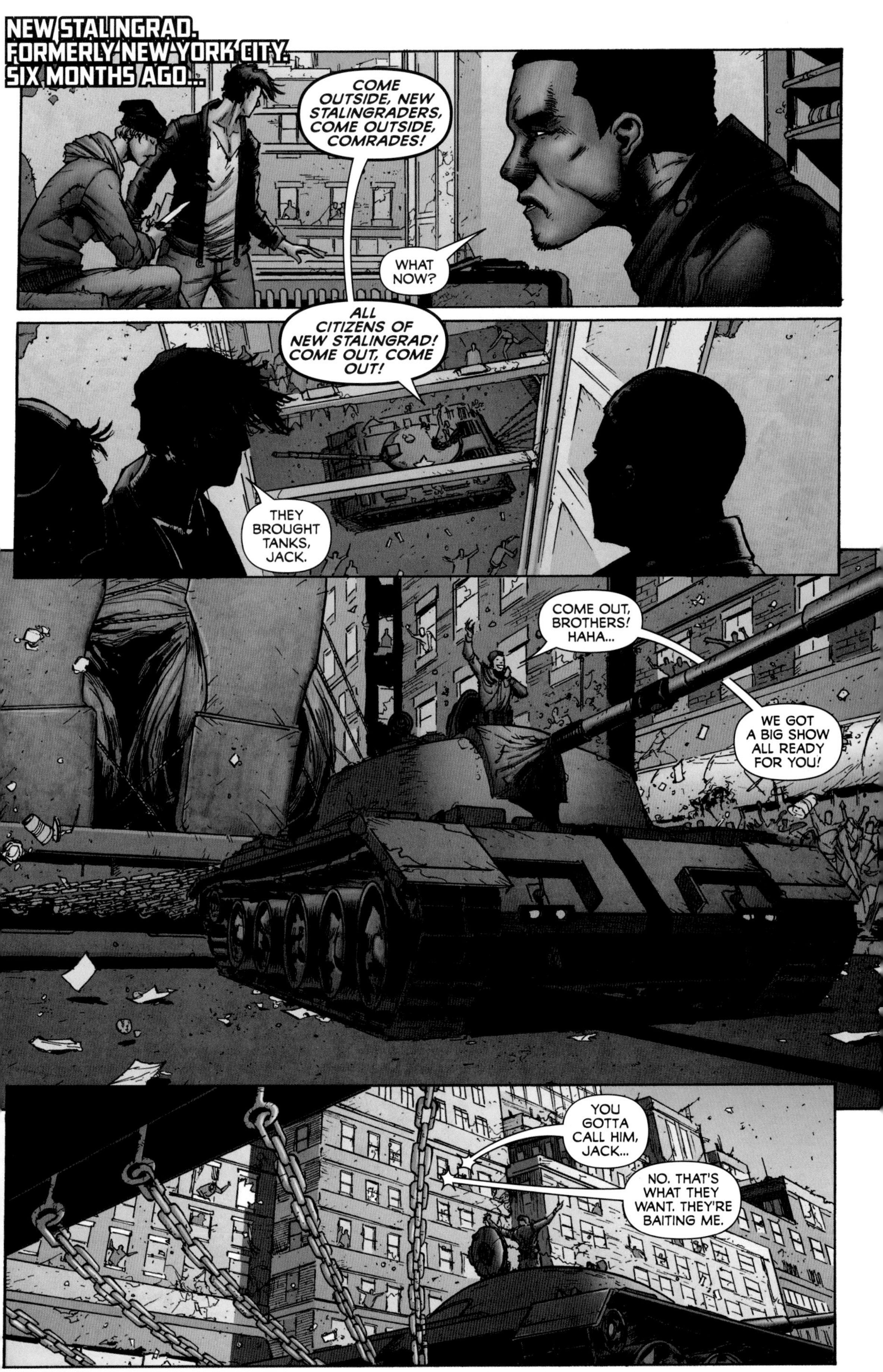
NEW STALINGRAD. FORMERLY NEW YORK CITY. SIX MONTHS AGO...
COME OUTSIDE, NEW STALINGRADERS, COME OUTSIDE, COMRADES!
WHAT NOW?
ALL CITIZENS OF NEW STALINGRAD! COME OUT, COME OUT!
THEY BROUGHT TANKS, JACK.
COME OUT, BROTHERS! HAHA...
WE GOT A BIG SHOW ALL READY FOR YOU!
YOU GOTTA CALL HIM, JACK...
NO. THAT'S WHAT THEY WANT. THEY'RE BAITING ME.

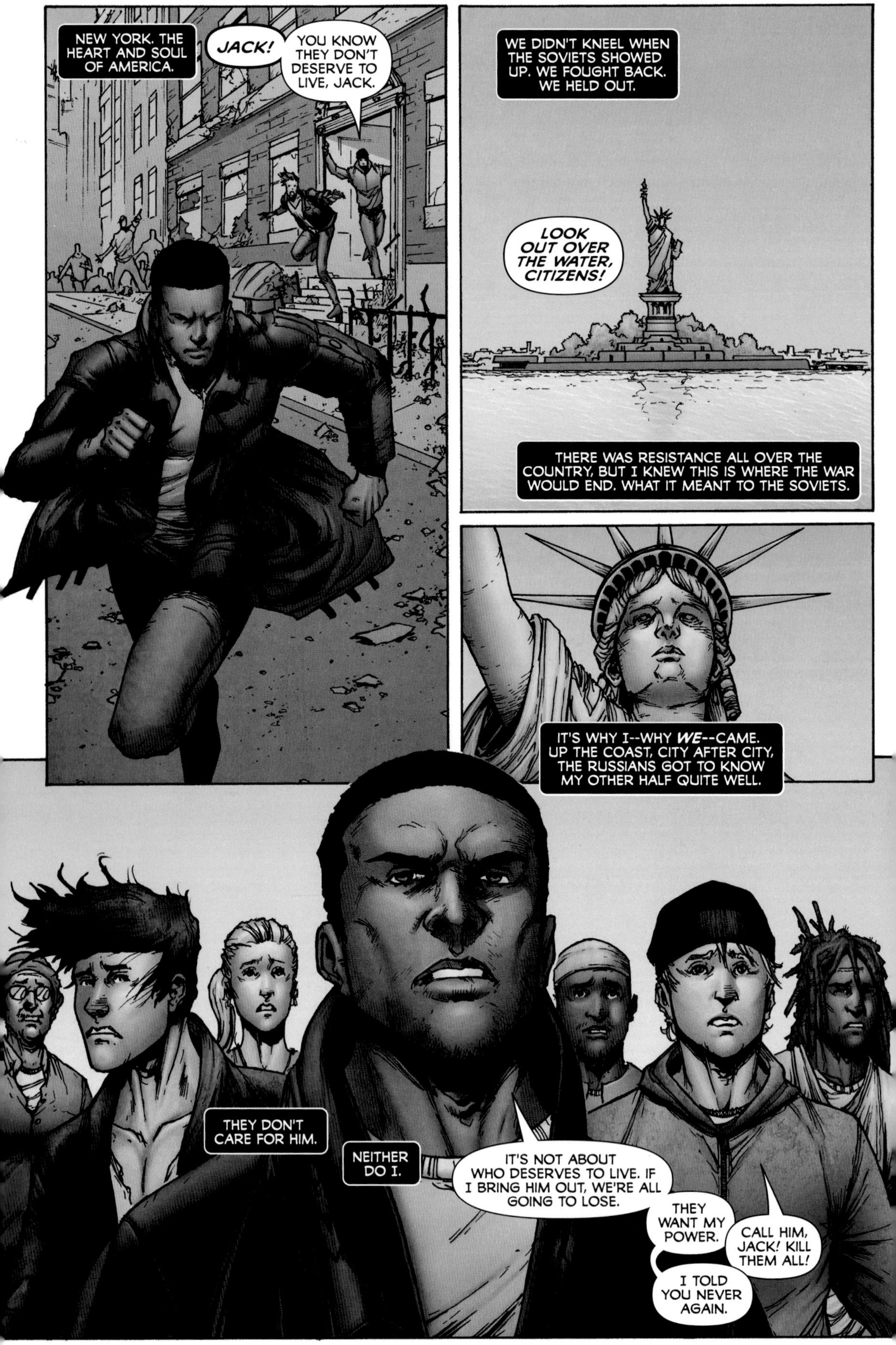
NEW YORK. THE HEART AND SOUL OF AMERICA.
JACK!
YOU KNOW THEY DON'T DESERVE TO LIVE, JACK.
WE DIDN'T KNEEL WHEN THE SOVIETS SHOWED UP. WE FOUGHT BACK. WE HELD OUT.
LOOK OUT OVER THE WATER, CITIZENS!
THERE WAS RESISTANCE ALL OVER THE COUNTRY, BUT I KNEW THIS IS WHERE THE WAR WOULD END. WHAT IT MEANT TO THE SOVIETS.
IT'S WHY I--WHY WE--CAME. UP THE COAST, CITY AFTER CITY, THE RUSSIANS GOT TO KNOW MY OTHER HALF QUITE WELL.
THEY DON'T CARE FOR HIM.
NEITHER DO I.
IT'S NOT ABOUT WHO DESERVES TO LIVE. IF I BRING HIM OUT, WE'RE ALL GOING TO LOSE.
THEY WANT MY POWER.
CALL HIM, JACK! KILL THEM ALL!
I TOLD YOU NEVER AGAIN.

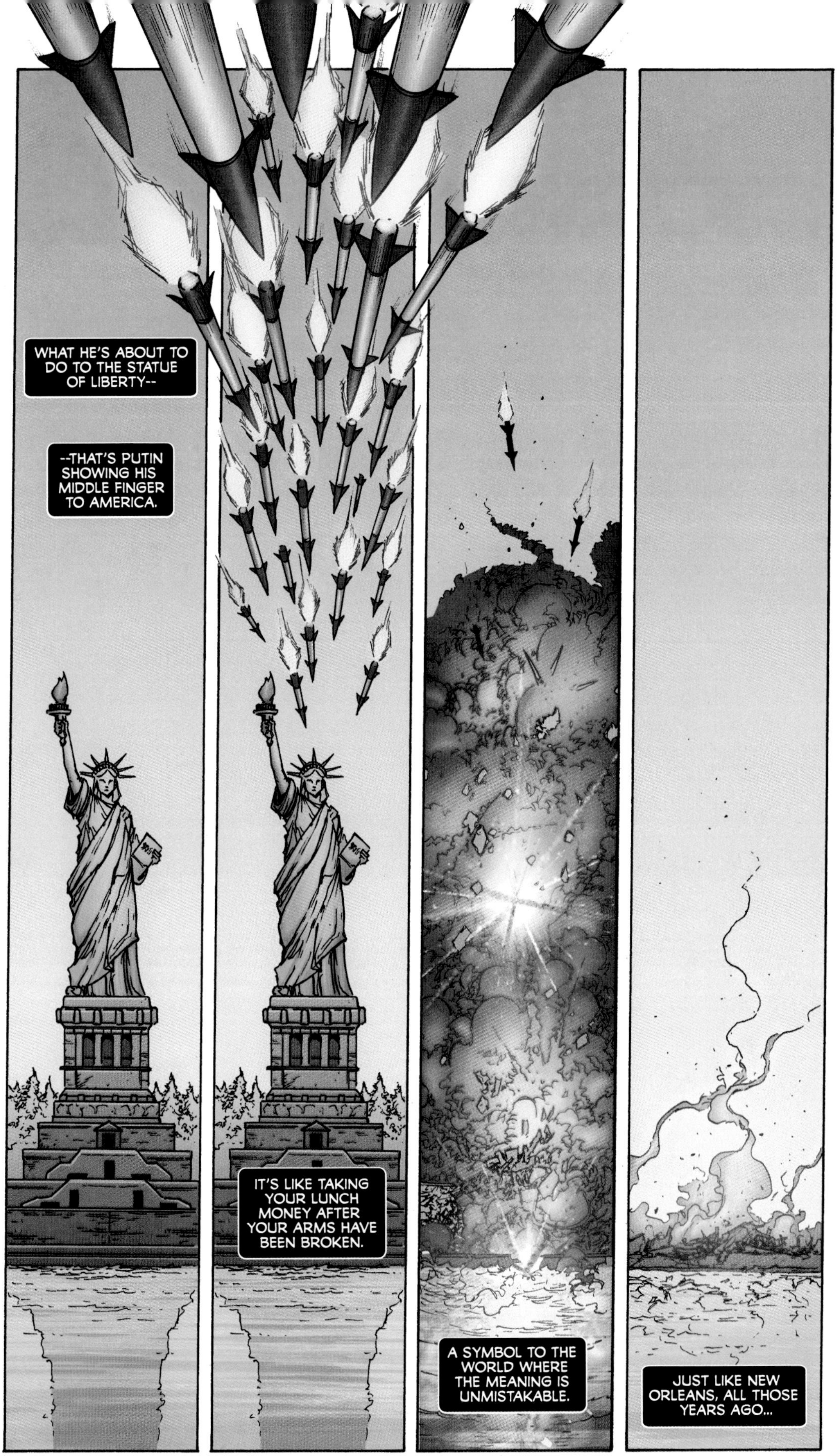
WHAT HE'S ABOUT TO DO TO THE STATUE OF LIBERTY--
--THAT'S PUTIN SHOWING HIS MIDDLE FINGER TO AMERICA.
IT'S LIKE TAKING YOUR LUNCH MONEY AFTER YOUR ARMS HAVE BEEN BROKEN.
A SYMBOL TO THE WORLD WHERE THE MEANING IS UNMISTAKABLE.
JUST LIKE NEW ORLEANS, ALL THOSE YEARS AGO...

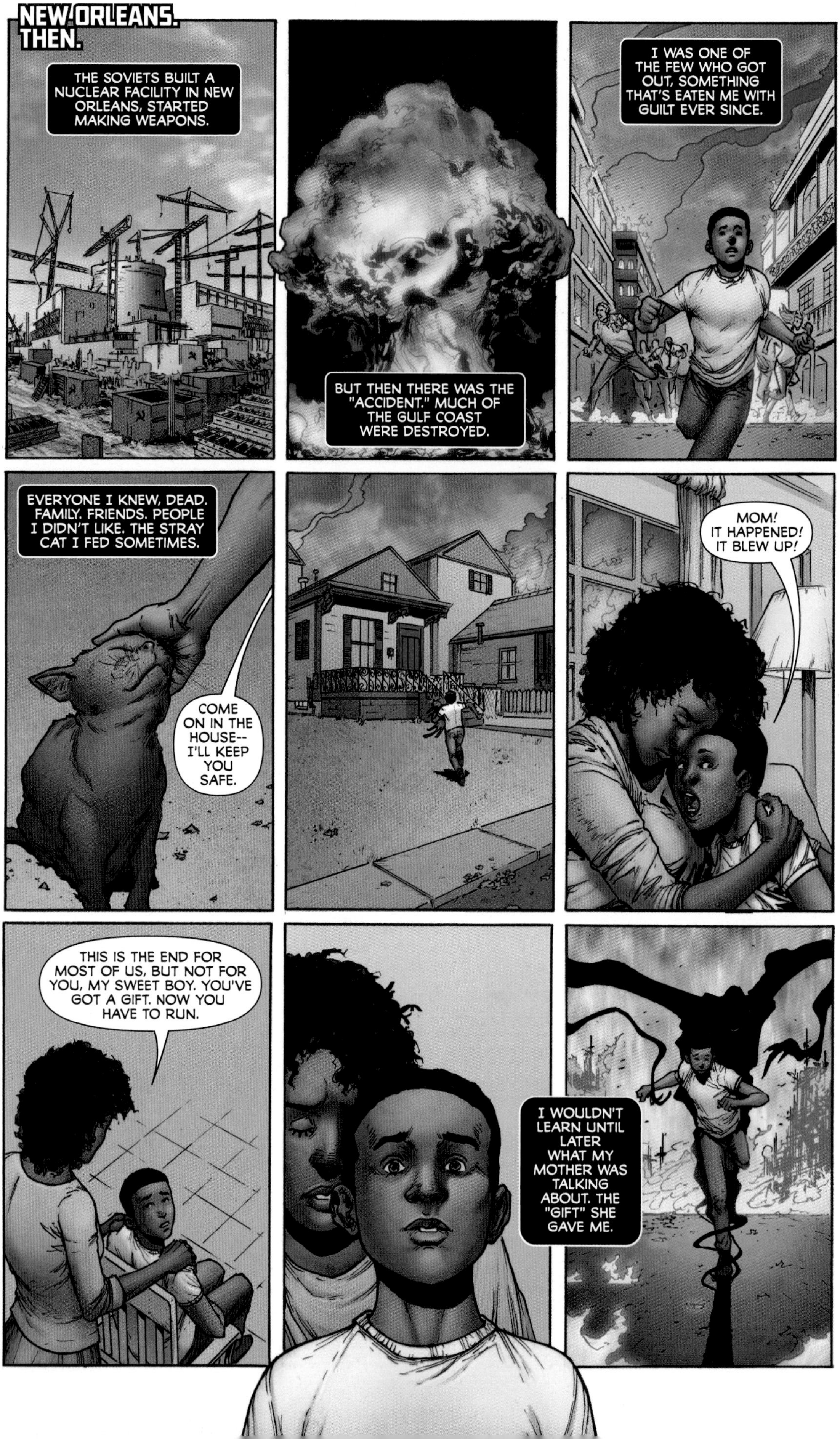
NEW ORLEANS. THEN.
THE SOVIETS BUILT A NUCLEAR FACILITY IN NEW ORLEANS, STARTED MAKING WEAPONS.
BUT THEN THERE WAS THE "ACCIDENT." MUCH OF THE GULF COAST WERE DESTROYED.
I WAS ONE OF THE FEW WHO GOT OUT, SOMETHING THAT'S EATEN ME WITH GUILT EVER SINCE.
EVERYONE I KNEW, DEAD. FAMILY. FRIENDS. PEOPLE I DIDN'T LIKE. THE STRAY CAT I FED SOMETIMES.
COME ON IN THE HOUSE-- I'LL KEEP YOU SAFE.
MOM! IT HAPPENED! IT BLEW UP!
THIS IS THE END FOR MOST OF US, BUT NOT FOR YOU, MY SWEET BOY. YOU'VE GOT A GIFT. NOW YOU HAVE TO RUN.
I WOULDN'T LEARN UNTIL LATER WHAT MY MOTHER WAS TALKING ABOUT. THE "GIFT" SHE GAVE ME.

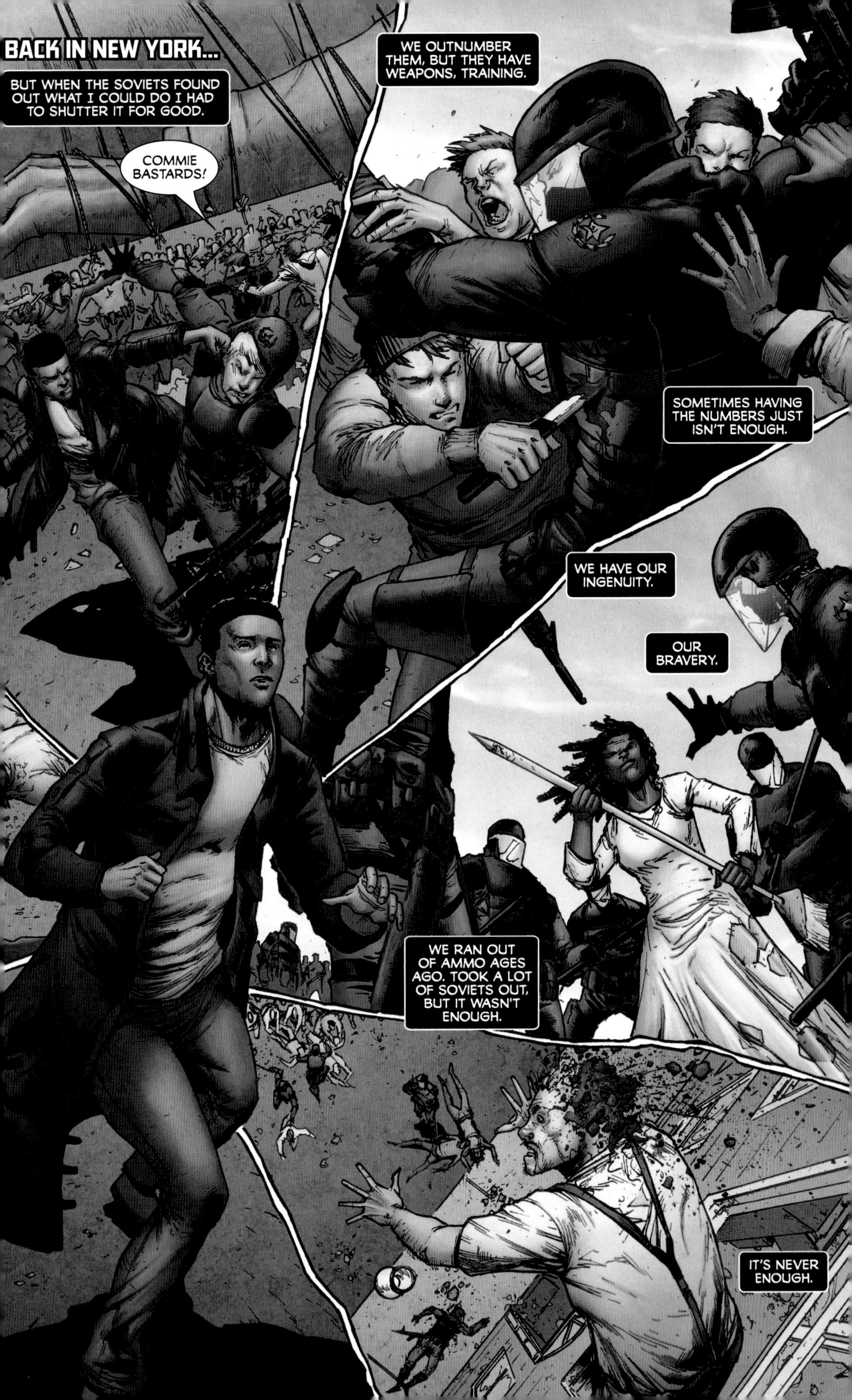
BACK IN NEW YORK...
BUT WHEN THE SOVIETS FOUND OUT WHAT I COULD DO I HAD TO SHUTTER IT FOR GOOD.
COMMIE BASTARDS!
WE OUTNUMBER THEM, BUT THEY HAVE WEAPONS, TRAINING.
SOMETIMES HAVING THE NUMBERS JUST ISN'T ENOUGH.
WE HAVE OUR INGENUITY.
OUR BRAVERY.
WE RAN OUT OF AMMO AGES AGO. TOOK A LOT OF SOVIETS OUT, BUT IT WASN'T ENOUGH.
IT'S NEVER ENOUGH.

I CALLED THAT STRAY CAT ZEKE. LOOKED LIKE A ZEKE.

DON'T SEE A LOT OF STRAYS THESE DAYS. PEOPLE ARE HUNGRY.

WE'RE FIGHTING WITH ANYTHING WE HAVE. THE SOVIETS' CONFIDENCE AND SWAGGER IS MAKING THEM...SADISTIC.

THERE'S NOTHING I WANT MORE THAN TO CALL MY OTHER HALF.

THE POWER USED TO SCARE ME. HOW IT MADE ME FEEL. WHAT I COULD DO WITH IT.

BUT NOW THE ONLY THING THAT SCARES ME IS WHAT THE SOVIETS WOULD DO WITH IT IF THEY TOOK CONTROL OF IT.

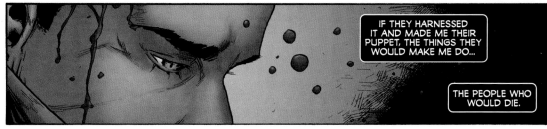

IF THEY HARNESSED IT AND MADE ME THEIR PUPPET, THE THINGS THEY WOULD MAKE ME DO...

THE PEOPLE WHO WOULD DIE.

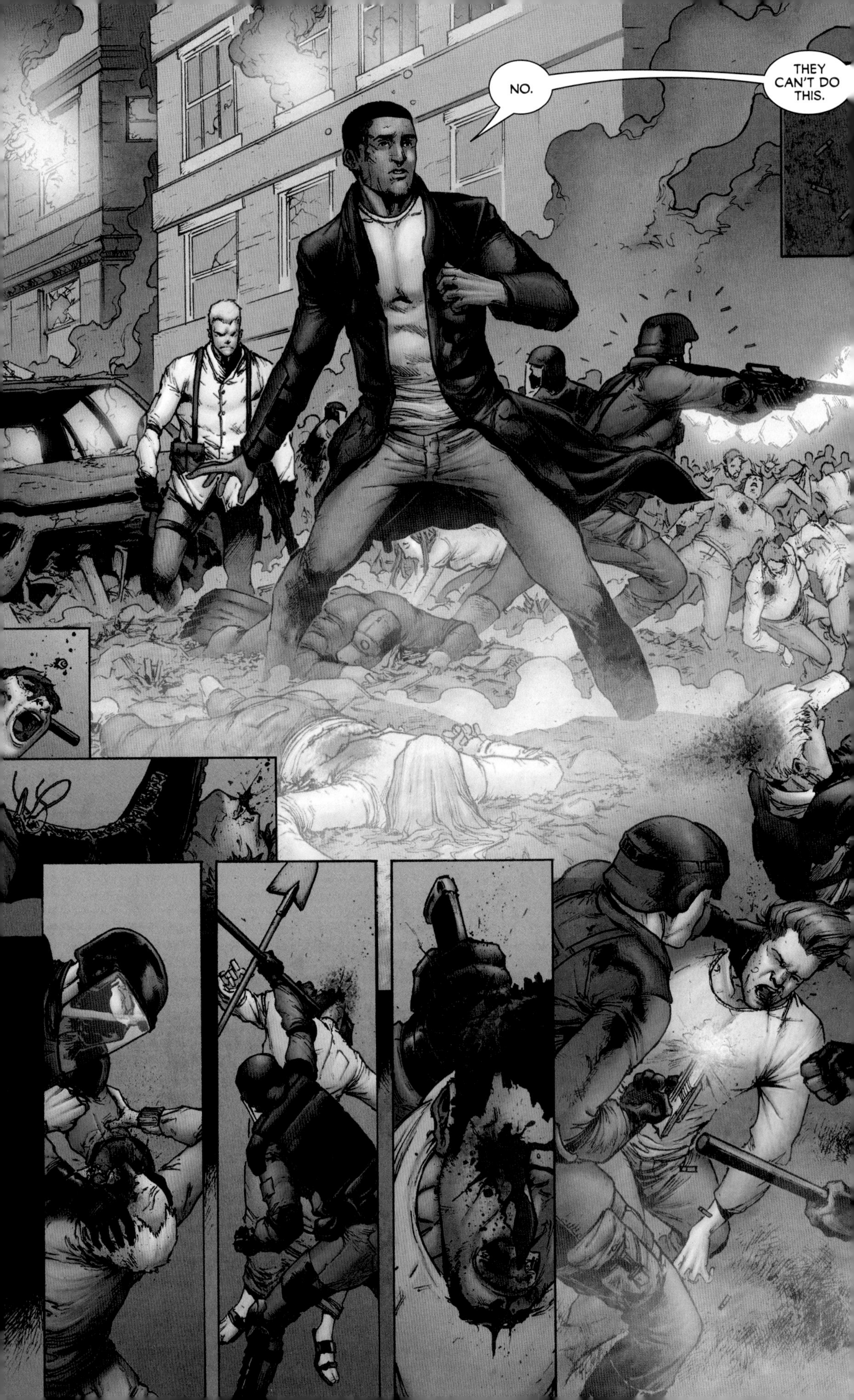
NO.
THEY CAN'T DO THIS.

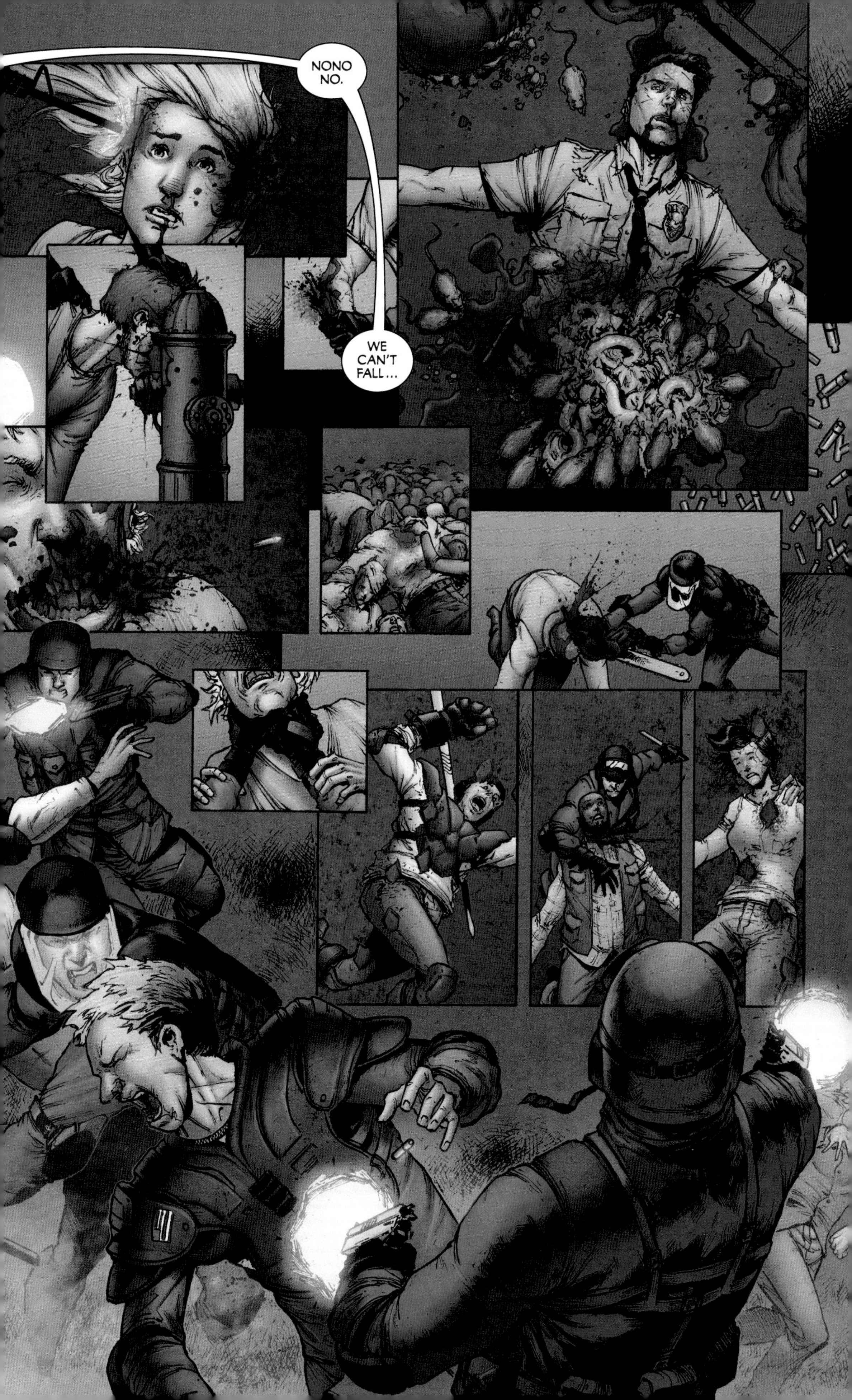
NONO NO.
WE CAN'T FALL...

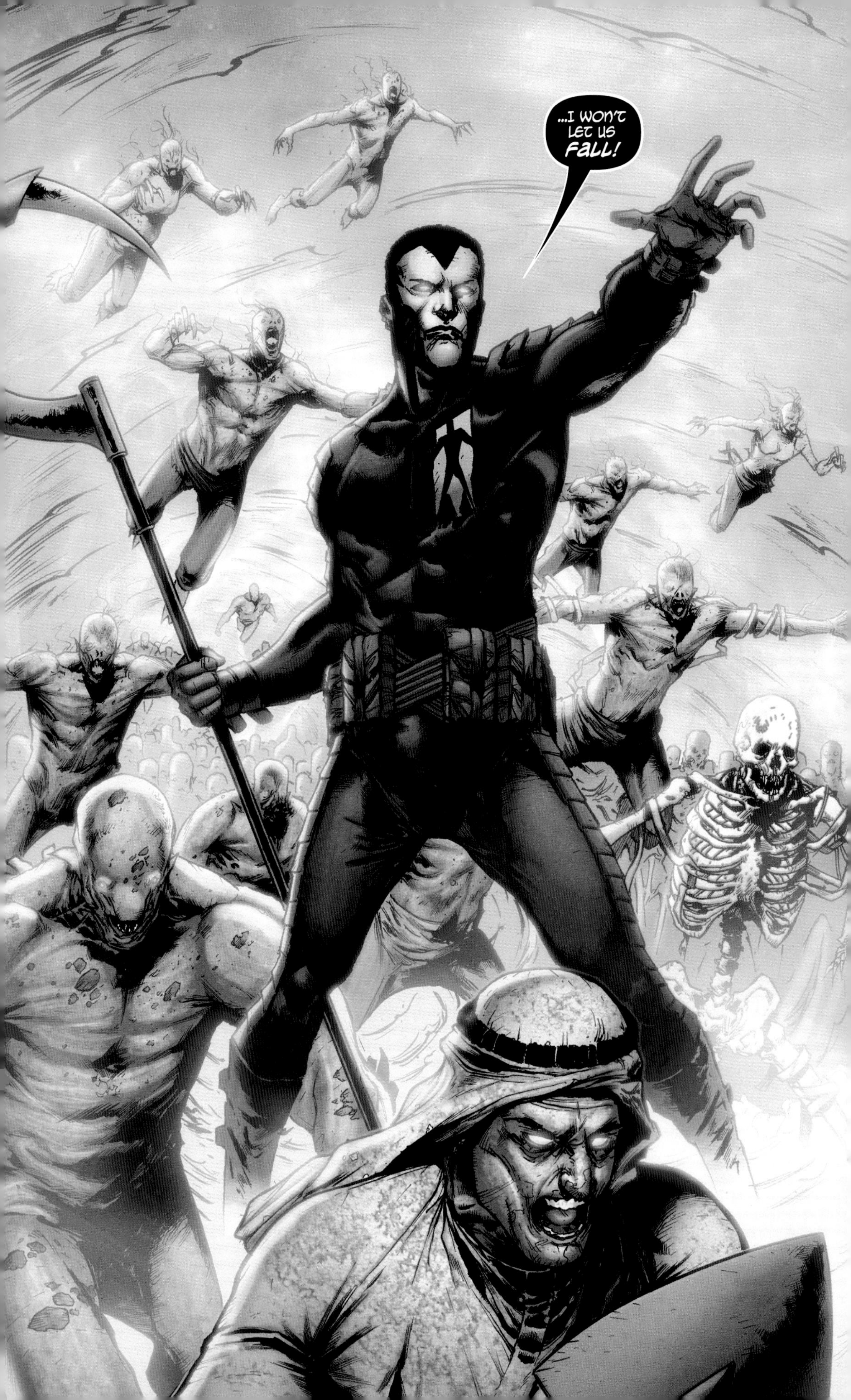
...I WON'T LET US FALL!

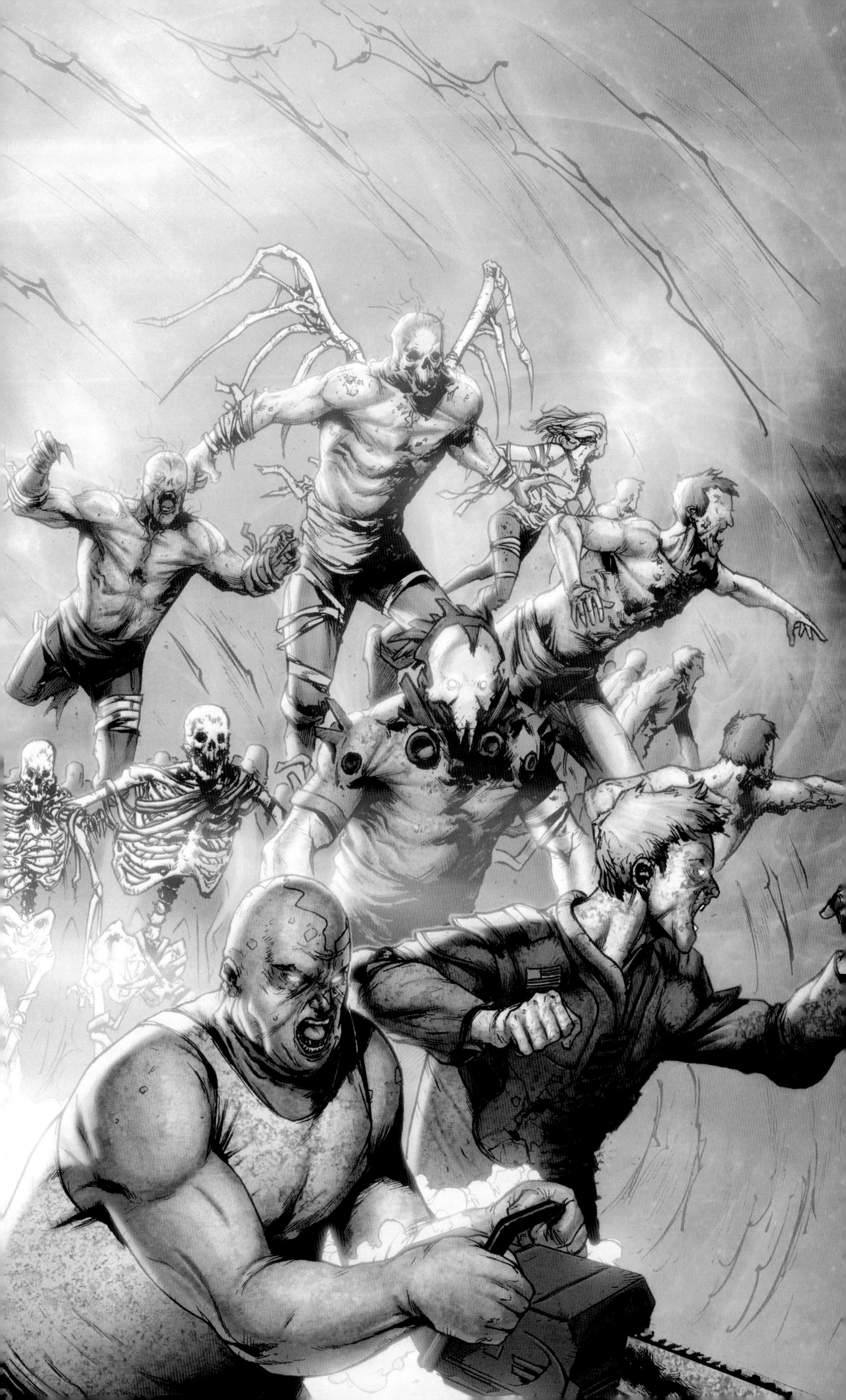

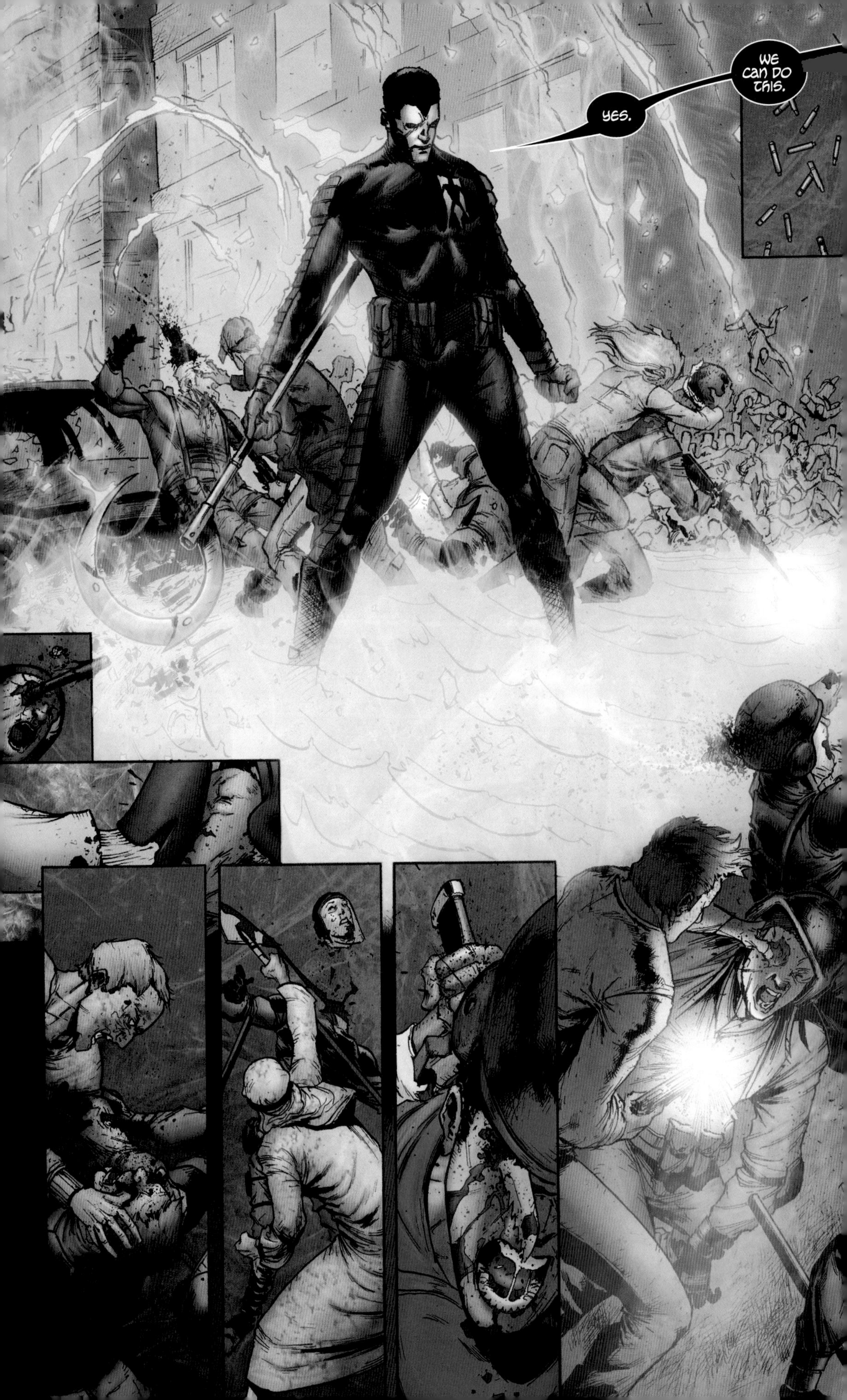
WE CAN DO THIS.
YES.

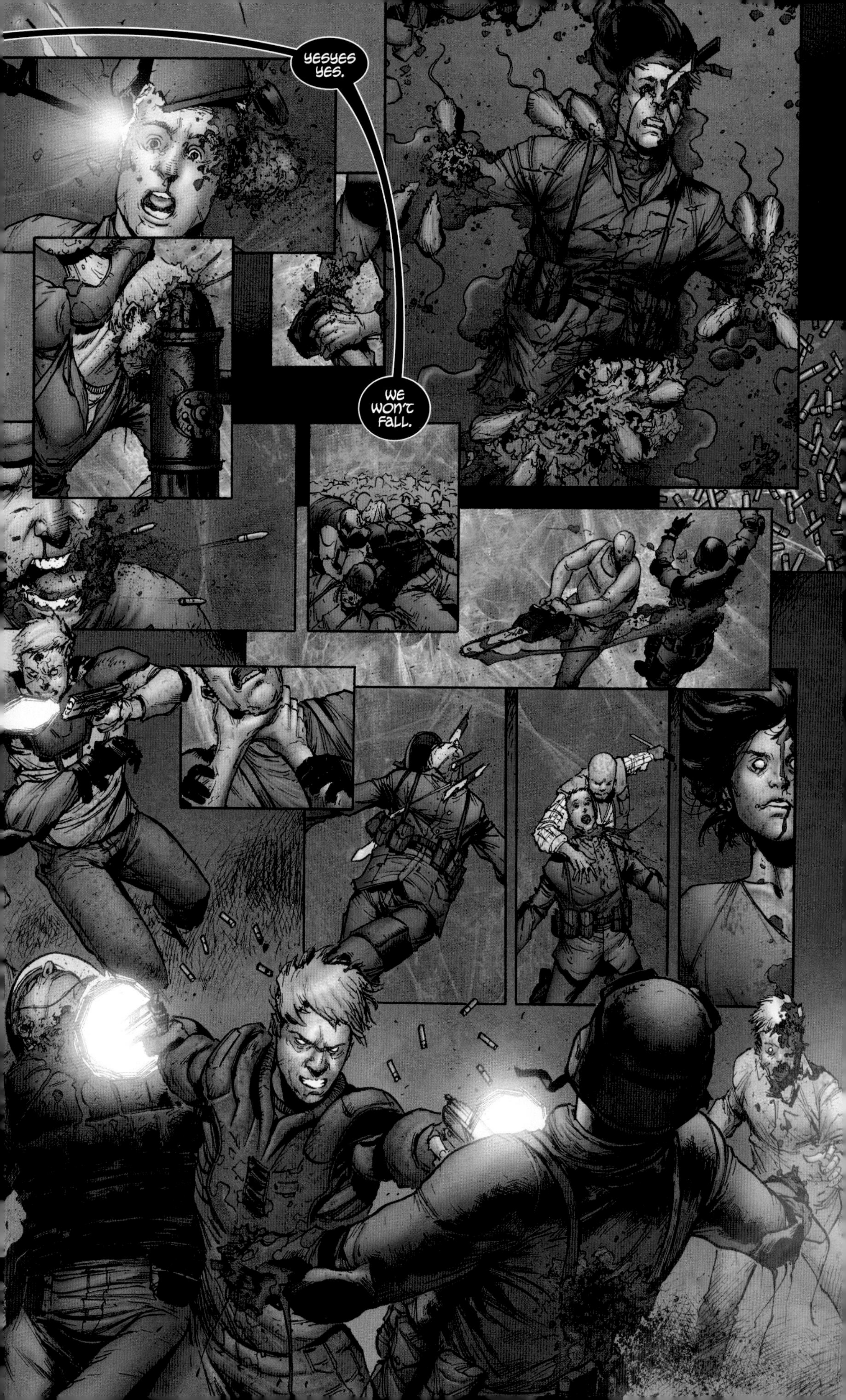
YESYES YES.
WE WON'T FALL.

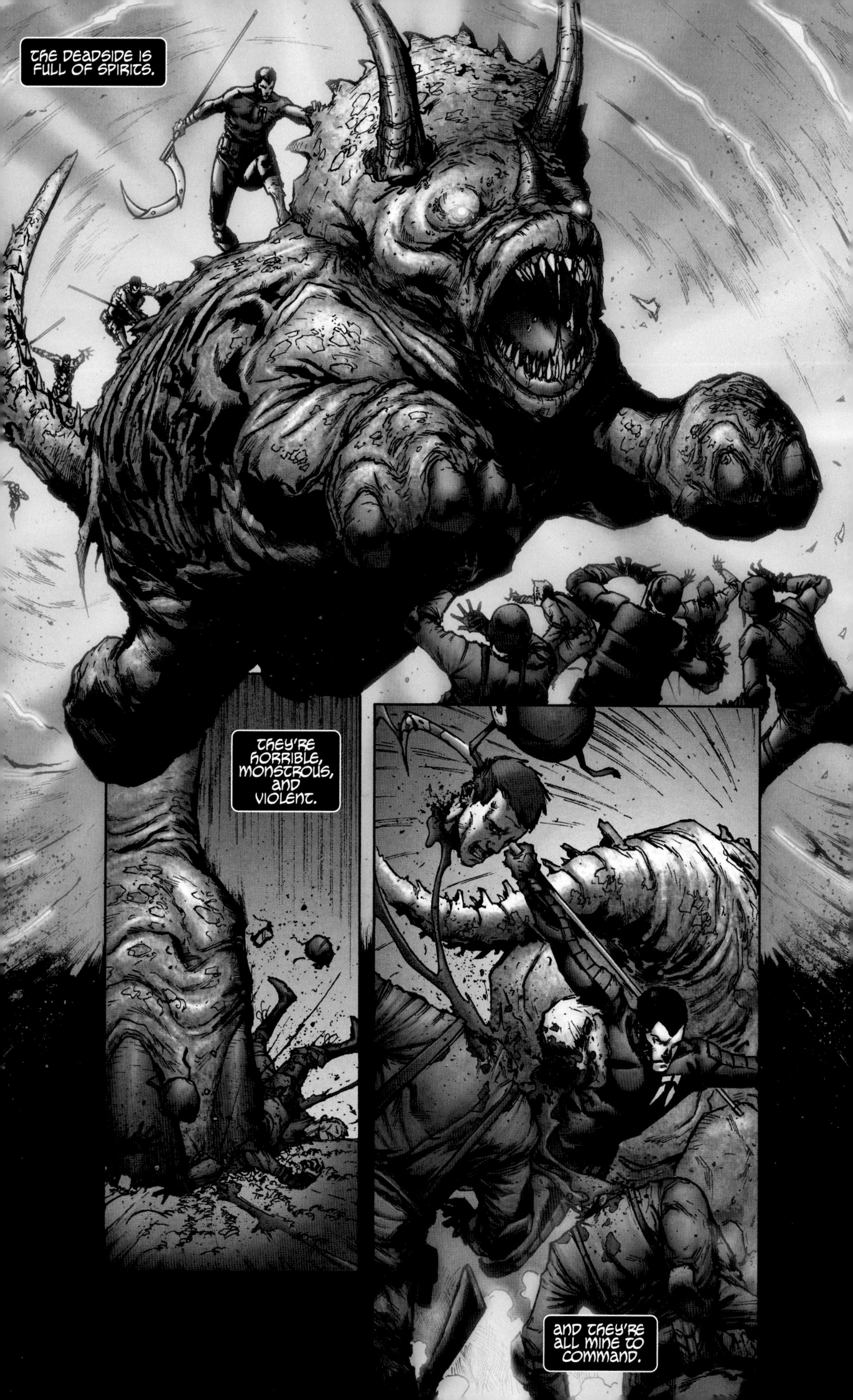
THE DEADSIDE IS FULL OF SPIRITS.
THEY'RE HORRIBLE, MONSTROUS, AND VIOLENT.
AND THEY'RE ALL MINE TO COMMAND.

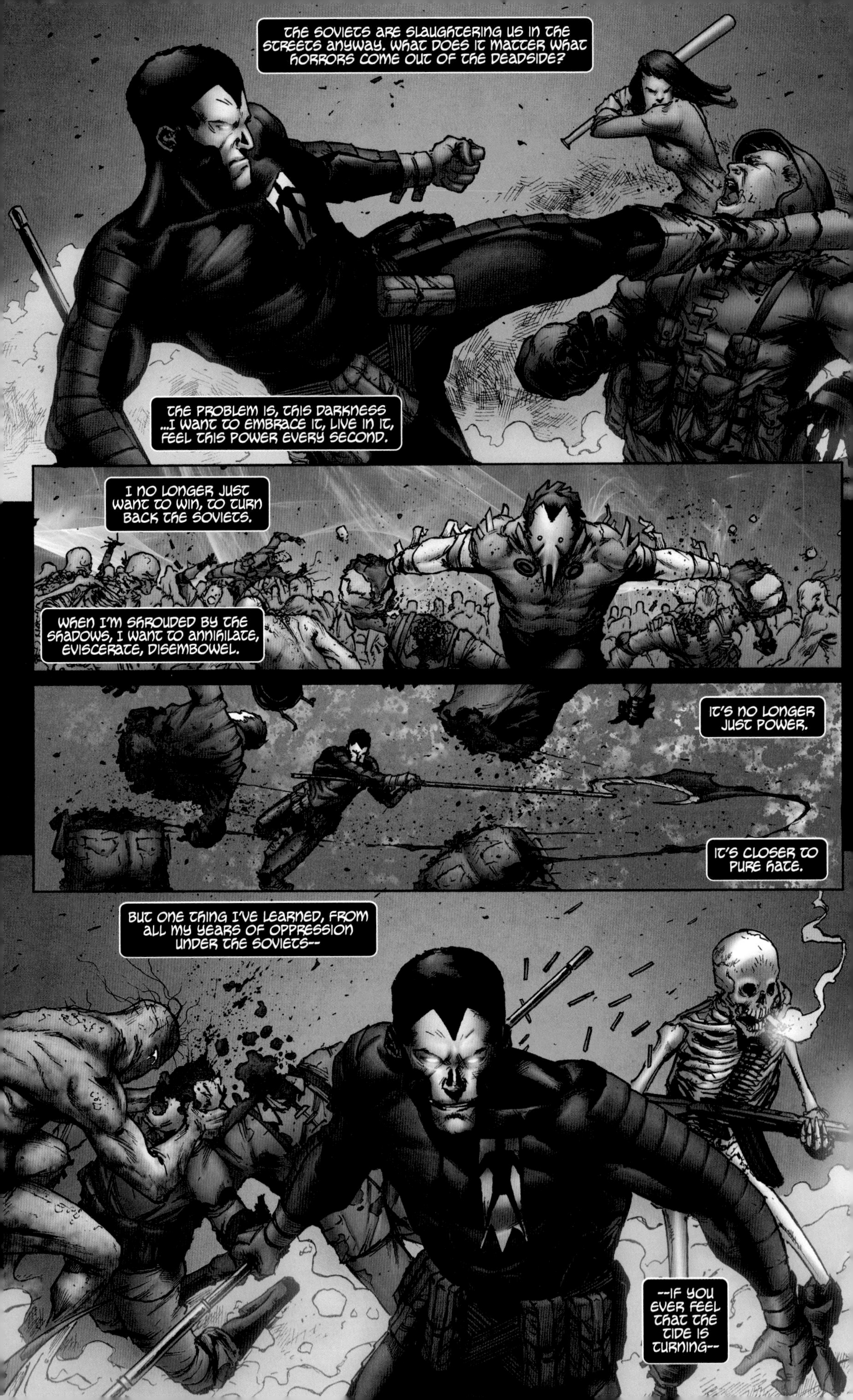
THE SOVIETS ARE SLAUGHTERING US IN THE STREETS ANYWAY. WHAT DOES IT MATTER WHAT HORRORS COME OUT OF THE DEADSIDE?
THE PROBLEM IS, THIS DARKNESS ...I WANT TO EMBRACE IT, LIVE IN IT, FEEL THIS POWER EVERY SECOND.
I NO LONGER JUST WANT TO WIN, TO TURN BACK THE SOVIETS.
WHEN I'M SHROUDED BY THE SHADOWS, I WANT TO ANNIHILATE, EVISCERATE, DISEMBOWEL.
IT'S NO LONGER JUST POWER.
IT'S CLOSER TO PURE HATE.
BUT ONE THING I'VE LEARNED, FROM ALL MY YEARS OF OPPRESSION UNDER THE SOVIETS--
--IF YOU EVER FEEL THAT THE TIDE IS TURNING--

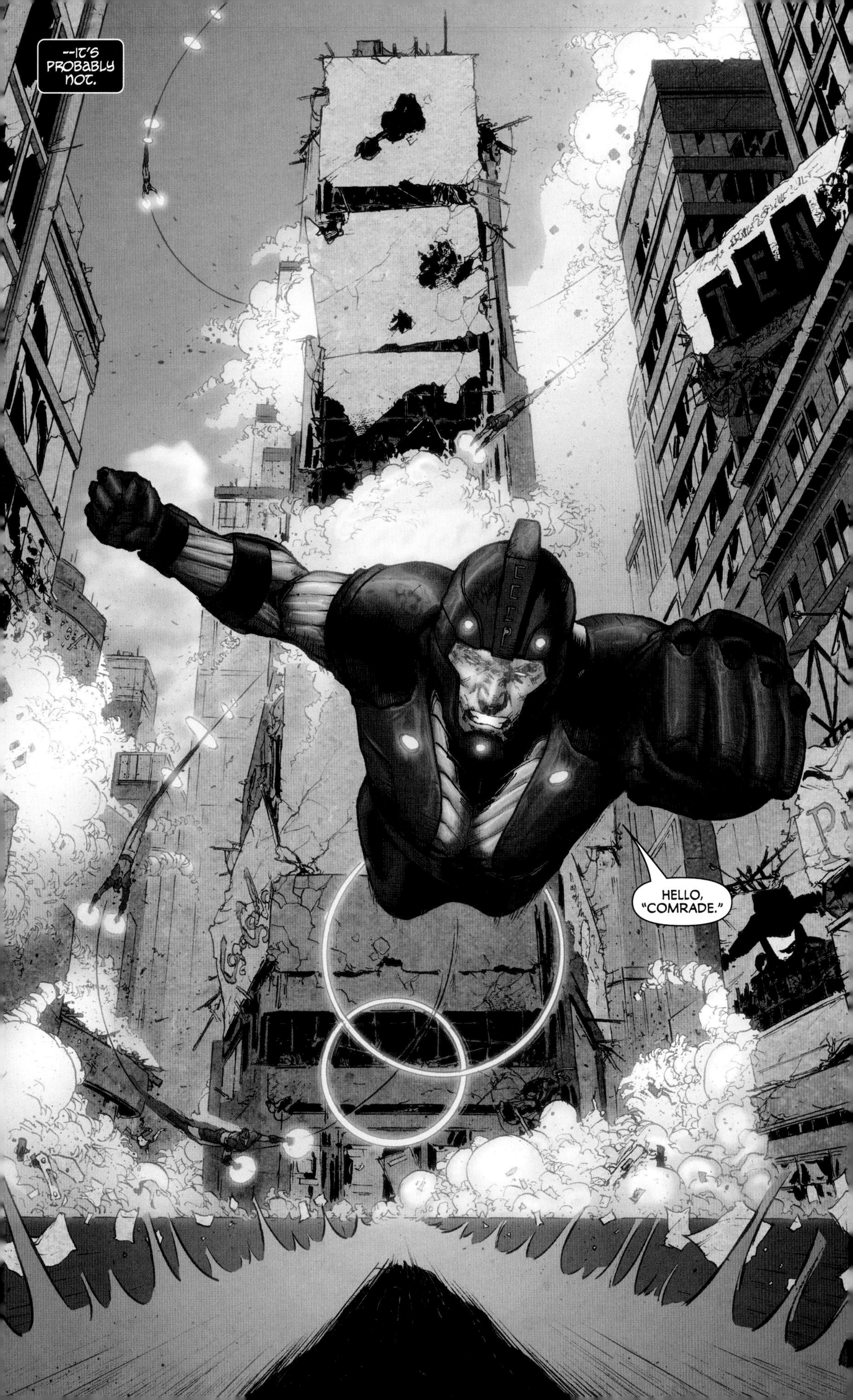
--IT'S PROBABLY NOT.
HELLO, "COMRADE."

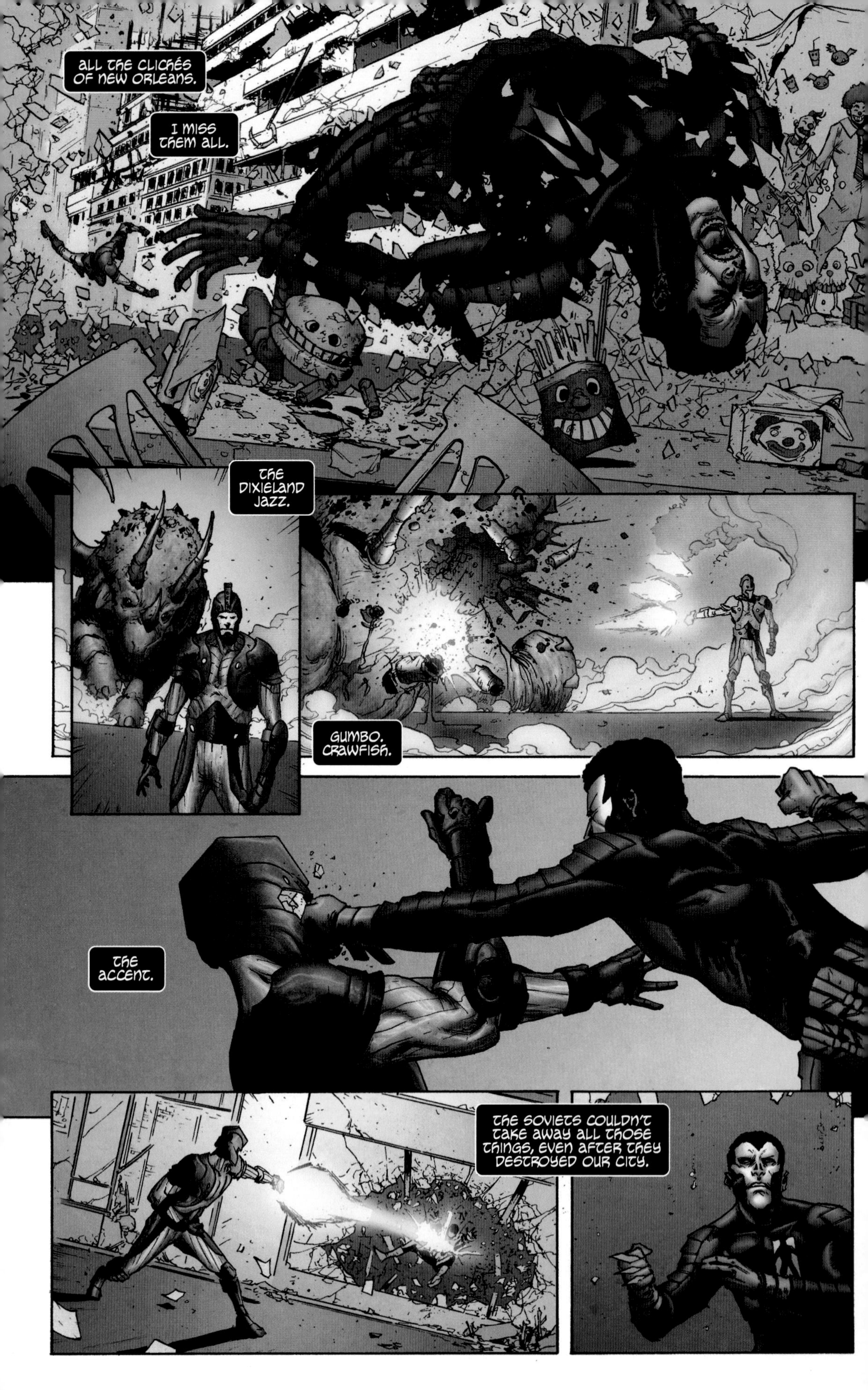
ALL THE CLICHÉS OF NEW ORLEANS.
I MISS THEM ALL.
THE DIXIELAND JAZZ.
GUMBO. CRAWFISH.
THE ACCENT.
THE SOVIETS COULDN'T TAKE AWAY ALL THOSE THINGS, EVEN AFTER THEY DESTROYED OUR CITY.

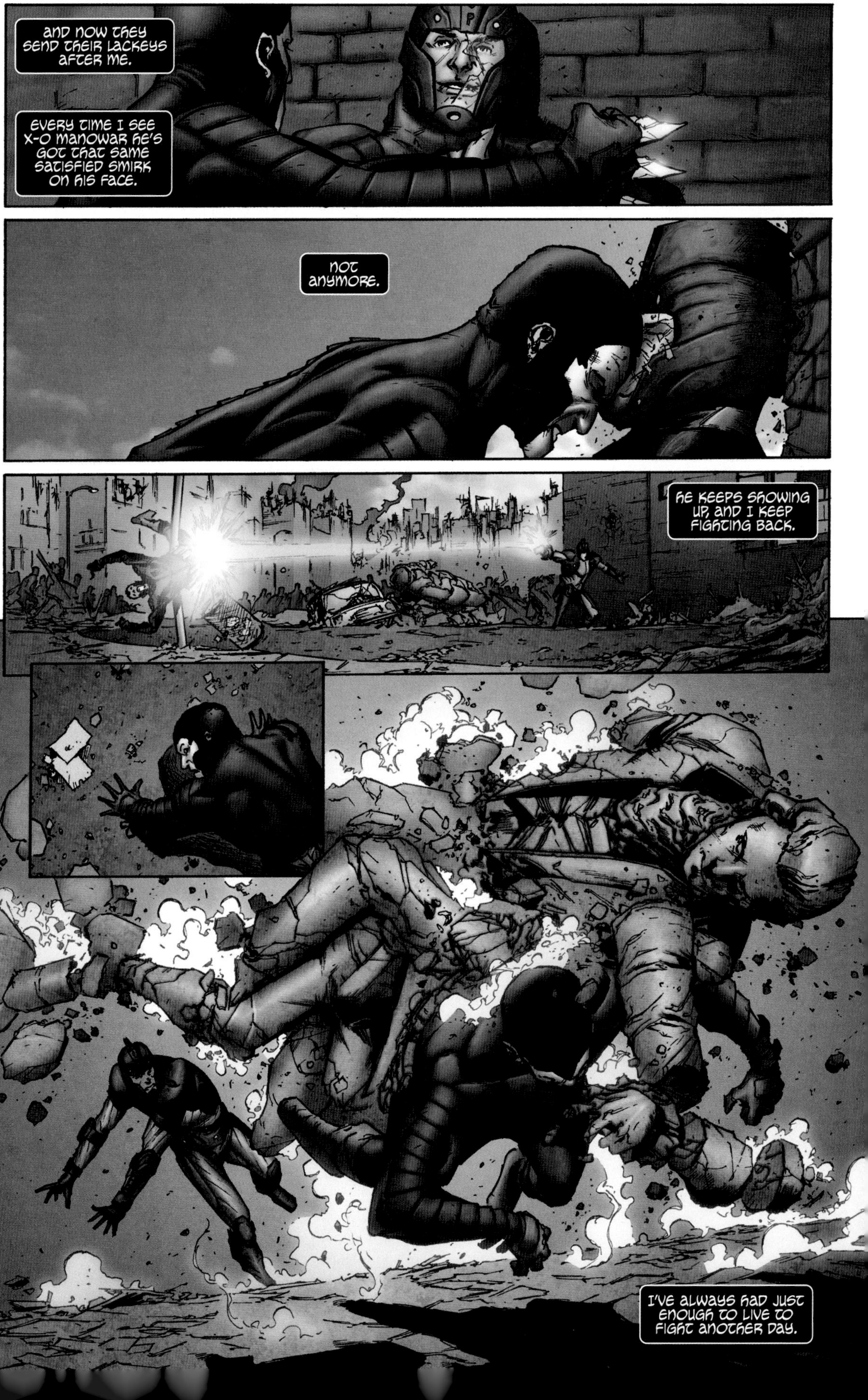
and now they send their lackeys after me.
Every time I see X-O Manowar he's got that same satisfied smirk on his face.
not anymore.
he keeps showing up, and I keep fighting back.
I've always had just enough to live to fight another day.

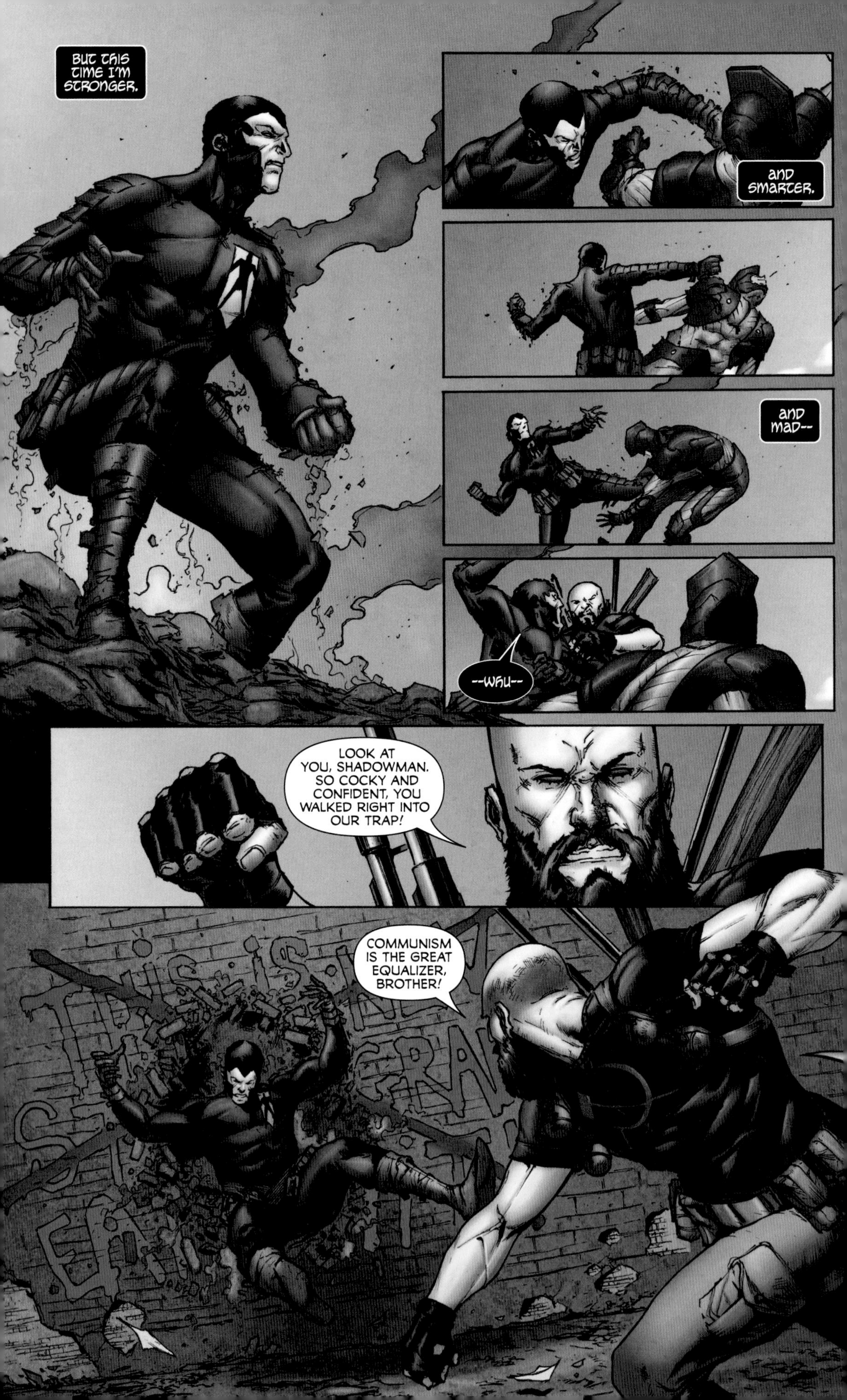
BUT THIS TIME I'M STRONGER.
AND SMARTER.
AND MAD--
--WHU--
LOOK AT YOU, SHADOWMAN. SO COCKY AND CONFIDENT, YOU WALKED RIGHT INTO OUR TRAP!
COMMUNISM IS THE GREAT EQUALIZER, BROTHER!

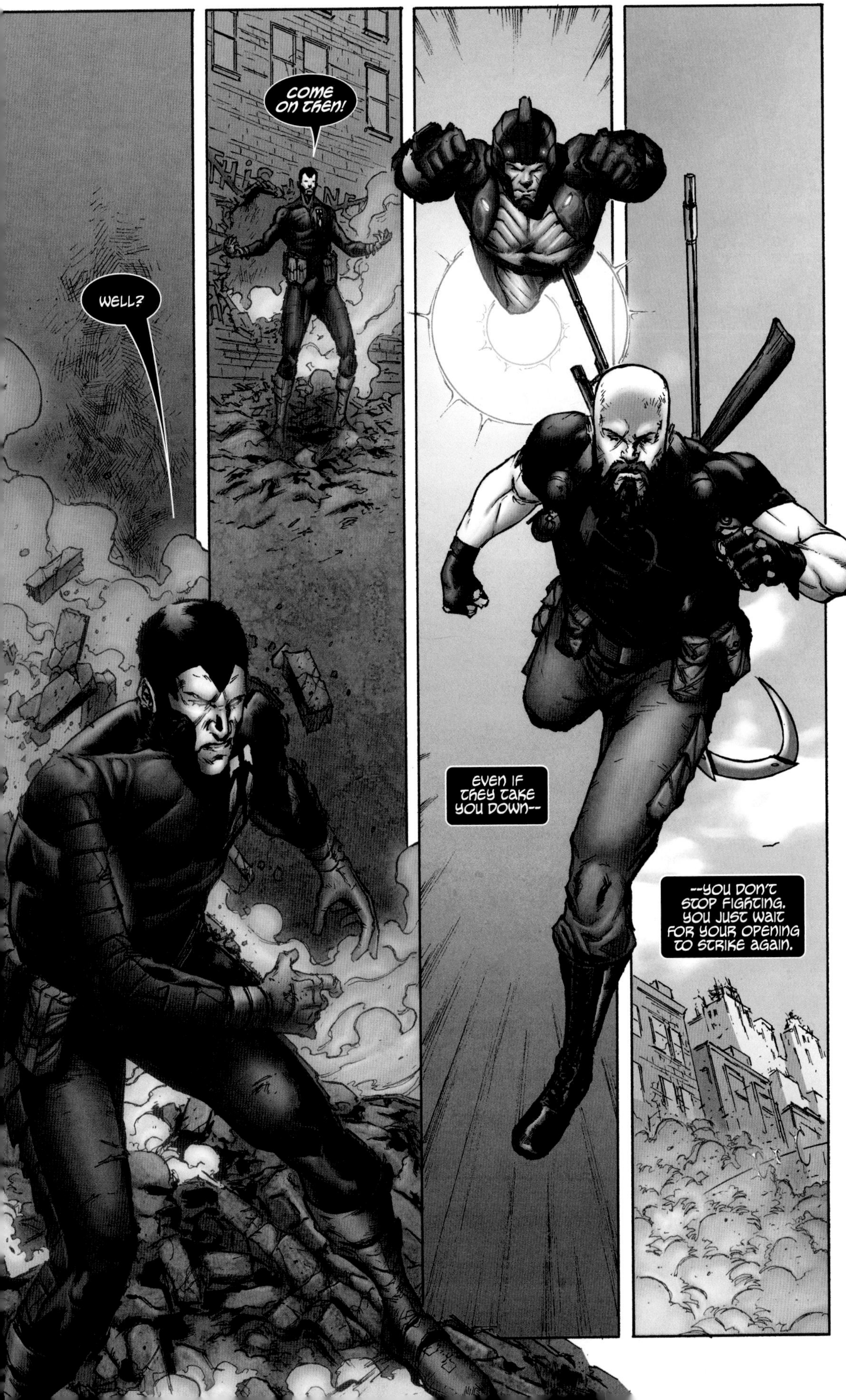
WELL?
COME ON THEN!
EVEN IF THEY TAKE YOU DOWN--
--YOU DON'T STOP FIGHTING. YOU JUST WAIT FOR YOUR OPENING TO STRIKE AGAIN.

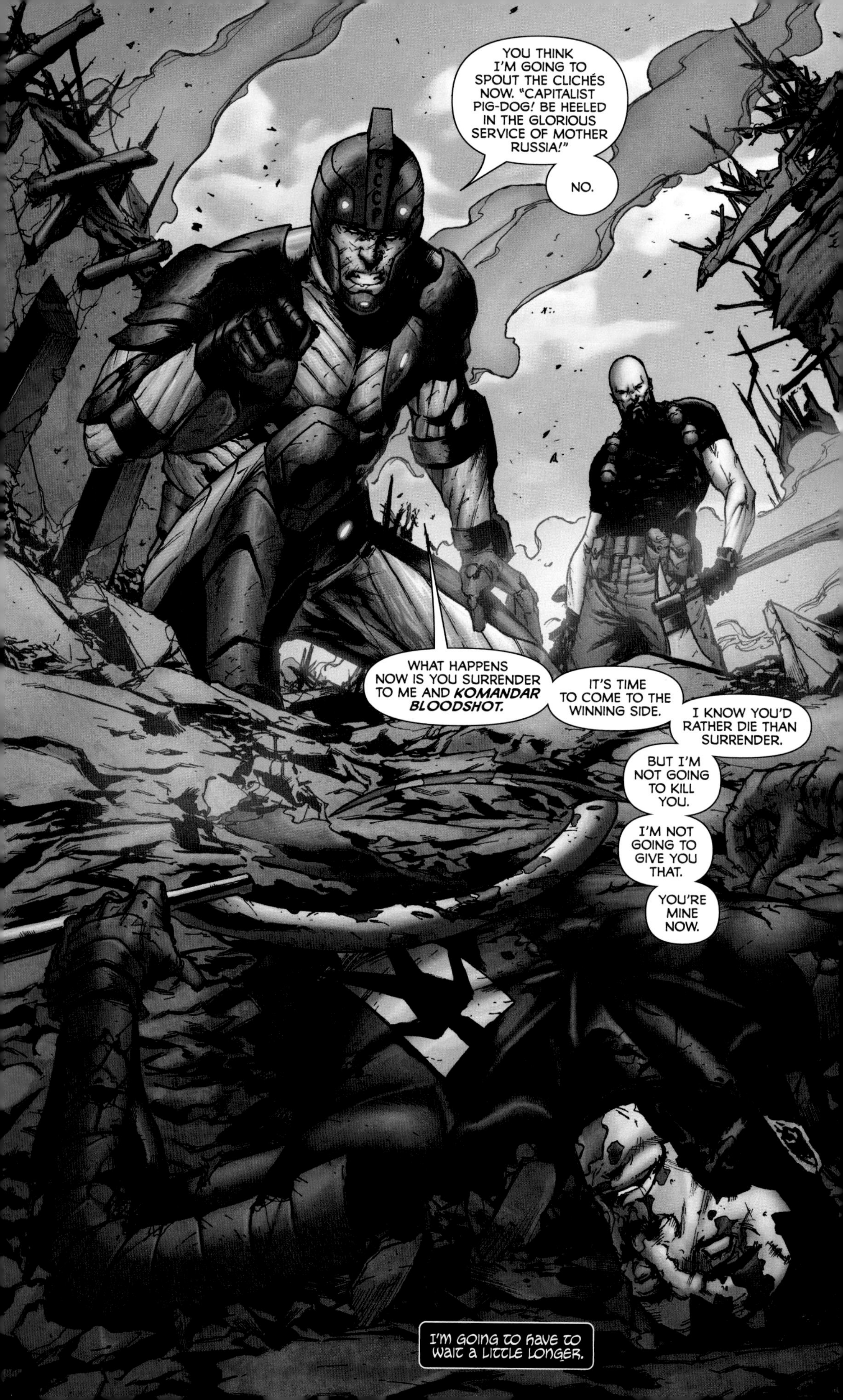
YOU THINK I'M GOING TO SPOUT THE CLICHÉS NOW. "CAPITALIST PIG-DOG! BE HEELED IN THE GLORIOUS SERVICE OF MOTHER RUSSIA!"
NO.
WHAT HAPPENS NOW IS YOU SURRENDER TO ME AND *KOMANDAR BLOODSHOT.*
IT'S TIME TO COME TO THE WINNING SIDE.
I KNOW YOU'D RATHER DIE THAN SURRENDER.
BUT I'M NOT GOING TO KILL YOU.
I'M NOT GOING TO GIVE YOU THAT.
YOU'RE MINE NOW.
I'M GOING TO HAVE TO WAIT A LITTLE LONGER.

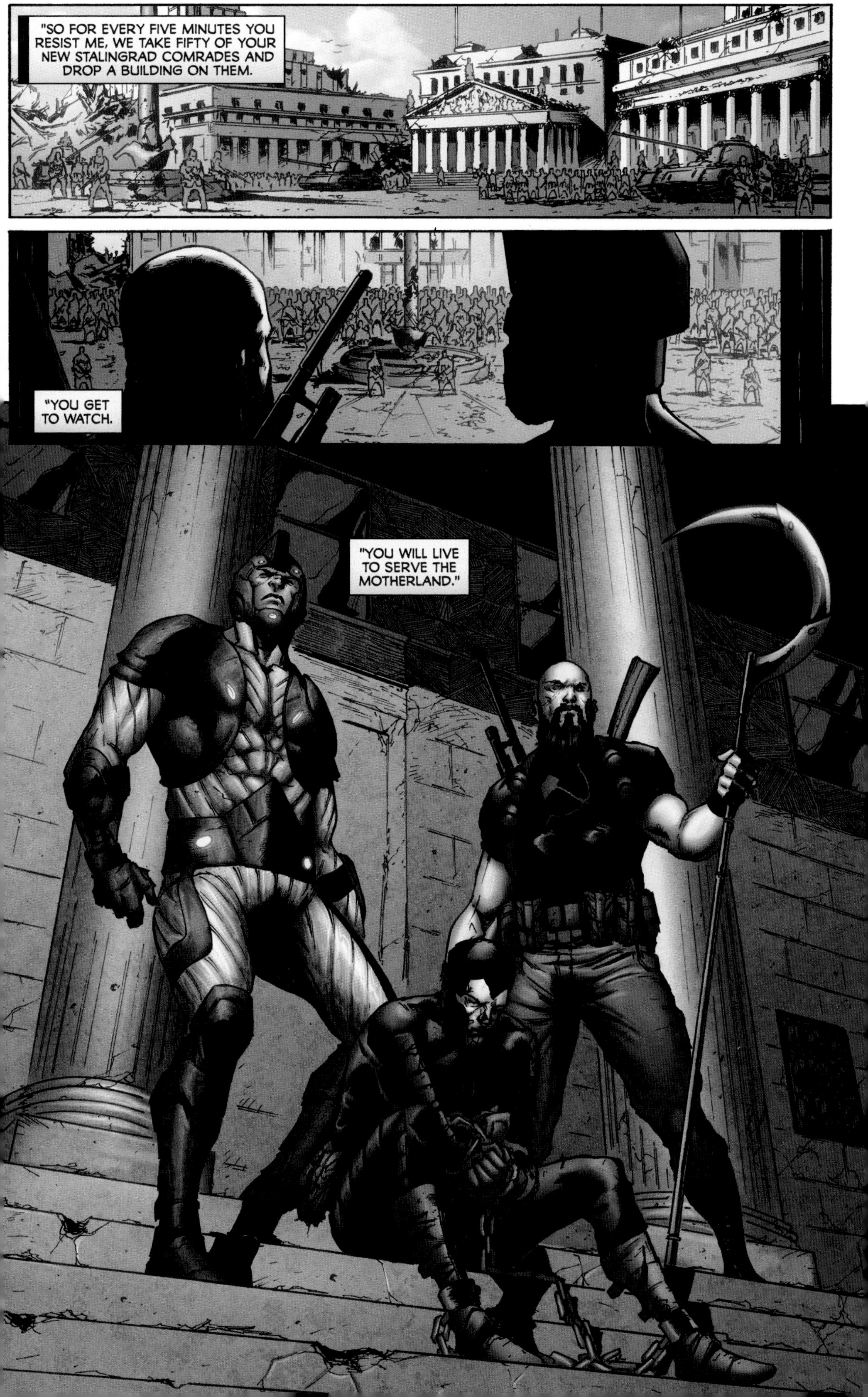
"SO FOR EVERY FIVE MINUTES YOU RESIST ME, WE TAKE FIFTY OF YOUR NEW STALINGRAD COMRADES AND DROP A BUILDING ON THEM.
"YOU GET TO WATCH.
"YOU WILL LIVE TO SERVE THE MOTHERLAND."

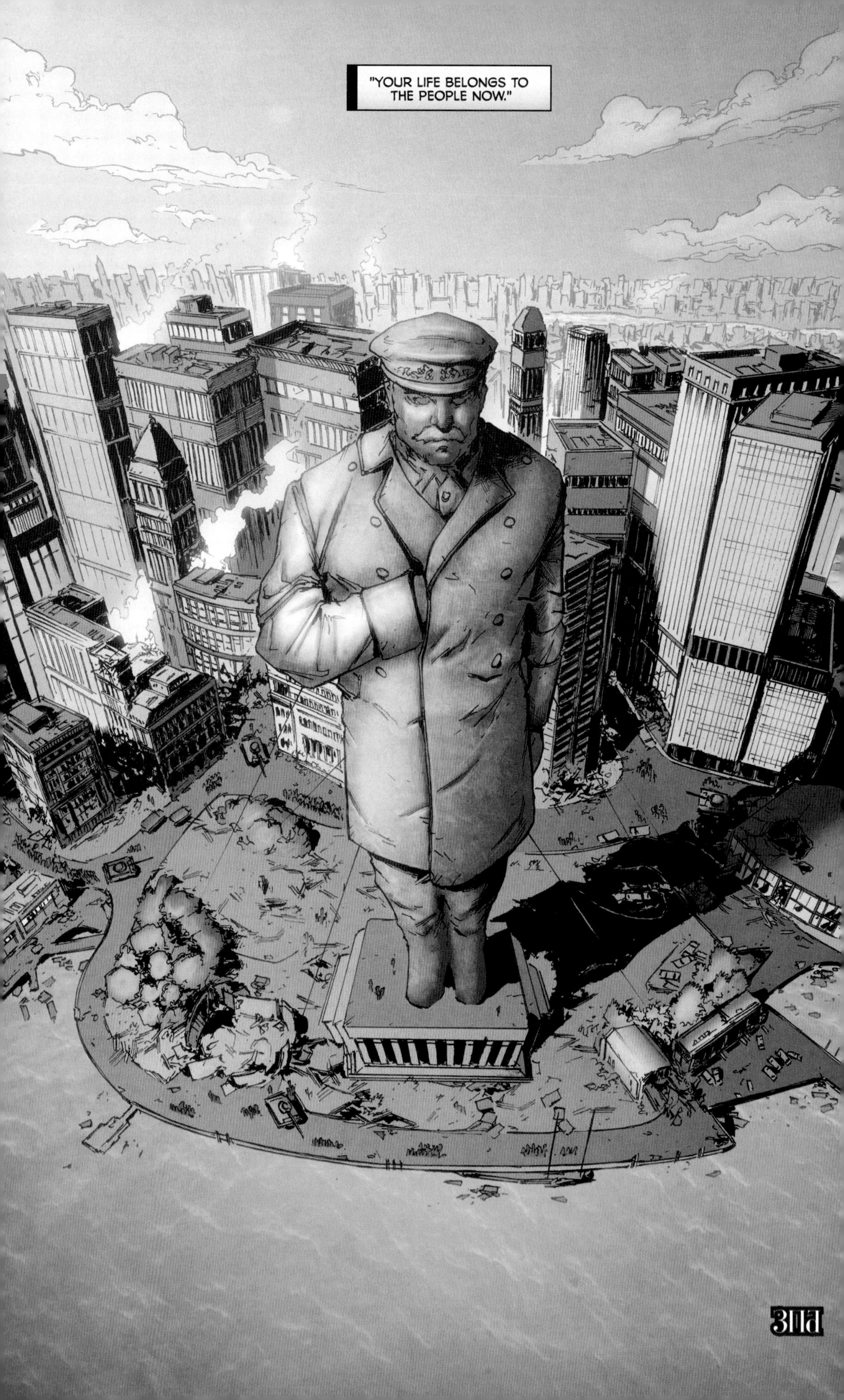
"YOUR LIFE BELONGS TO THE PEOPLE NOW."

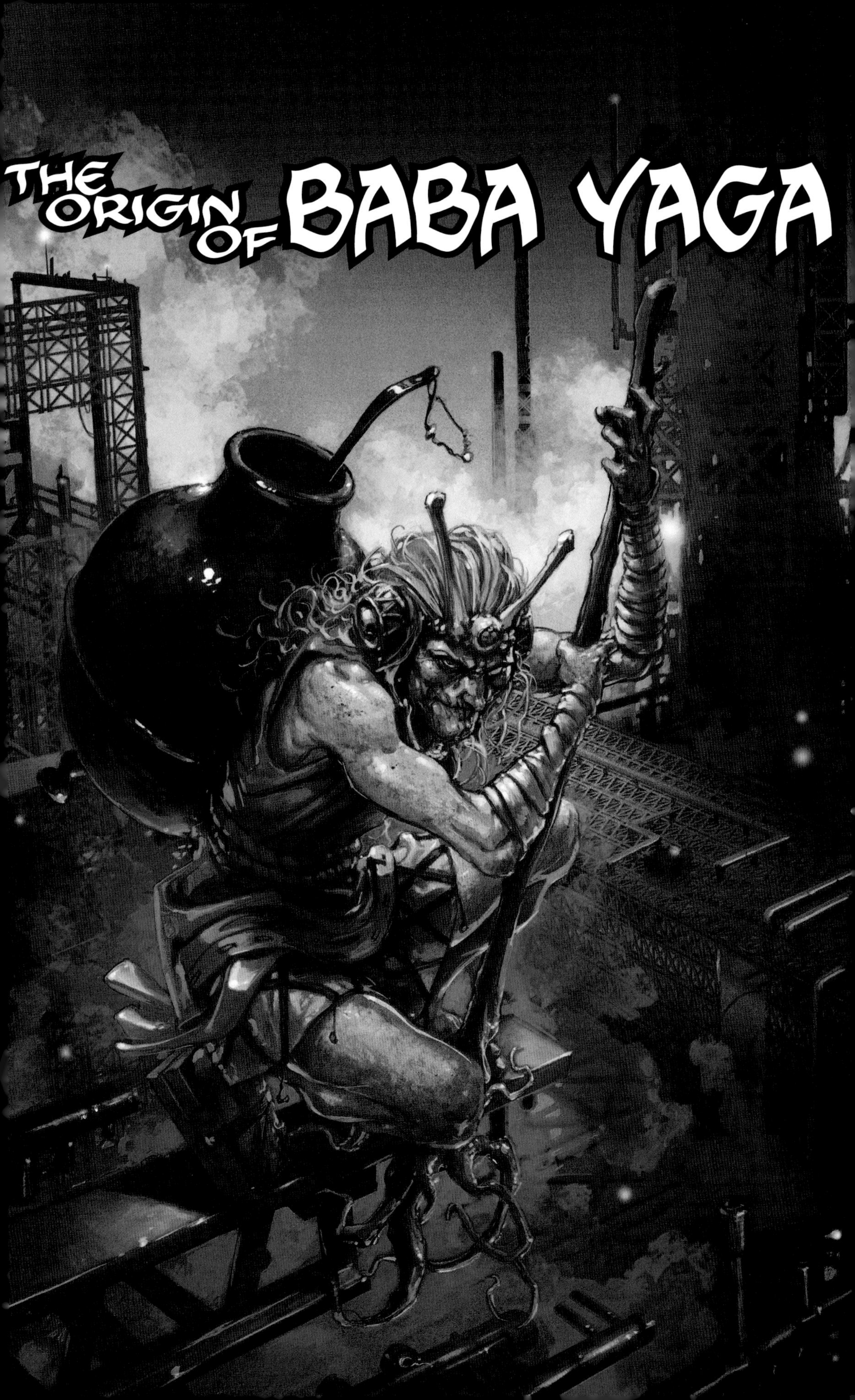
THE ORIGIN OF BABA YAGA

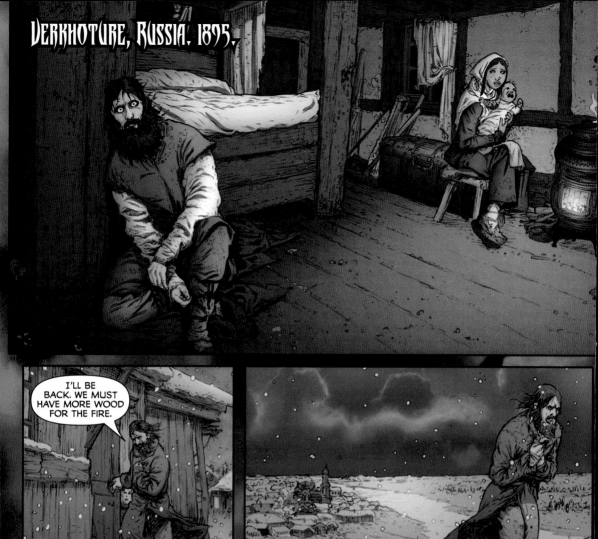

I'LL BE BACK. WE MUST HAVE MORE WOOD FOR THE FIRE.

"THAT WAS THE YEAR THAT GRIGORI RASPUTIN LEFT HIS WIFE AND CHILD.

"THAT WAS THE YEAR GRIGORI TRAVELED SOUTH TO THE HOLY LAND."

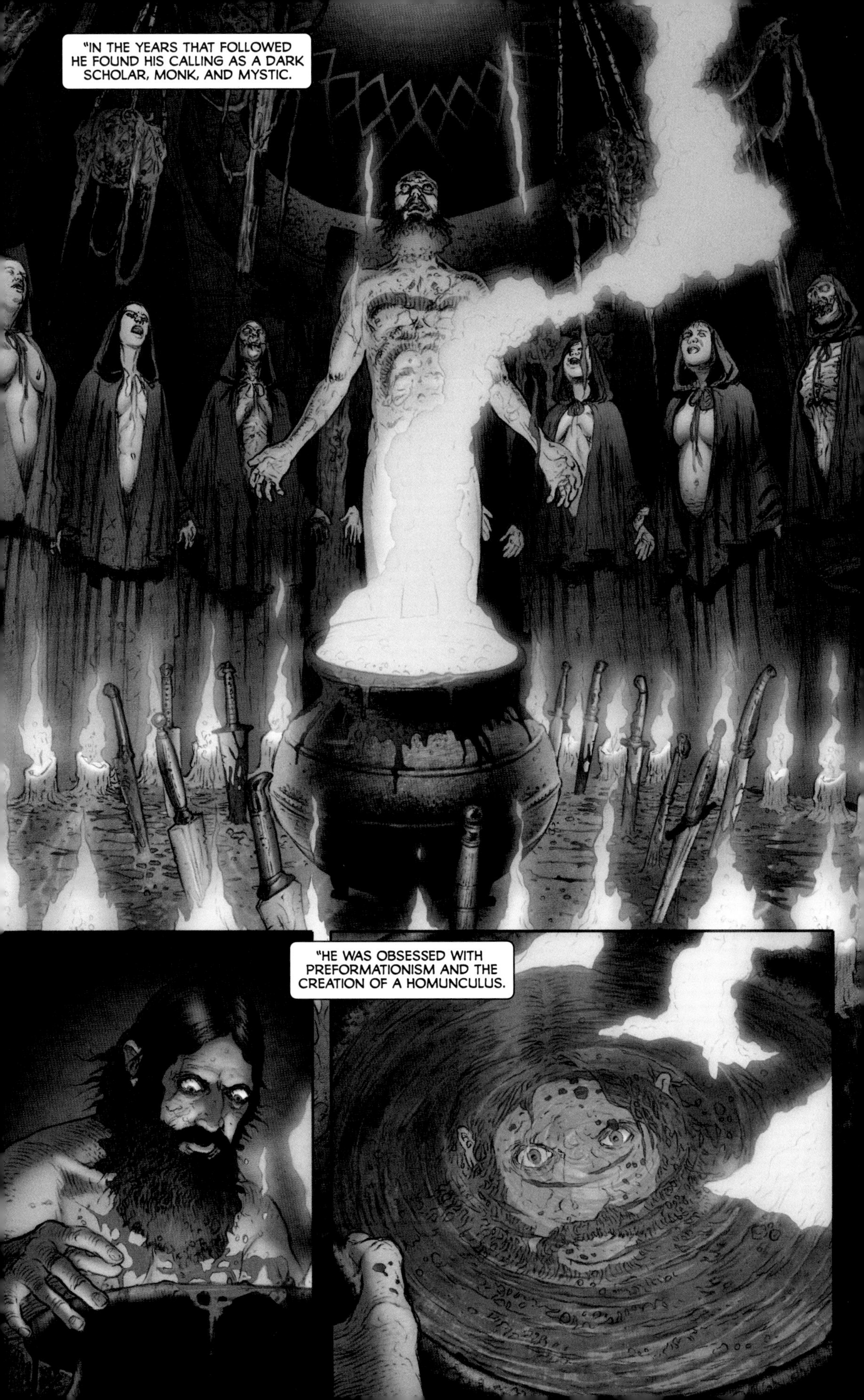
"IN THE YEARS THAT FOLLOWED HE FOUND HIS CALLING AS A DARK SCHOLAR, MONK, AND MYSTIC.
"HE WAS OBSESSED WITH PREFORMATIONISM AND THE CREATION OF A HOMUNCULUS.

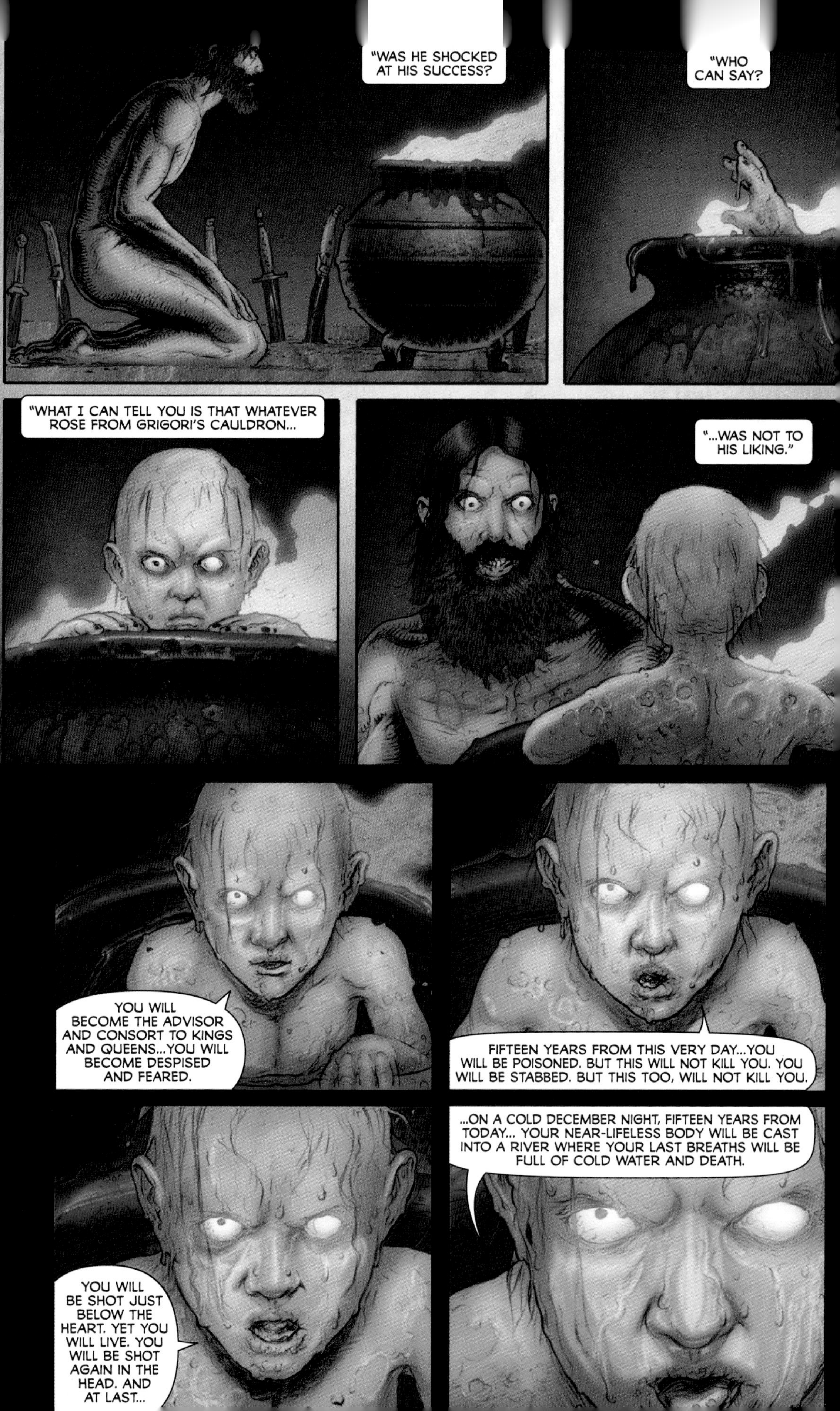
"WAS HE SHOCKED AT HIS SUCCESS?
"WHO CAN SAY?
"WHAT I CAN TELL YOU IS THAT WHATEVER ROSE FROM GRIGORI'S CAULDRON...
"...WAS NOT TO HIS LIKING."
YOU WILL BECOME THE ADVISOR AND CONSORT TO KINGS AND QUEENS...YOU WILL BECOME DESPISED AND FEARED.
FIFTEEN YEARS FROM THIS VERY DAY...YOU WILL BE POISONED. BUT THIS WILL NOT KILL YOU. YOU WILL BE STABBED. BUT THIS TOO, WILL NOT KILL YOU.
YOU WILL BE SHOT JUST BELOW THE HEART. YET YOU WILL LIVE. YOU WILL BE SHOT AGAIN IN THE HEAD. AND AT LAST...
...ON A COLD DECEMBER NIGHT, FIFTEEN YEARS FROM TODAY... YOUR NEAR-LIFELESS BODY WILL BE CAST INTO A RIVER WHERE YOUR LAST BREATHS WILL BE FULL OF COLD WATER AND DEATH.

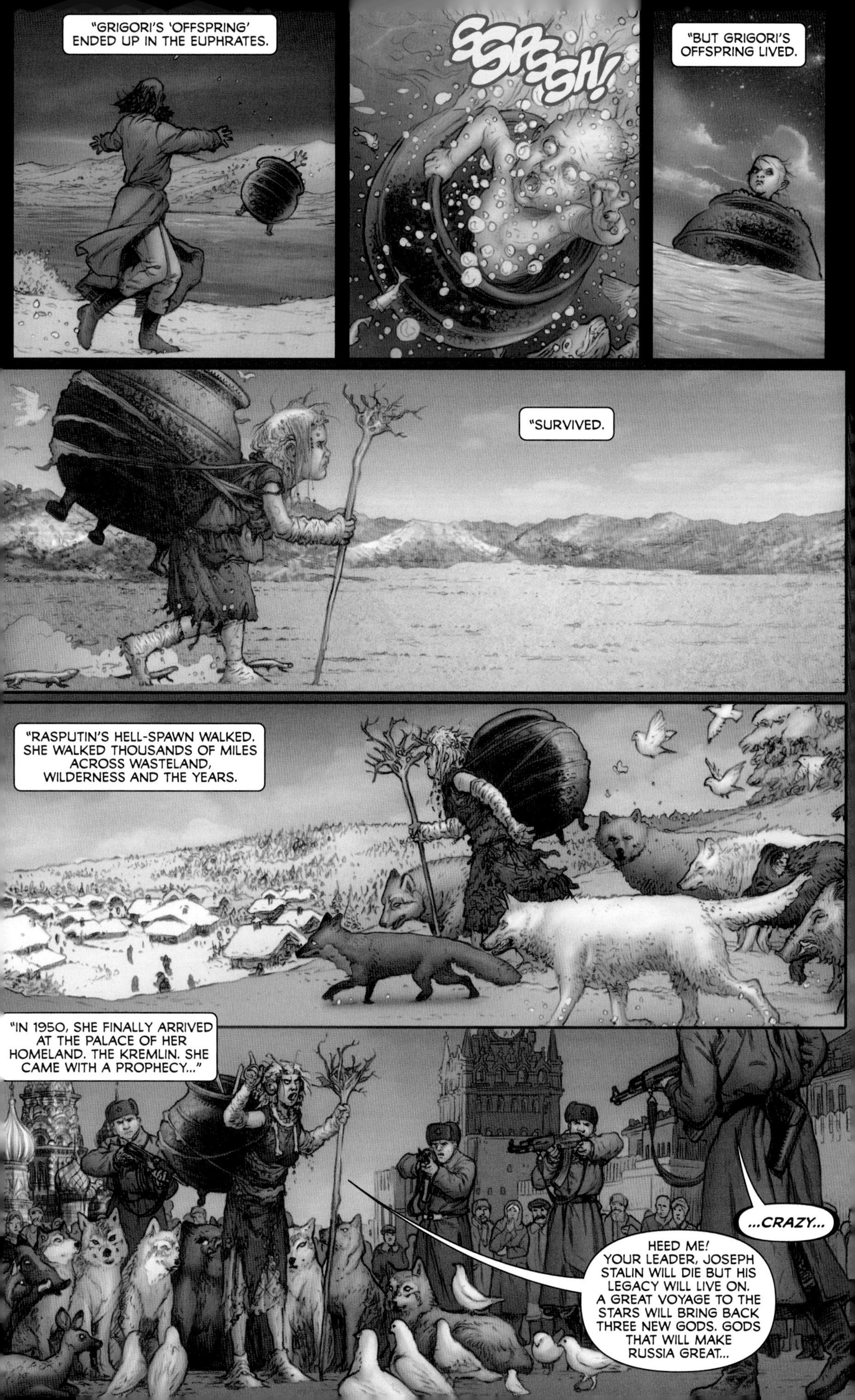
"GRIGORI'S 'OFFSPRING' ENDED UP IN THE EUPHRATES.
SSPSSH!
"BUT GRIGORI'S OFFSPRING LIVED.
"SURVIVED.
"RASPUTIN'S HELL-SPAWN WALKED. SHE WALKED THOUSANDS OF MILES ACROSS WASTELAND, WILDERNESS AND THE YEARS.
"IN 1950, SHE FINALLY ARRIVED AT THE PALACE OF HER HOMELAND. THE KREMLIN. SHE CAME WITH A PROPHECY..."
...CRAZY...
HEED ME! YOUR LEADER, JOSEPH STALIN WILL DIE BUT HIS LEGACY WILL LIVE ON. A GREAT VOYAGE TO THE STARS WILL BRING BACK THREE NEW GODS. GODS THAT WILL MAKE RUSSIA GREAT...

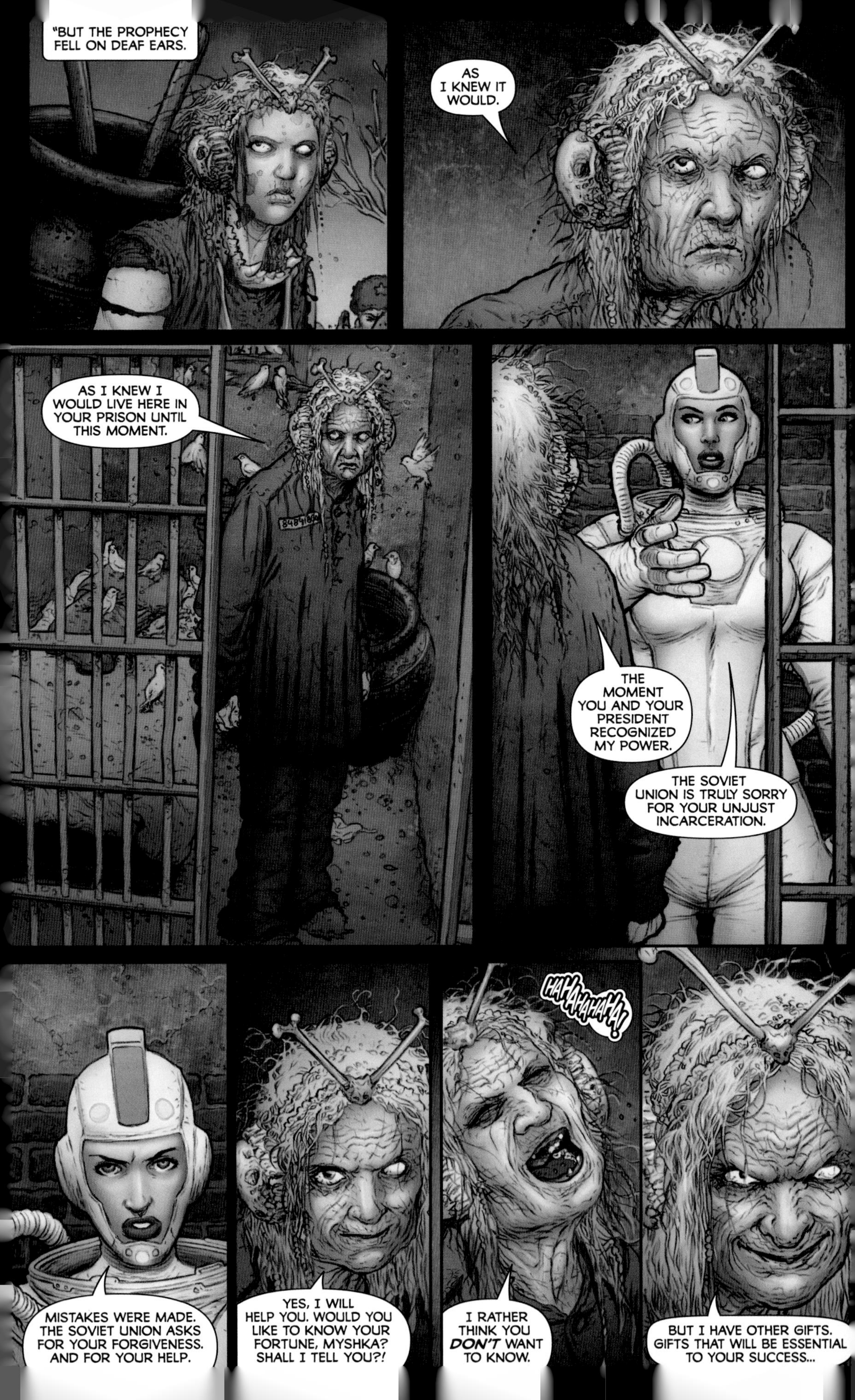
"BUT THE PROPHECY FELL ON DEAF EARS.
AS I KNEW IT WOULD.
AS I KNEW I WOULD LIVE HERE IN YOUR PRISON UNTIL THIS MOMENT.
THE MOMENT YOU AND YOUR PRESIDENT RECOGNIZED MY POWER.
THE SOVIET UNION IS TRULY SORRY FOR YOUR UNJUST INCARCERATION.
MISTAKES WERE MADE. THE SOVIET UNION ASKS FOR YOUR FORGIVENESS. AND FOR YOUR HELP.
YES, I WILL HELP YOU. WOULD YOU LIKE TO KNOW YOUR FORTUNE, MYSHKA? SHALL I TELL YOU?!
HAHAHAHAHA!
I RATHER THINK YOU *DON'T* WANT TO KNOW.
BUT I HAVE OTHER GIFTS. GIFTS THAT WILL BE ESSENTIAL TO YOUR SUCCESS...

VALIANT
STALINVERSE #1
DIVINITY III
ESCAPE FROM
GULAG 396
ELIOT RAHAL | FRANCIS PORTELA | ANDREW DALHOUSE
PLUS: THE ORIGIN OF
THE PIONEER

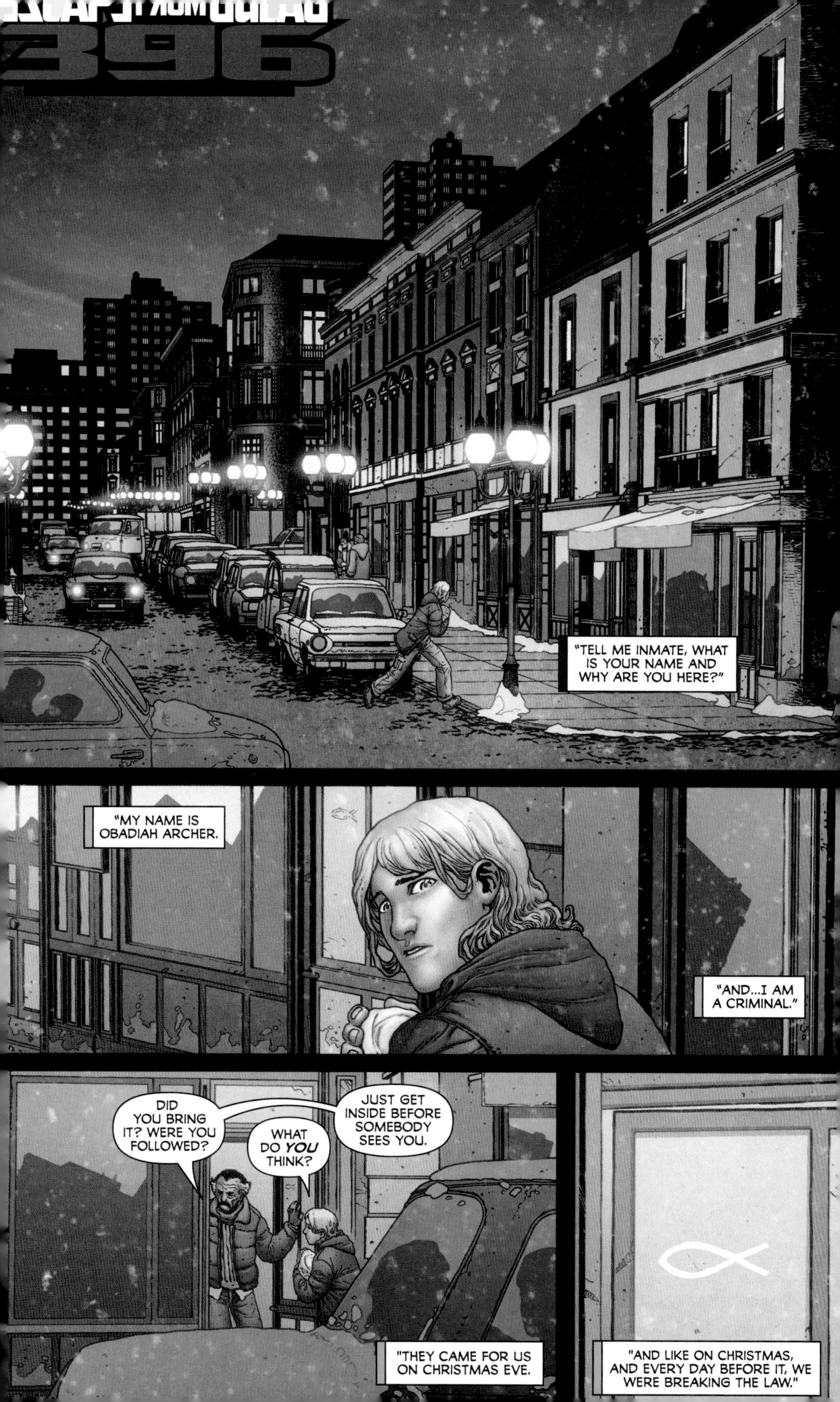
ESCAPE FROM GULAG 396
"TELL ME INMATE, WHAT IS YOUR NAME AND WHY ARE YOU HERE?"
"MY NAME IS OBADIAH ARCHER.
"AND...I AM A CRIMINAL."
DID YOU BRING IT? WERE YOU FOLLOWED?
WHAT DO *YOU* THINK?
JUST GET INSIDE BEFORE SOMEBODY SEES YOU.
"THEY CAME FOR US ON CHRISTMAS EVE.
"AND LIKE ON CHRISTMAS, AND EVERY DAY BEFORE IT, WE WERE BREAKING THE LAW."

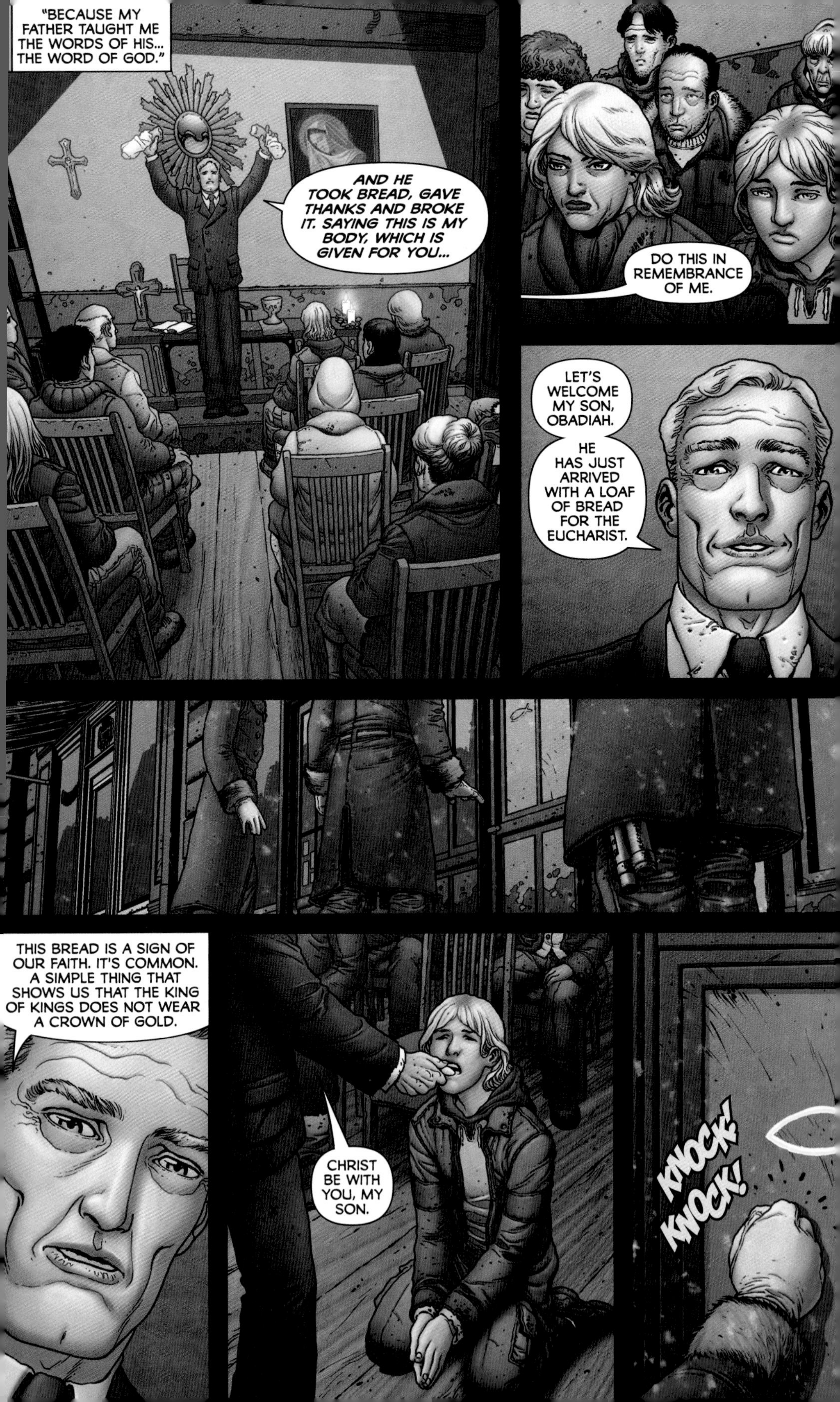
"BECAUSE MY FATHER TAUGHT ME THE WORDS OF HIS... THE WORD OF GOD."
AND HE TOOK BREAD, GAVE THANKS AND BROKE IT. SAYING THIS IS MY BODY, WHICH IS GIVEN FOR YOU...
DO THIS IN REMEMBRANCE OF ME.
LET'S WELCOME MY SON, OBADIAH.
HE HAS JUST ARRIVED WITH A LOAF OF BREAD FOR THE EUCHARIST.
THIS BREAD IS A SIGN OF OUR FAITH. IT'S COMMON. A SIMPLE THING THAT SHOWS US THAT THE KING OF KINGS DOES NOT WEAR A CROWN OF GOLD.
CHRIST BE WITH YOU, MY SON.
KNOCK! KNOCK!

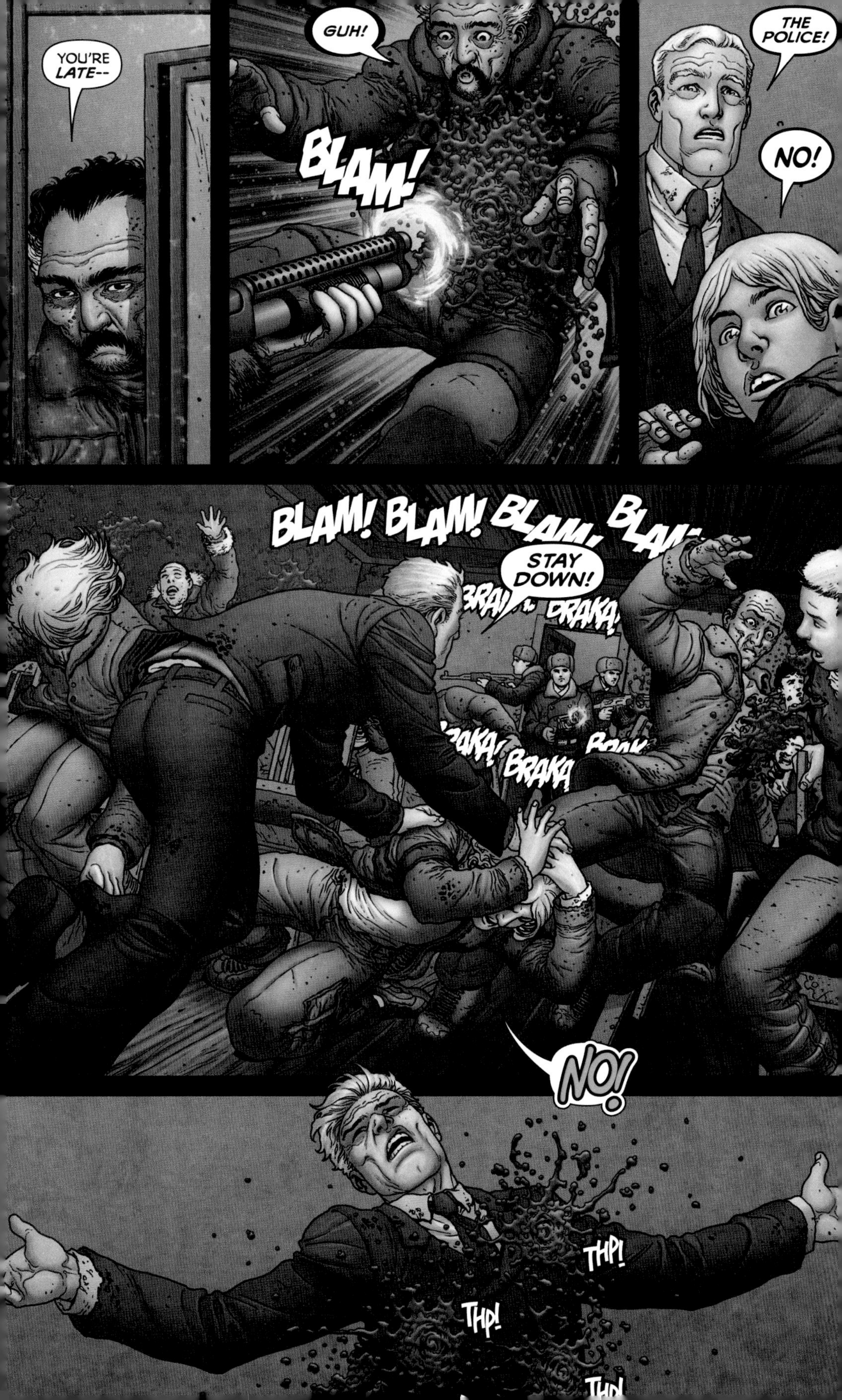
YOU'RE LATE--
GUH!
BLAM!
THE POLICE!
NO!
BLAM! BLAM!
STAY DOWN!
BRAKA
NO!
THP!
THP!

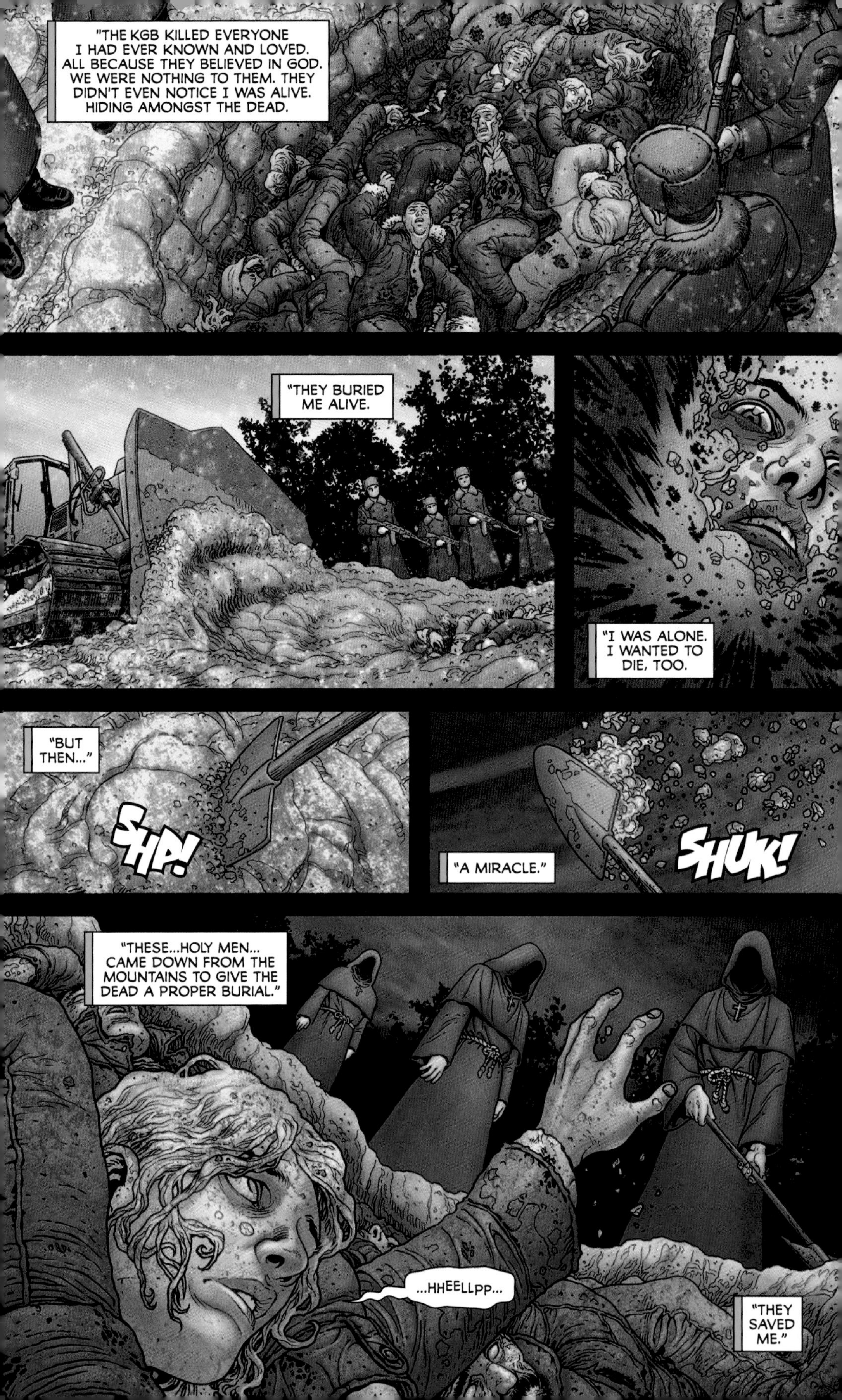
"THE KGB KILLED EVERYONE I HAD EVER KNOWN AND LOVED. ALL BECAUSE THEY BELIEVED IN GOD. WE WERE NOTHING TO THEM. THEY DIDN'T EVEN NOTICE I WAS ALIVE. HIDING AMONGST THE DEAD.
"THEY BURIED ME ALIVE.
"I WAS ALONE. I WANTED TO DIE, TOO.
"BUT THEN..."
SHP!
"A MIRACLE."
SHUK!
"THESE...HOLY MEN... CAME DOWN FROM THE MOUNTAINS TO GIVE THE DEAD A PROPER BURIAL."
...HHEELLPP...
"THEY SAVED ME."

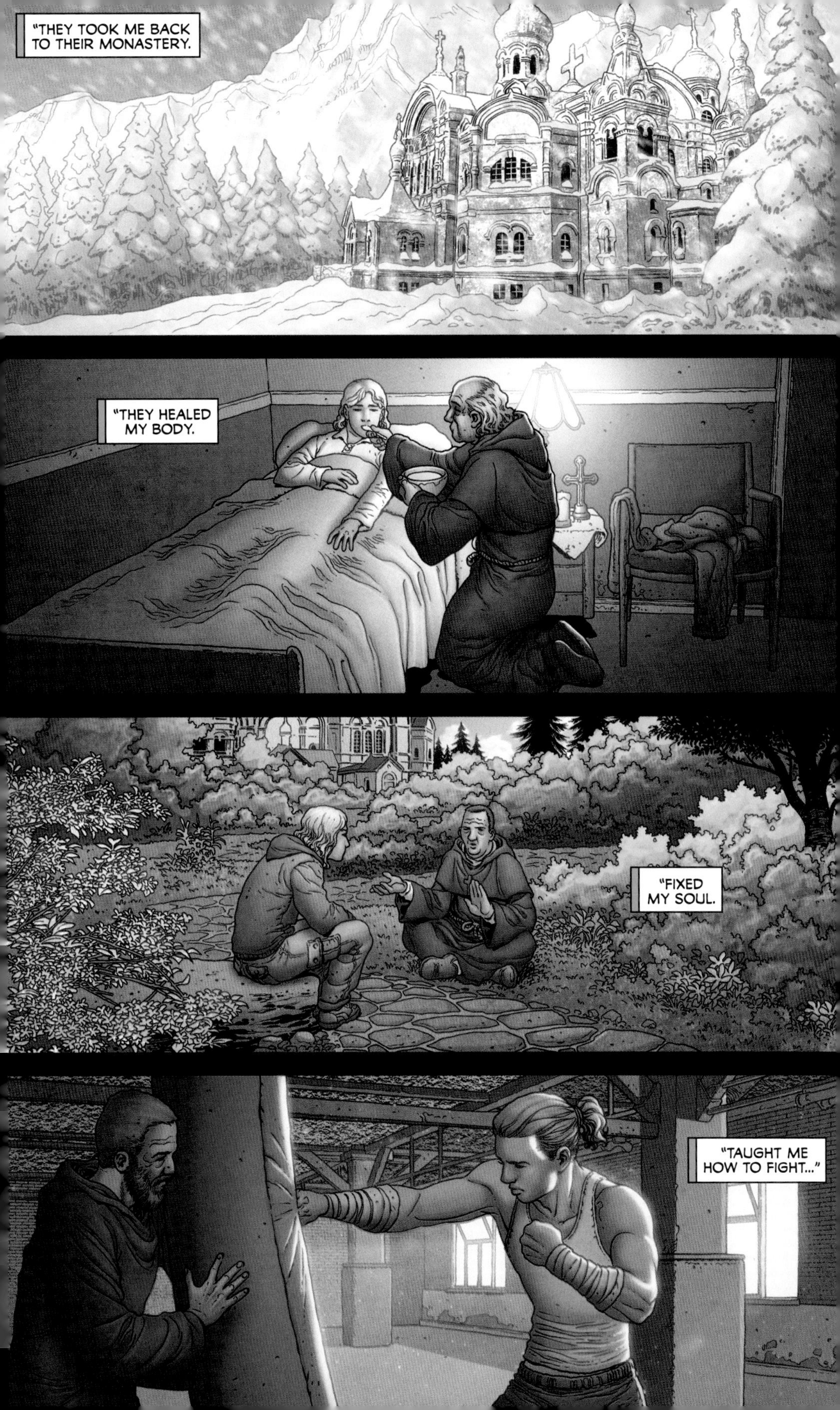
"THEY TOOK ME BACK TO THEIR MONASTERY.
"THEY HEALED MY BODY.
"FIXED MY SOUL.
"TAUGHT ME HOW TO FIGHT..."

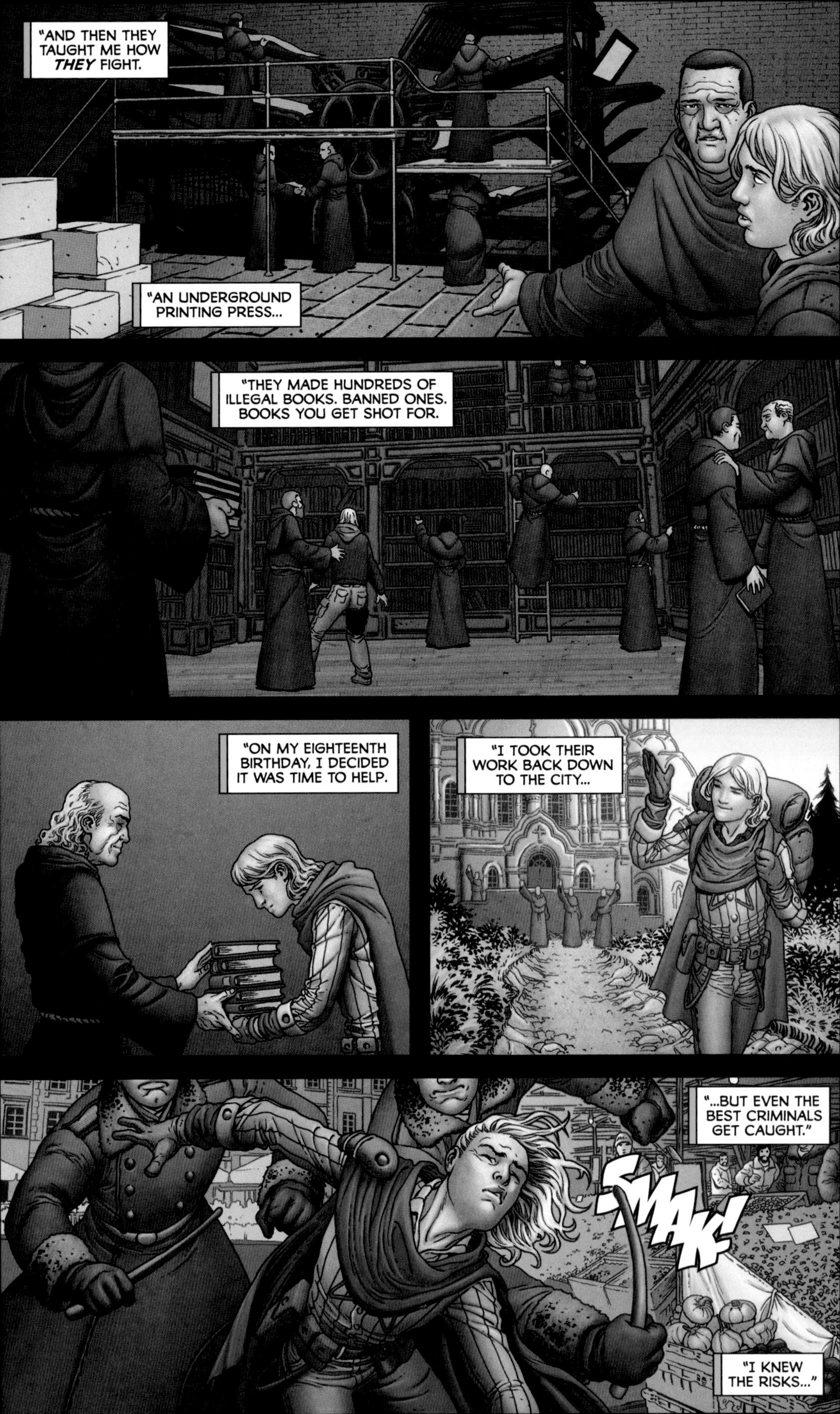
"AND THEN THEY TAUGHT ME HOW *THEY* FIGHT.
"AN UNDERGROUND PRINTING PRESS...
"THEY MADE HUNDREDS OF ILLEGAL BOOKS. BANNED ONES. BOOKS YOU GET SHOT FOR.
"ON MY EIGHTEENTH BIRTHDAY, I DECIDED IT WAS TIME TO HELP.
"I TOOK THEIR WORK BACK DOWN TO THE CITY...
"...BUT EVEN THE BEST CRIMINALS GET CAUGHT."
SMAK!
"I KNEW THE RISKS..."

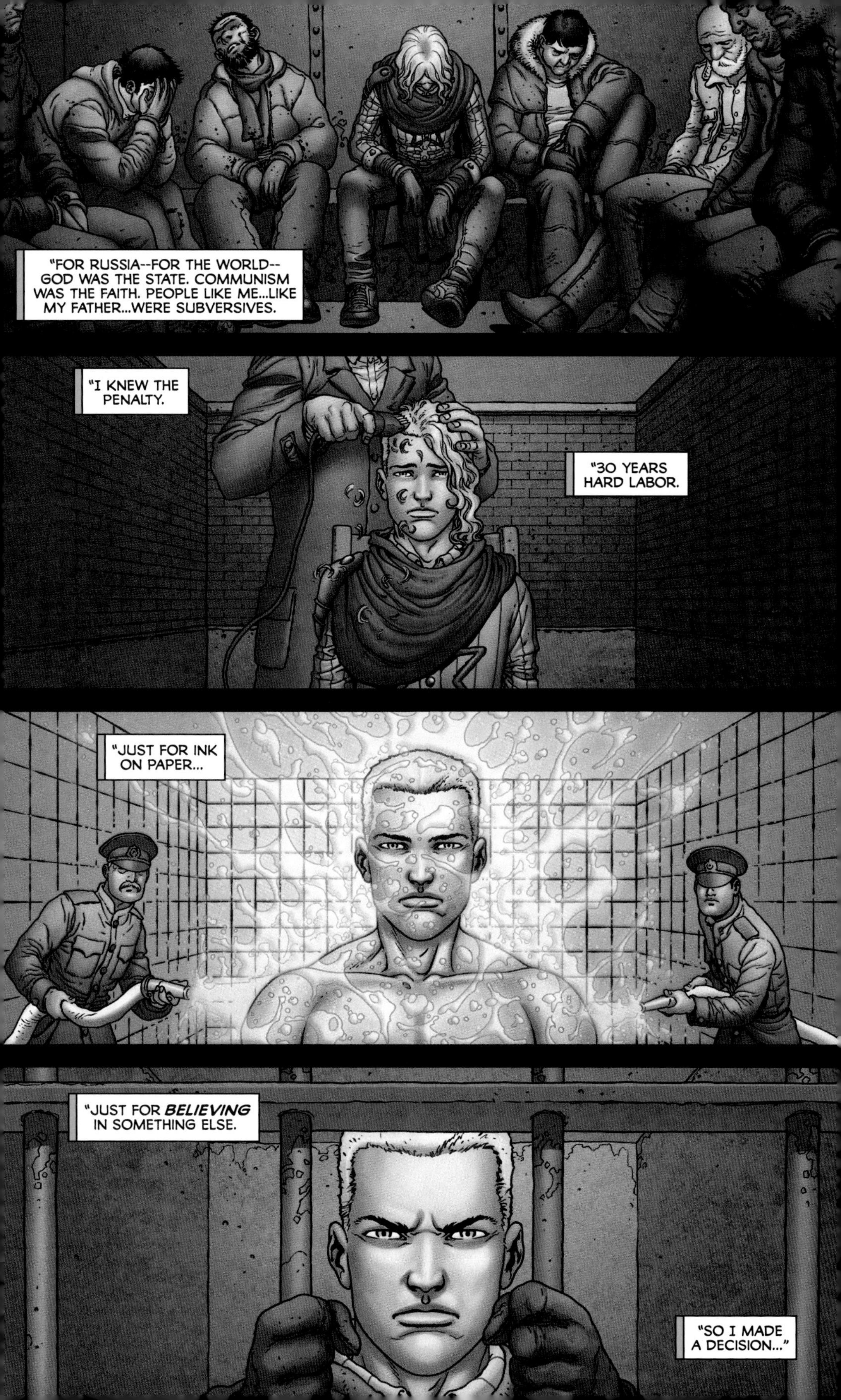
"FOR RUSSIA--FOR THE WORLD-- GOD WAS THE STATE. COMMUNISM WAS THE FAITH. PEOPLE LIKE ME...LIKE MY FATHER...WERE SUBVERSIVES.
"I KNEW THE PENALTY.
"30 YEARS HARD LABOR.
"JUST FOR INK ON PAPER...
"JUST FOR *BELIEVING* IN SOMETHING ELSE.
"SO I MADE A DECISION..."

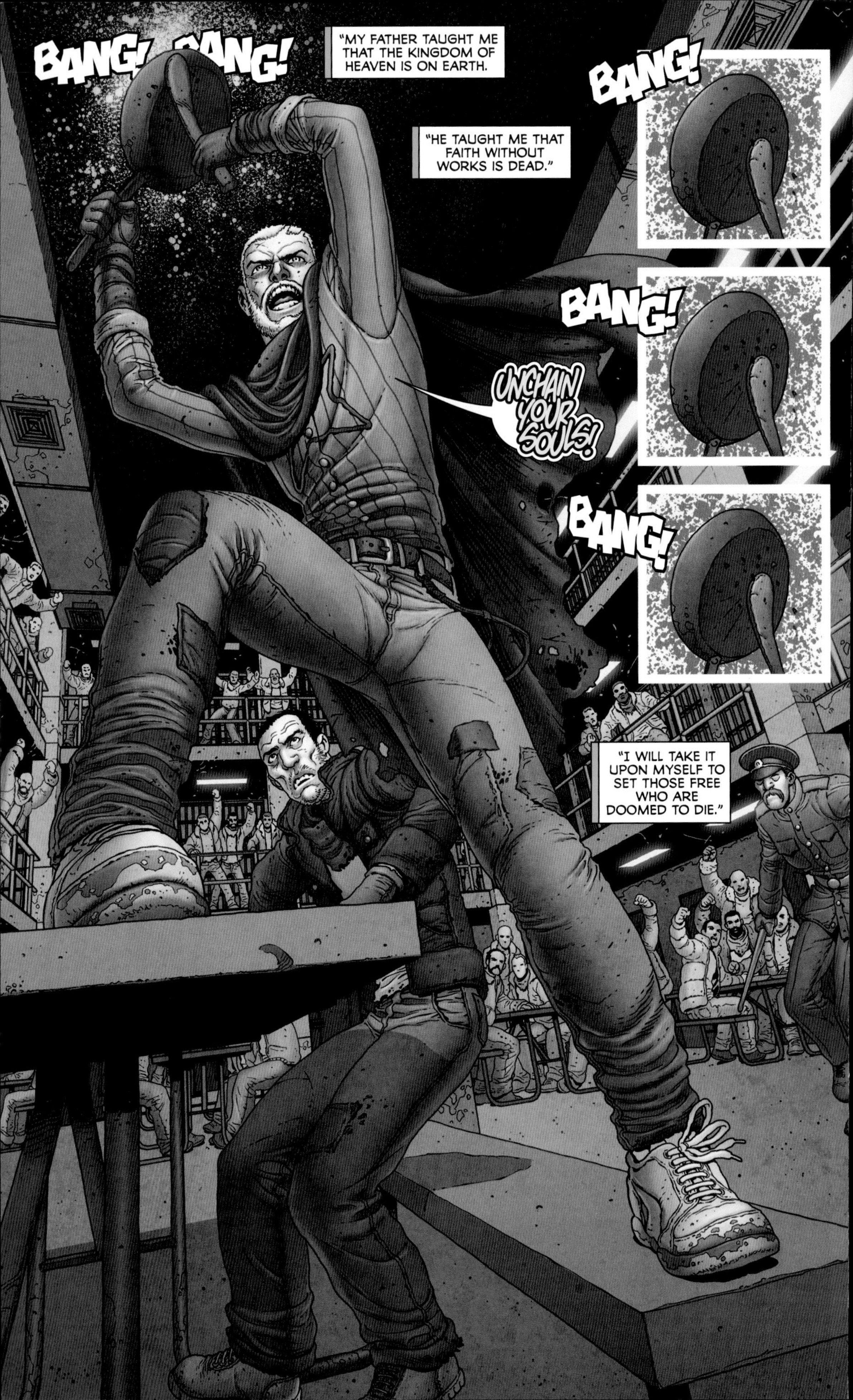
BANG! BANG!
"MY FATHER TAUGHT ME THAT THE KINGDOM OF HEAVEN IS ON EARTH.
"HE TAUGHT ME THAT FAITH WITHOUT WORKS IS DEAD."
BANG!
BANG!
UNCHAIN YOUR SOULS!
BANG!
"I WILL TAKE IT UPON MYSELF TO SET THOSE FREE WHO ARE DOOMED TO DIE."

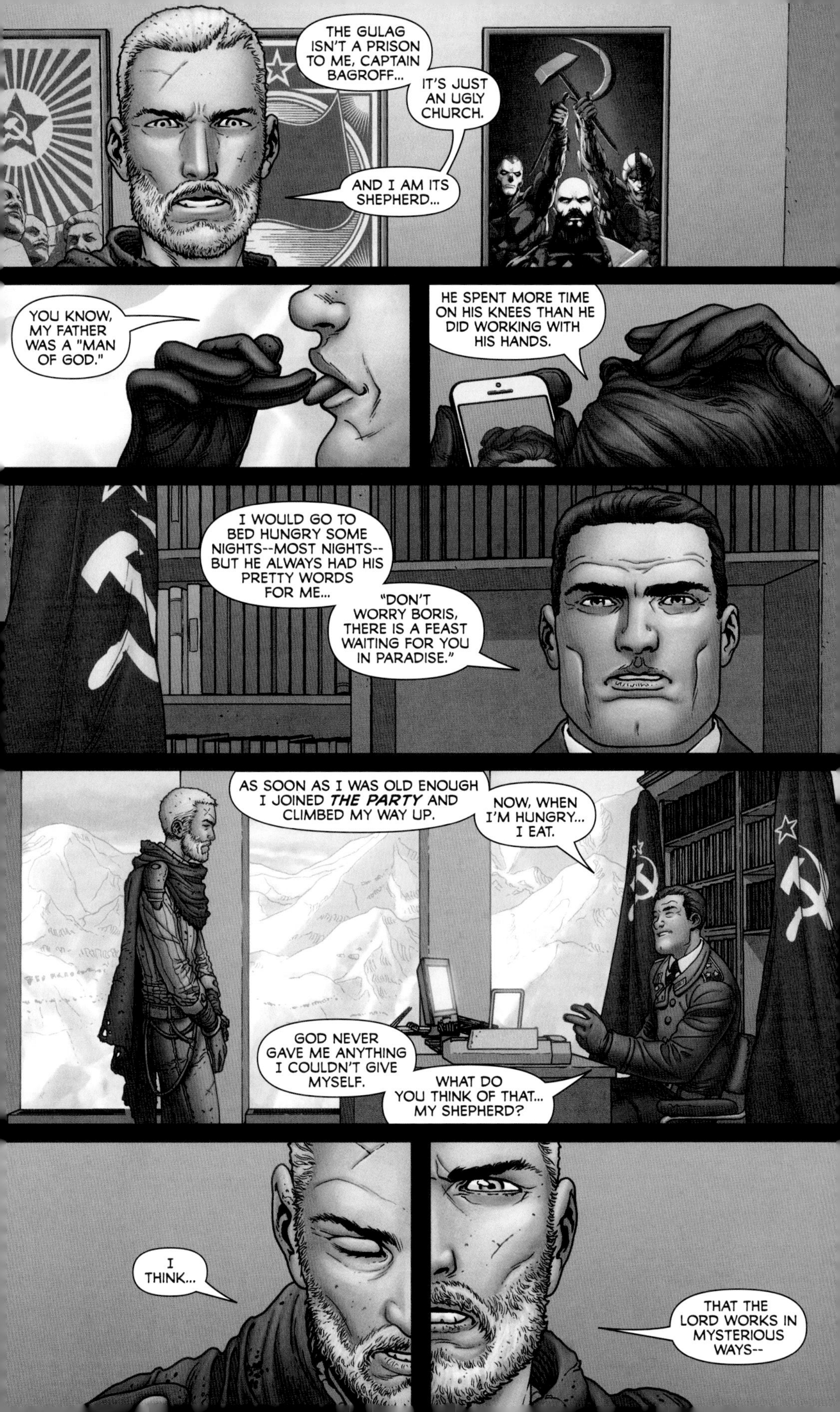
THE GULAG ISN'T A PRISON TO ME, CAPTAIN BAGROFF...
IT'S JUST AN UGLY CHURCH.
AND I AM ITS SHEPHERD...
YOU KNOW, MY FATHER WAS A "MAN OF GOD."
HE SPENT MORE TIME ON HIS KNEES THAN HE DID WORKING WITH HIS HANDS.
I WOULD GO TO BED HUNGRY SOME NIGHTS--MOST NIGHTS--BUT HE ALWAYS HAD HIS PRETTY WORDS FOR ME...
"DON'T WORRY BORIS, THERE IS A FEAST WAITING FOR YOU IN PARADISE."
AS SOON AS I WAS OLD ENOUGH I JOINED *THE PARTY* AND CLIMBED MY WAY UP.
NOW, WHEN I'M HUNGRY... I EAT.
GOD NEVER GAVE ME ANYTHING I COULDN'T GIVE MYSELF.
WHAT DO YOU THINK OF THAT... MY SHEPHERD?
I THINK...
THAT THE LORD WORKS IN MYSTERIOUS WAYS--

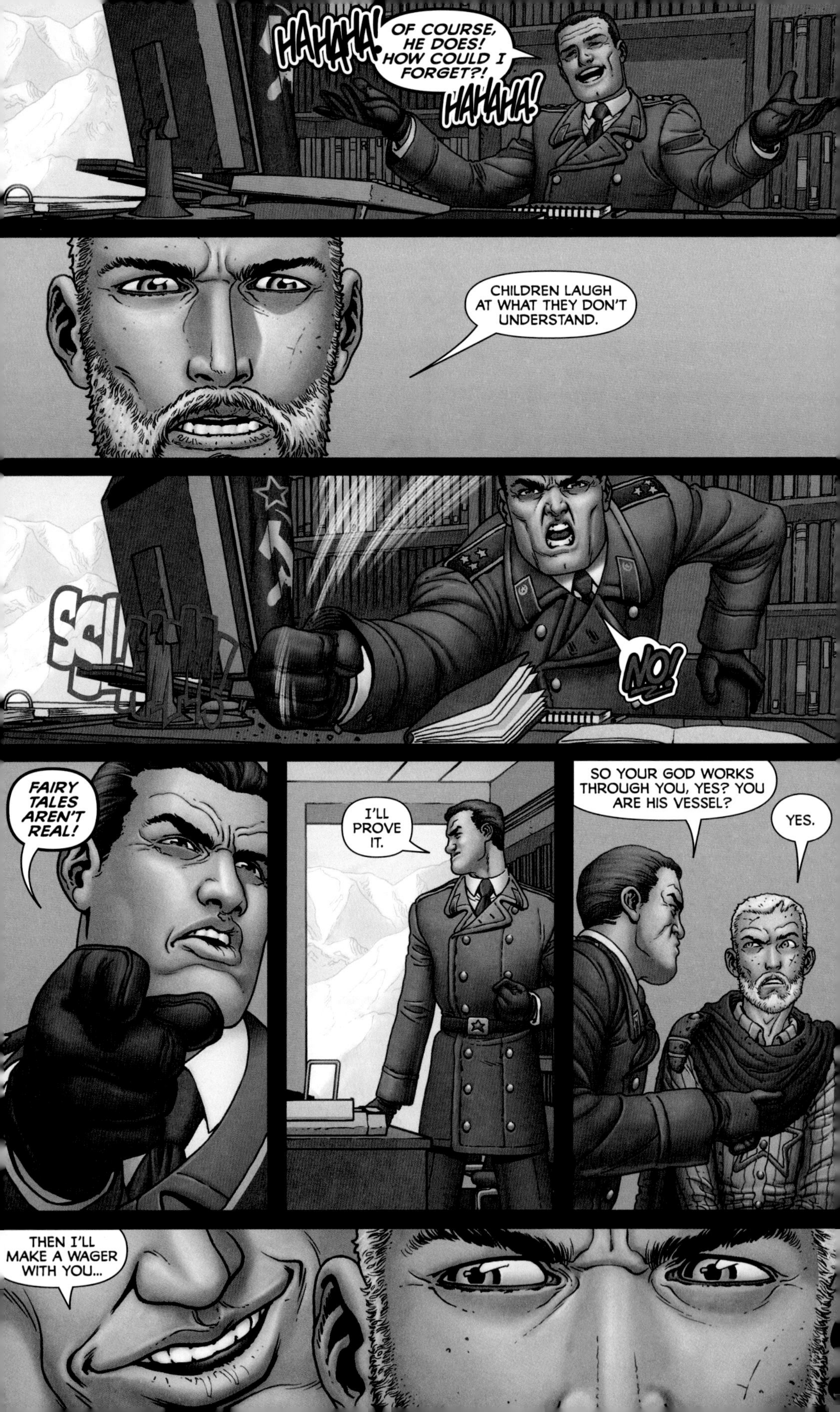
HAHAHA!
OF COURSE, HE DOES! HOW COULD I FORGET?!
HAHAHA!
CHILDREN LAUGH AT WHAT THEY DON'T UNDERSTAND.
NO!
FAIRY TALES AREN'T REAL!
I'LL PROVE IT.
SO YOUR GOD WORKS THROUGH YOU, YES? YOU ARE HIS VESSEL?
YES.
THEN I'LL MAKE A WAGER WITH YOU...

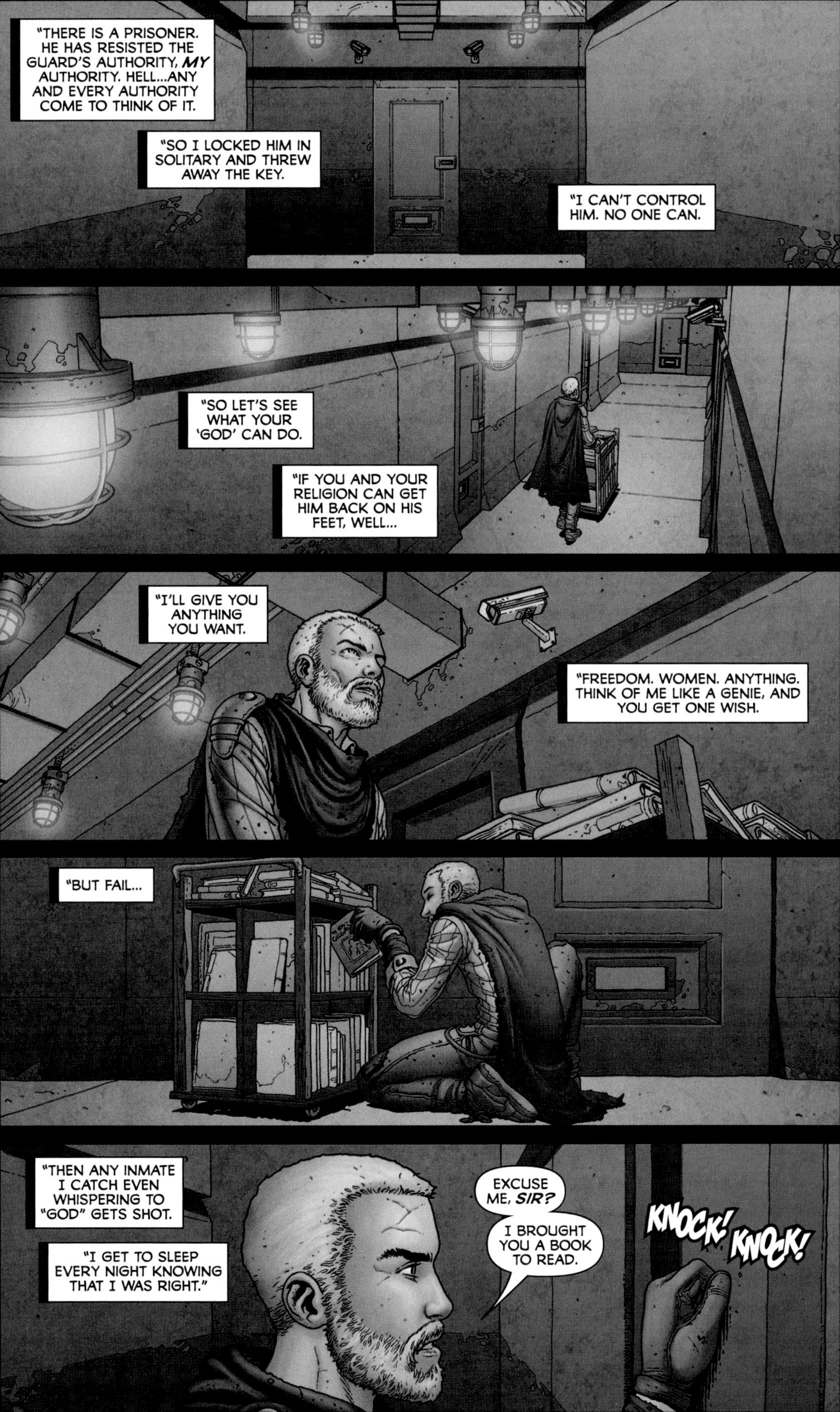
"THERE IS A PRISONER. HE HAS RESISTED THE GUARD'S AUTHORITY, *MY* AUTHORITY. HELL...ANY AND EVERY AUTHORITY COME TO THINK OF IT.
"SO I LOCKED HIM IN SOLITARY AND THREW AWAY THE KEY.
"I CAN'T CONTROL HIM. NO ONE CAN.
"SO LET'S SEE WHAT YOUR 'GOD' CAN DO.
"IF YOU AND YOUR RELIGION CAN GET HIM BACK ON HIS FEET, WELL...
"I'LL GIVE YOU ANYTHING YOU WANT.
"FREEDOM. WOMEN. ANYTHING. THINK OF ME LIKE A GENIE, AND YOU GET ONE WISH.
"BUT FAIL...
"THEN ANY INMATE I CATCH EVEN WHISPERING TO "GOD" GETS SHOT.
"I GET TO SLEEP EVERY NIGHT KNOWING THAT I WAS RIGHT."
KNOCK! KNOCK!
EXCUSE ME, *SIR?*
I BROUGHT YOU A BOOK TO READ.

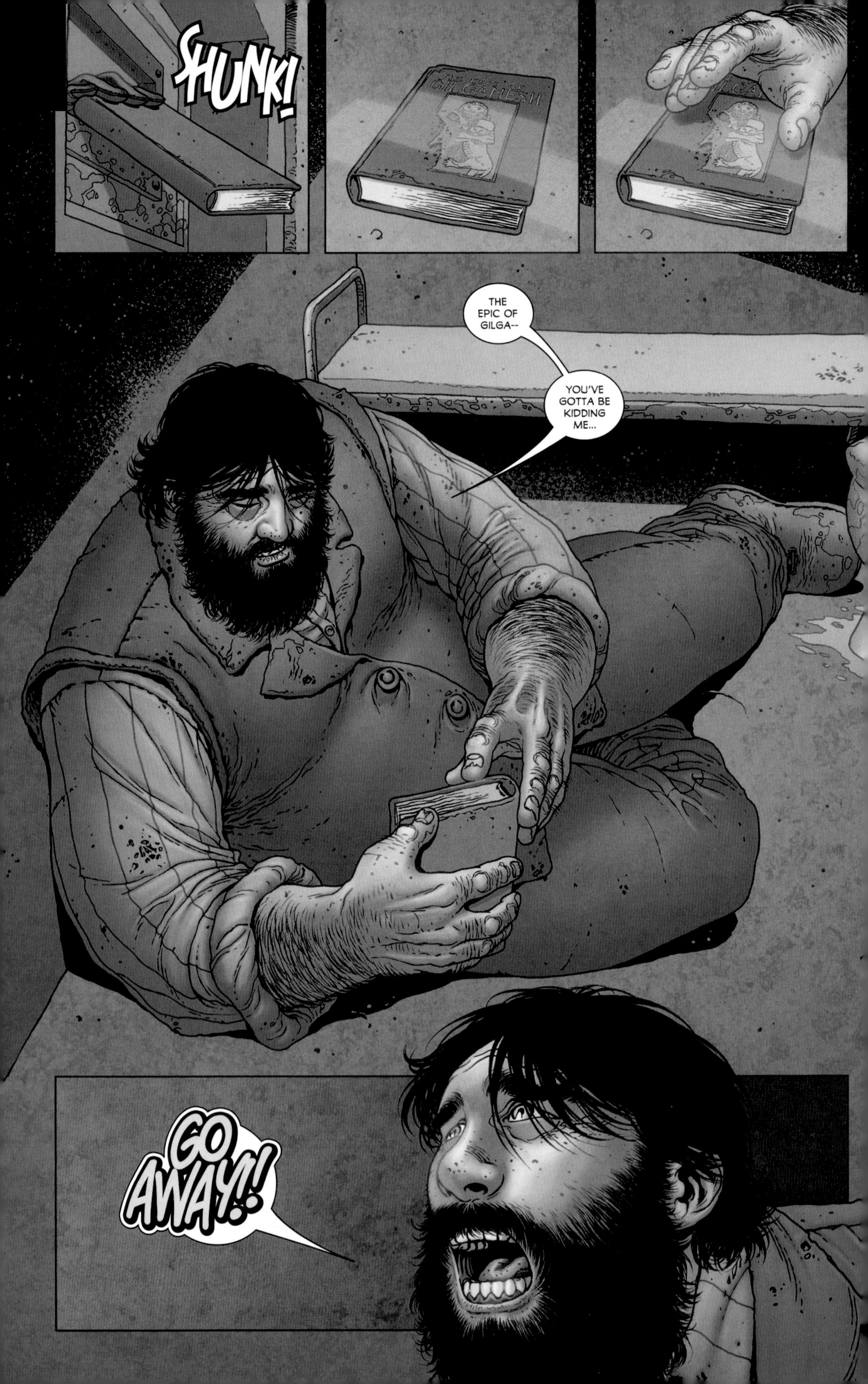
SHUNK!
THE EPIC OF GILGAMESH
THE EPIC OF GILGA--
YOU'VE GOTTA BE KIDDING ME...
GO AWAY!!

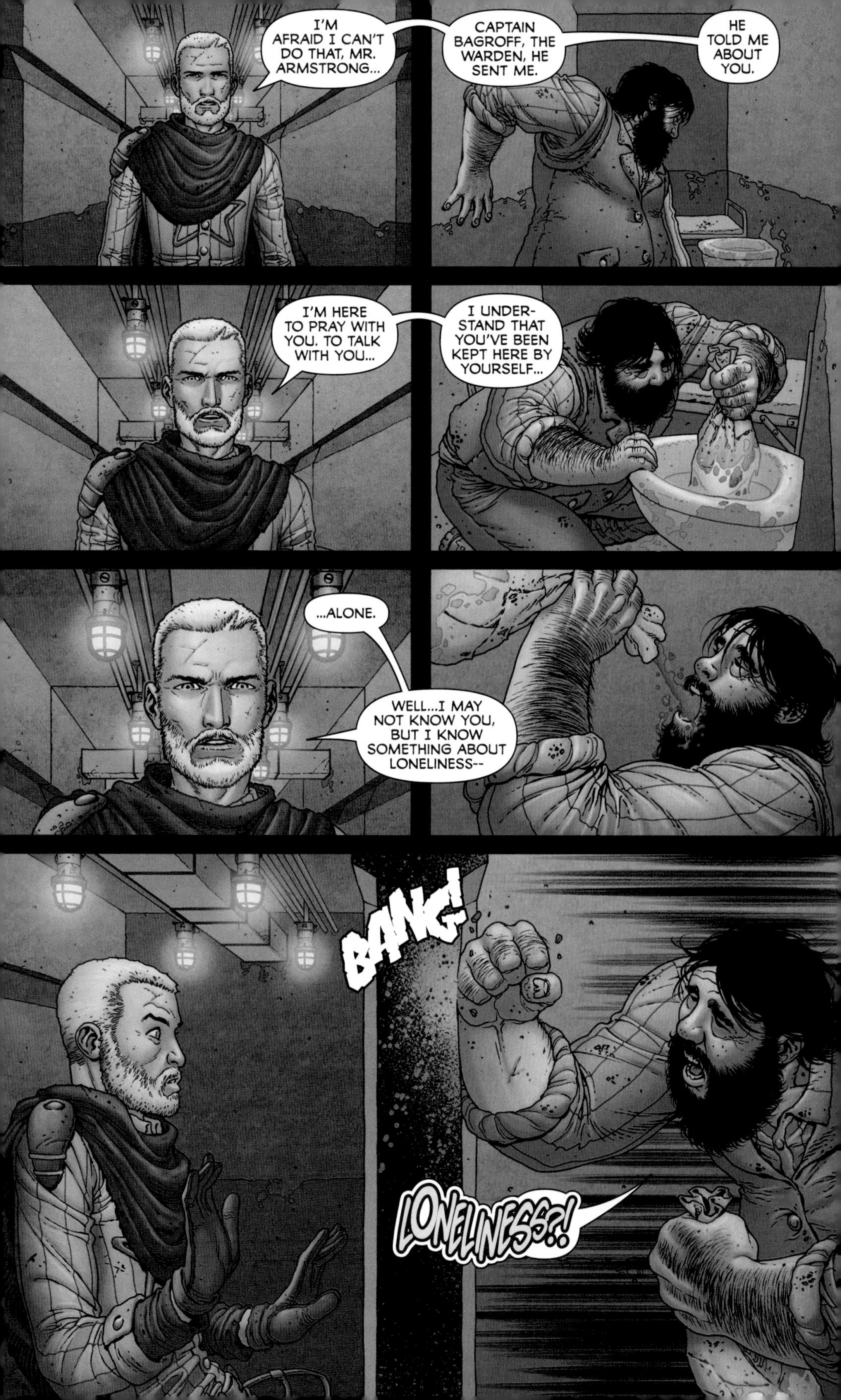
I'M AFRAID I CAN'T DO THAT, MR. ARMSTRONG...
CAPTAIN BAGROFF, THE WARDEN, HE SENT ME.
HE TOLD ME ABOUT YOU.
I'M HERE TO PRAY WITH YOU. TO TALK WITH YOU...
I UNDER-STAND THAT YOU'VE BEEN KEPT HERE BY YOURSELF...
...ALONE.
WELL...I MAY NOT KNOW YOU, BUT I KNOW SOMETHING ABOUT LONELINESS--
BANG!
LONELINESS?!

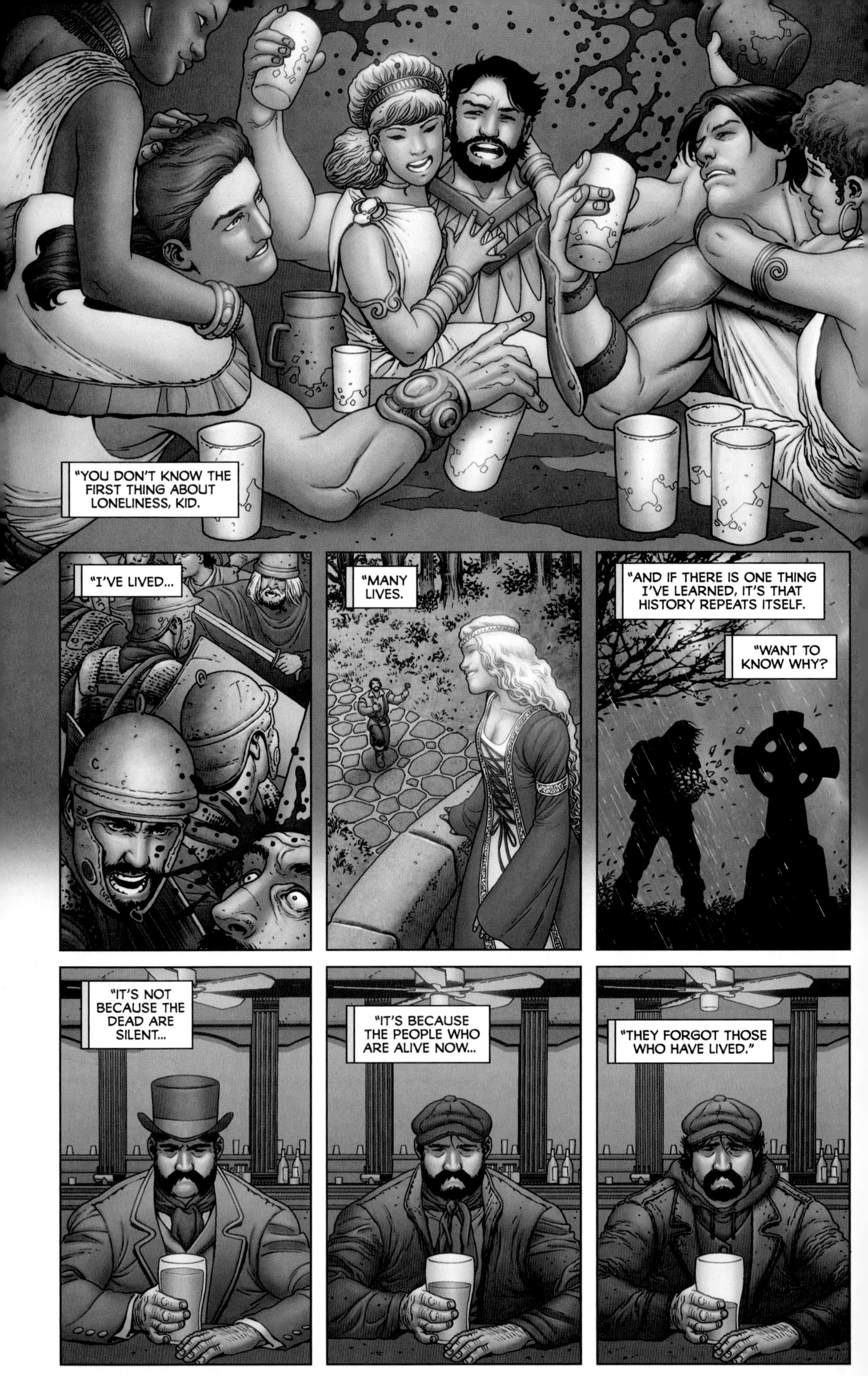
"YOU DON'T KNOW THE FIRST THING ABOUT LONELINESS, KID.
"I'VE LIVED...
"MANY LIVES.
"AND IF THERE IS ONE THING I'VE LEARNED, IT'S THAT HISTORY REPEATS ITSELF.
"WANT TO KNOW WHY?
"IT'S NOT BECAUSE THE DEAD ARE SILENT...
"IT'S BECAUSE THE PEOPLE WHO ARE ALIVE NOW...
"THEY FORGOT THOSE WHO HAVE LIVED."

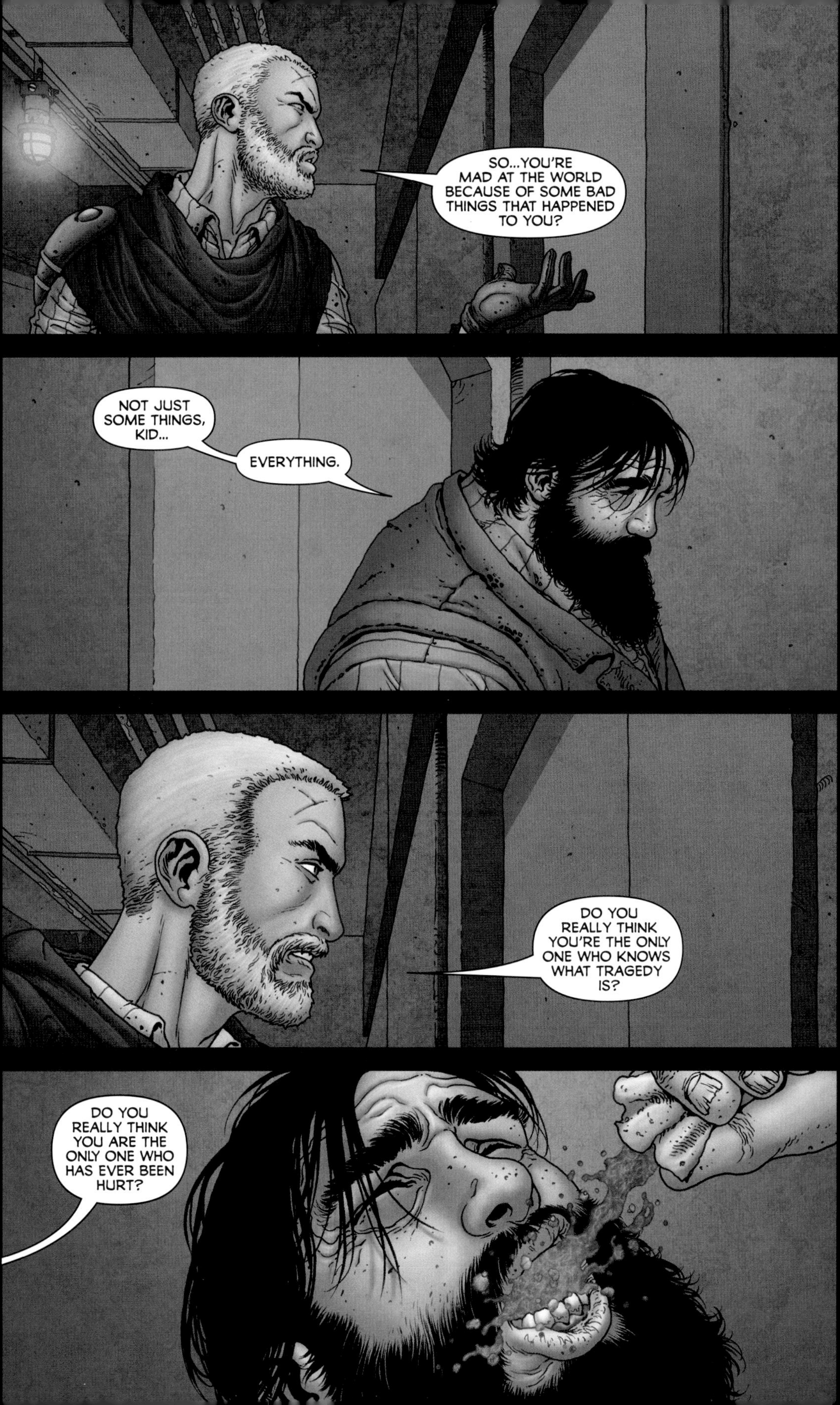
SO...YOU'RE MAD AT THE WORLD BECAUSE OF SOME BAD THINGS THAT HAPPENED TO YOU?
NOT JUST SOME THINGS, KID...
EVERYTHING.
DO YOU REALLY THINK YOU'RE THE ONLY ONE WHO KNOWS WHAT TRAGEDY IS?
DO YOU REALLY THINK YOU ARE THE ONLY ONE WHO HAS EVER BEEN HURT?

MY FATHER TAUGHT ME THAT HOPE IS WHERE THE HOPELESS ARE.
SHUNK!
"THAT TRUE COMPASSION TAKES COURAGE.
"AND EVEN OUR WORST ENEMIES ARE JUST PEOPLE..."
SHUNK!

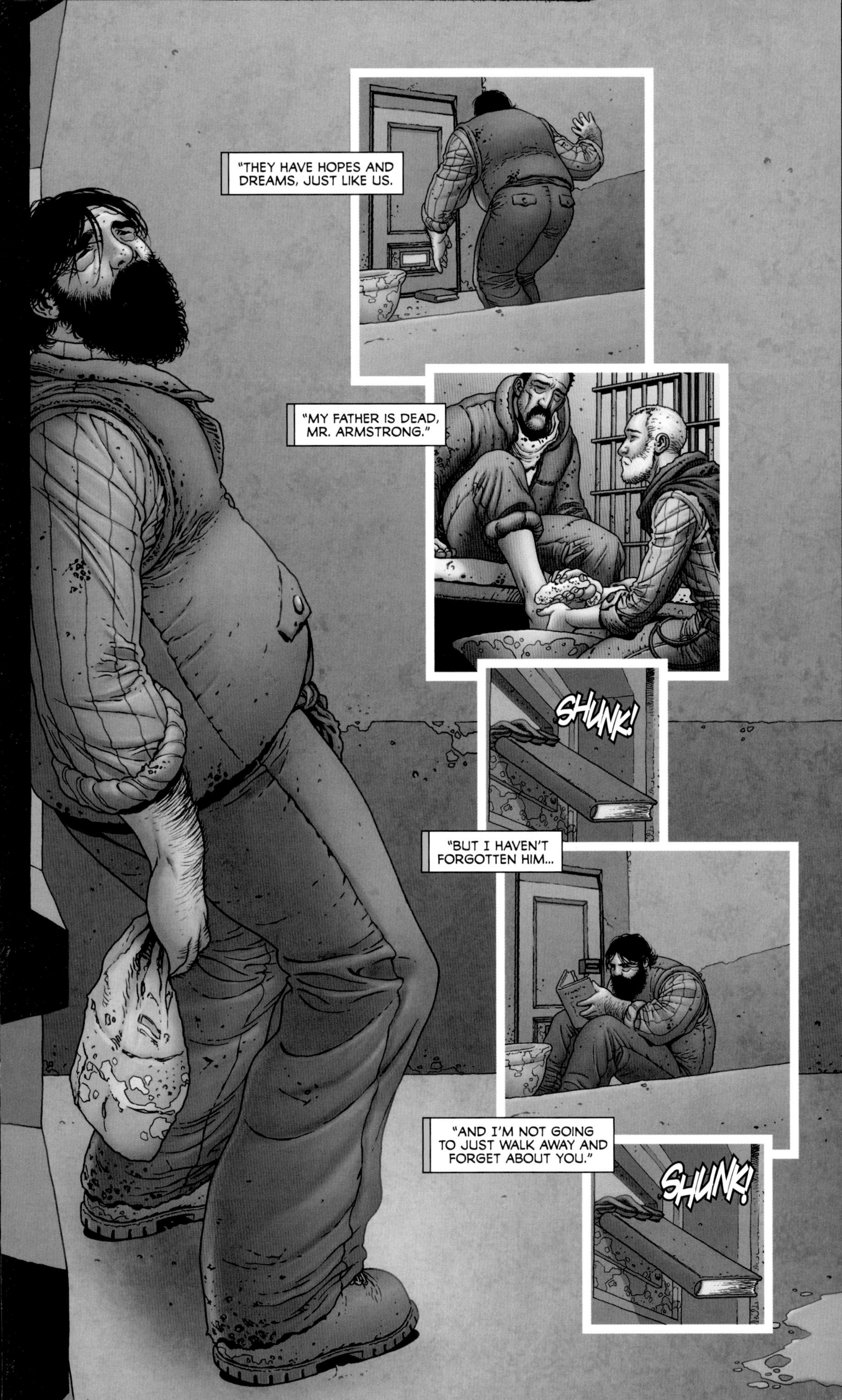
"THEY HAVE HOPES AND DREAMS, JUST LIKE US.
"MY FATHER IS DEAD, MR. ARMSTRONG."
SHUNK!
"BUT I HAVEN'T FORGOTTEN HIM...
"AND I'M NOT GOING TO JUST WALK AWAY AND FORGET ABOUT YOU."
SHUNK!

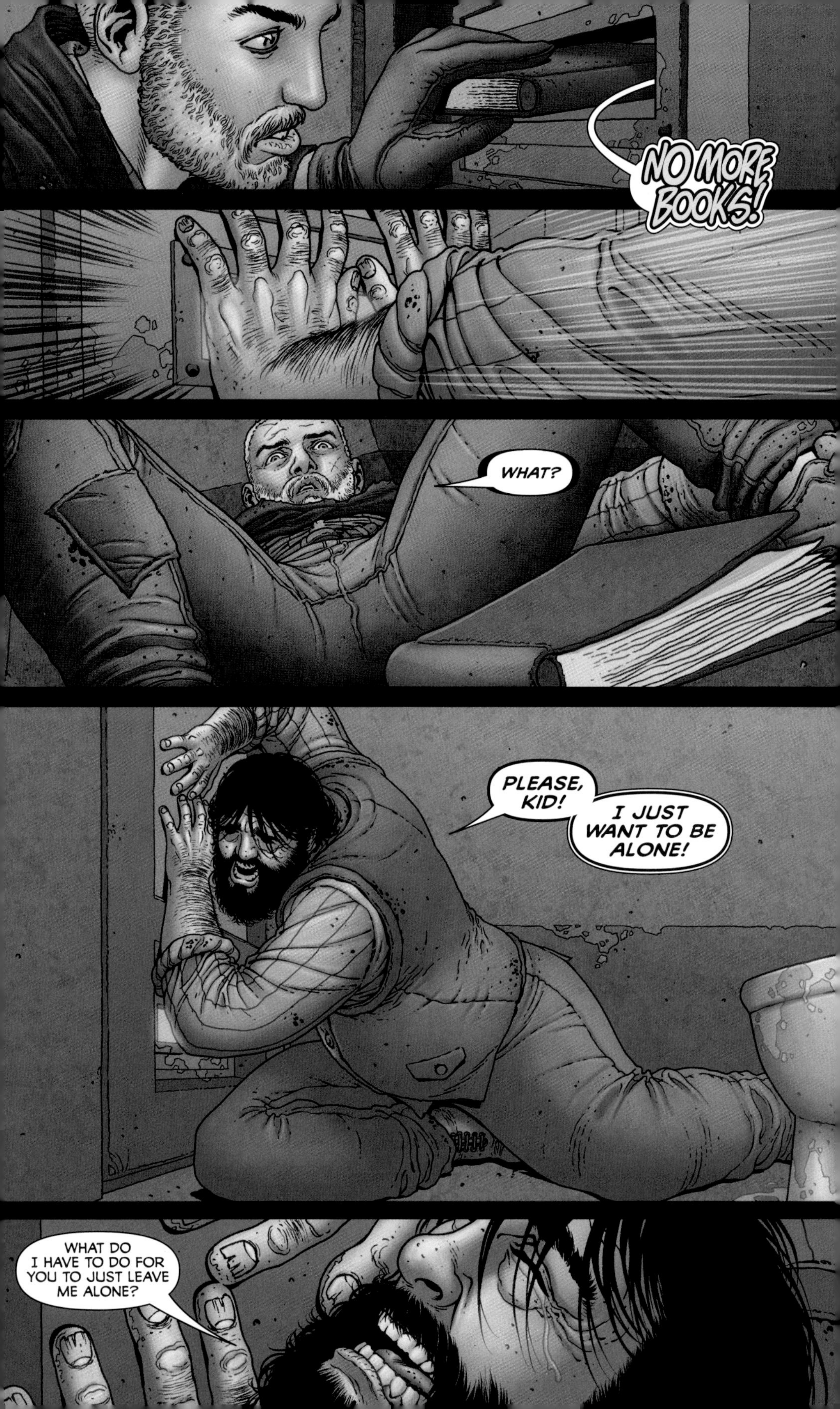
NO MORE BOOKS!
WHAT?
PLEASE, KID!
I JUST WANT TO BE ALONE!
WHAT DO I HAVE TO DO FOR YOU TO JUST LEAVE ME ALONE?

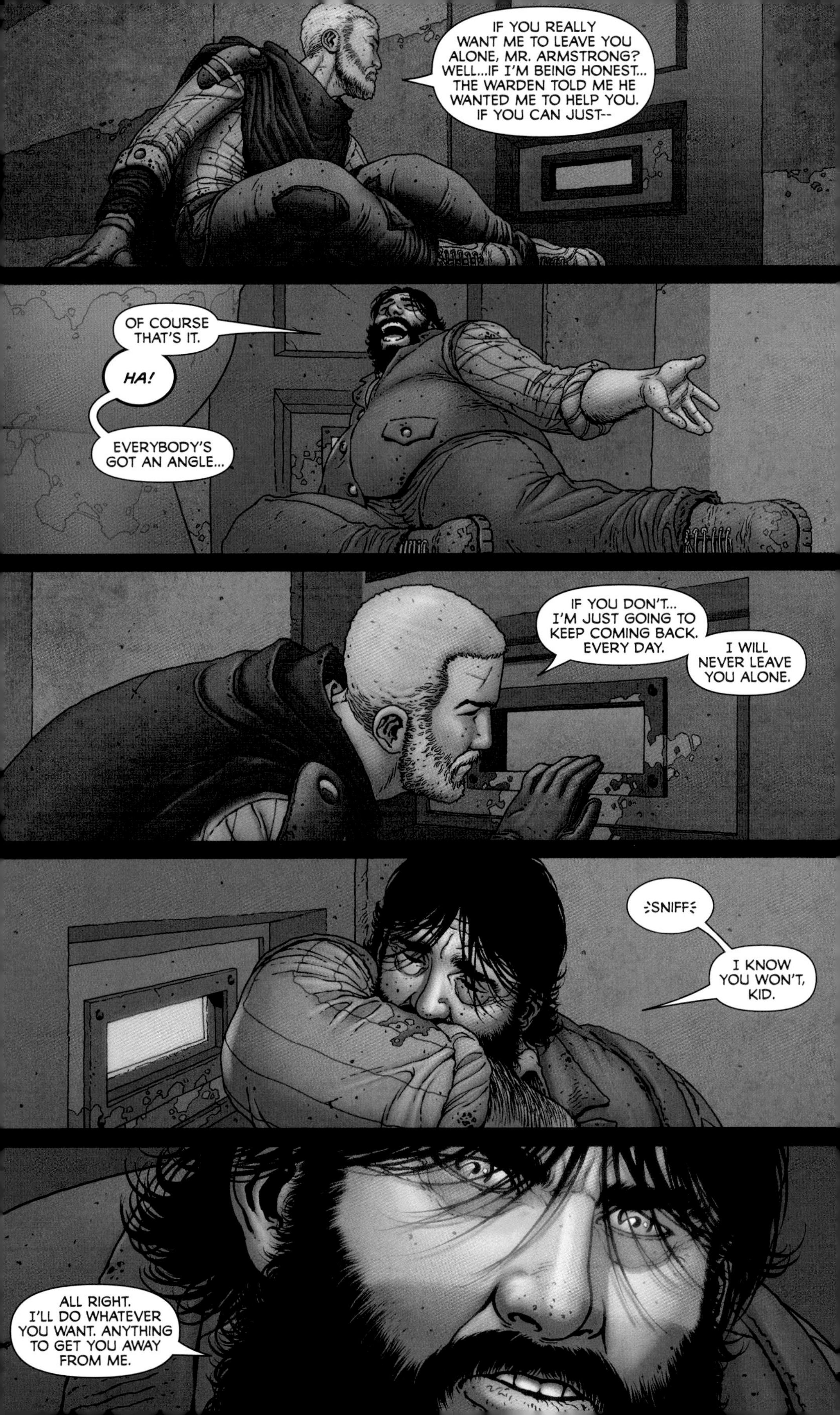
IF YOU REALLY WANT ME TO LEAVE YOU ALONE, MR. ARMSTRONG? WELL...IF I'M BEING HONEST... THE WARDEN TOLD ME HE WANTED ME TO HELP YOU. IF YOU CAN JUST--
OF COURSE THAT'S IT.
HA!
EVERYBODY'S GOT AN ANGLE...
IF YOU DON'T... I'M JUST GOING TO KEEP COMING BACK. EVERY DAY.
I WILL NEVER LEAVE YOU ALONE.
SNIFF
I KNOW YOU WON'T, KID.
ALL RIGHT. I'LL DO WHATEVER YOU WANT. ANYTHING TO GET YOU AWAY FROM ME.

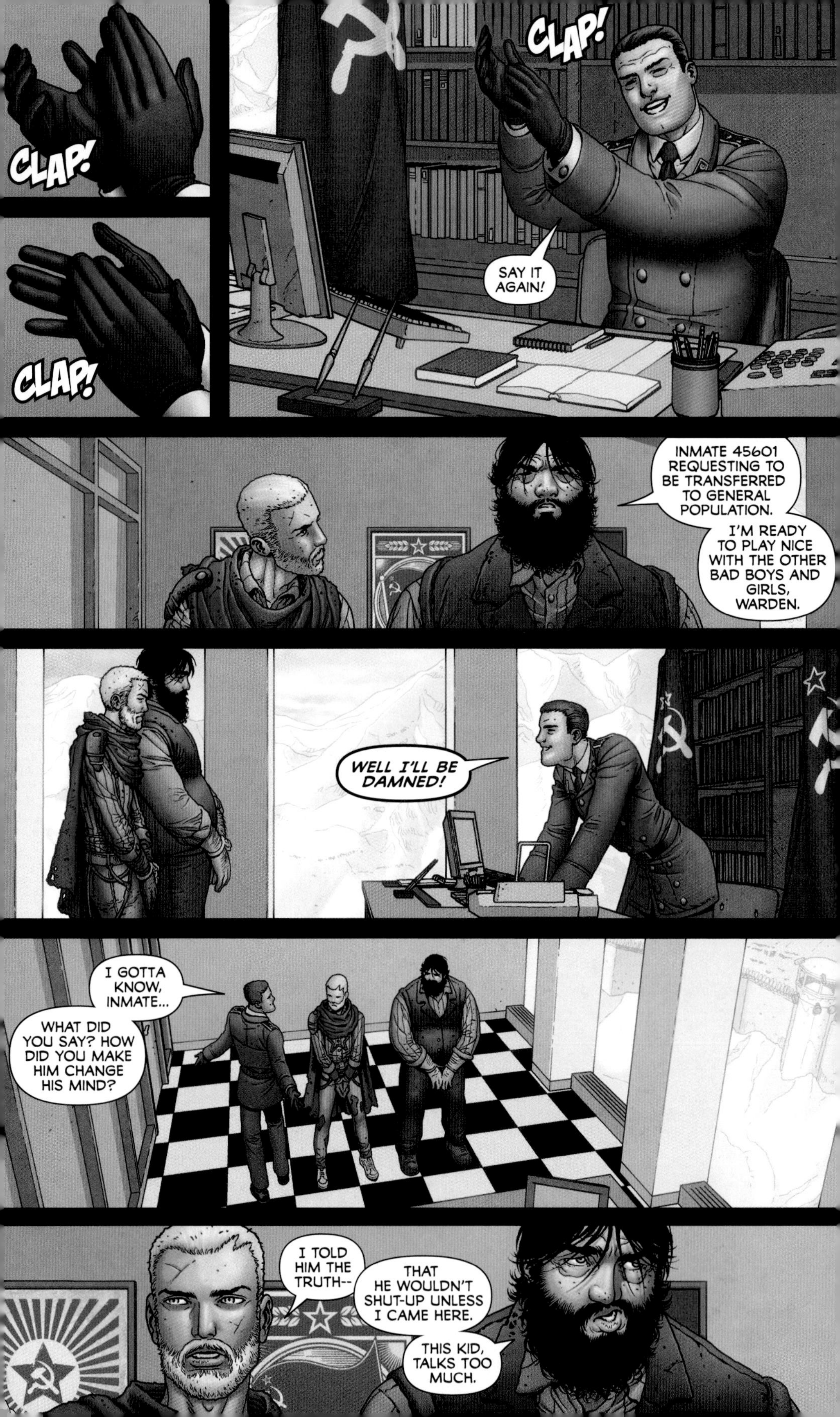
CLAP!
CLAP!
CLAP!
SAY IT AGAIN!
INMATE 45601 REQUESTING TO BE TRANSFERRED TO GENERAL POPULATION.
I'M READY TO PLAY NICE WITH THE OTHER BAD BOYS AND GIRLS, WARDEN.
WELL I'LL BE DAMNED!
I GOTTA KNOW, INMATE...
WHAT DID YOU SAY? HOW DID YOU MAKE HIM CHANGE HIS MIND?
I TOLD HIM THE TRUTH--
THAT HE WOULDN'T SHUT-UP UNLESS I CAME HERE.
THIS KID, TALKS TOO MUCH.

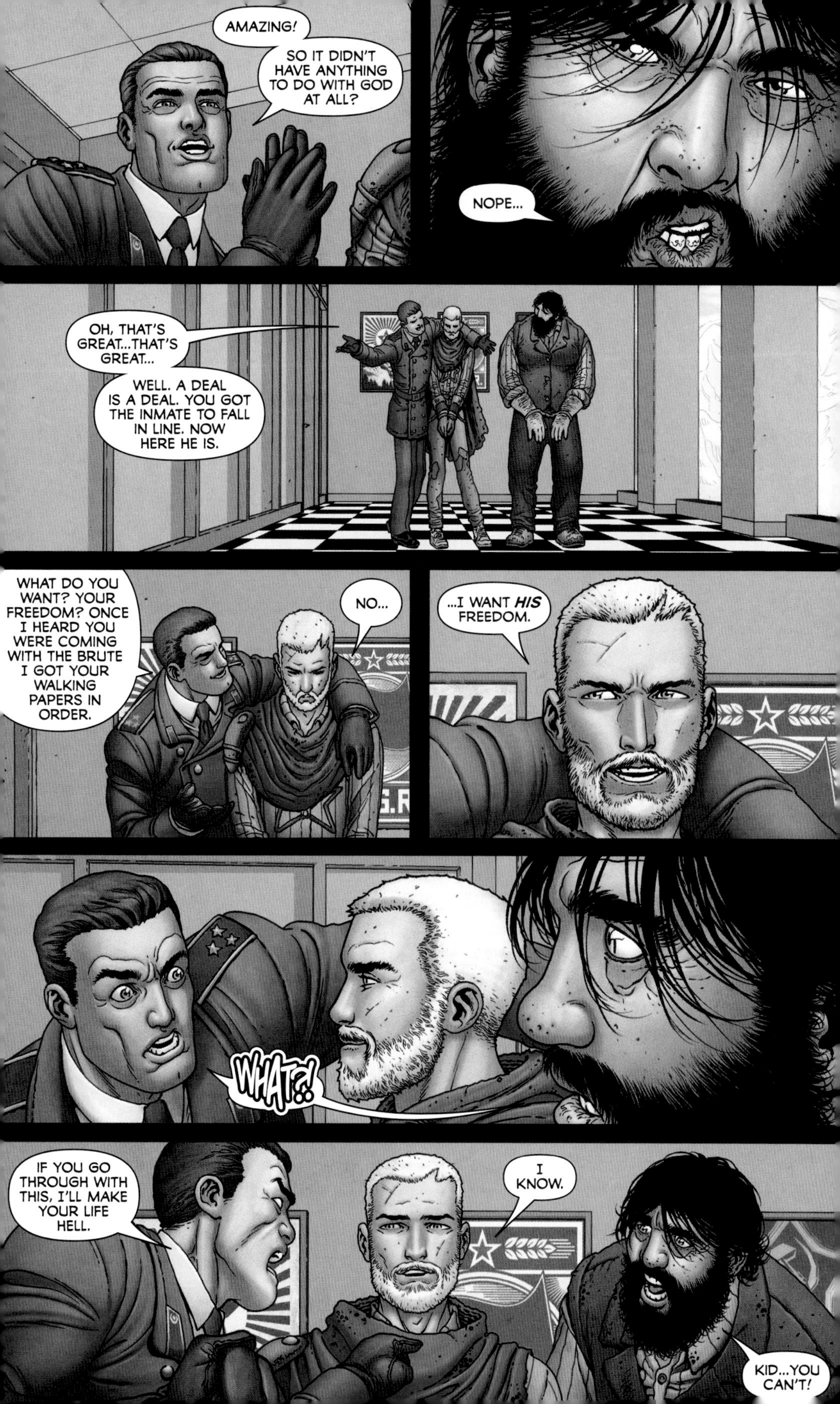
AMAZING!
SO IT DIDN'T HAVE ANYTHING TO DO WITH GOD AT ALL?
NOPE...
OH, THAT'S GREAT...THAT'S GREAT...
WELL. A DEAL IS A DEAL. YOU GOT THE INMATE TO FALL IN LINE. NOW HERE HE IS.
WHAT DO YOU WANT? YOUR FREEDOM? ONCE I HEARD YOU WERE COMING WITH THE BRUTE I GOT YOUR WALKING PAPERS IN ORDER.
NO...
...I WANT *HIS* FREEDOM.
WHAT?!
IF YOU GO THROUGH WITH THIS, I'LL MAKE YOUR LIFE HELL.
I KNOW.
KID...YOU CAN'T!

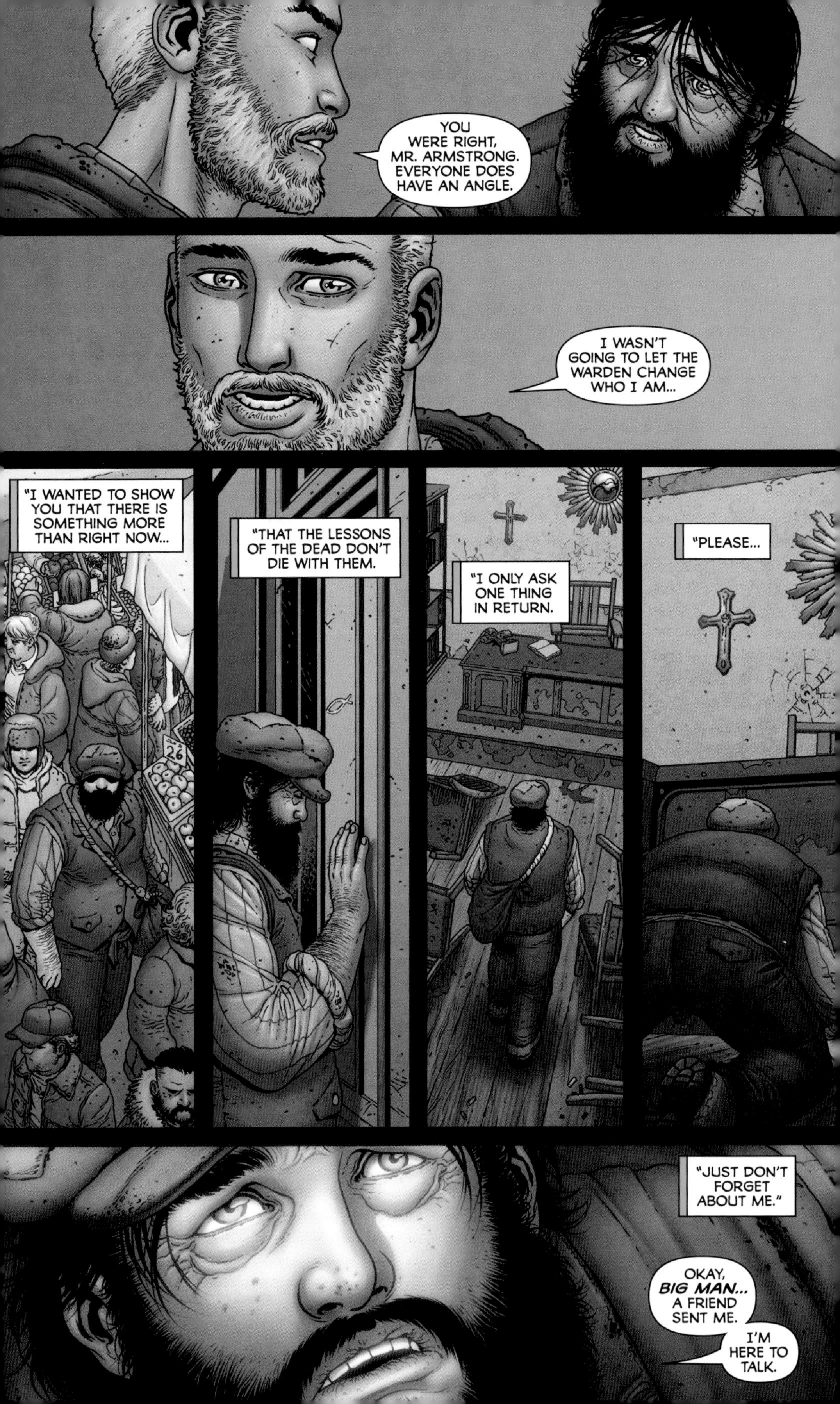
YOU WERE RIGHT, MR. ARMSTRONG. EVERYONE DOES HAVE AN ANGLE.
I WASN'T GOING TO LET THE WARDEN CHANGE WHO I AM...
"I WANTED TO SHOW YOU THAT THERE IS SOMETHING MORE THAN RIGHT NOW...
26
"THAT THE LESSONS OF THE DEAD DON'T DIE WITH THEM.
"I ONLY ASK ONE THING IN RETURN.
"PLEASE...
"JUST DON'T FORGET ABOUT ME."
OKAY, *BIG MAN...* A FRIEND SENT ME.
I'M HERE TO TALK.

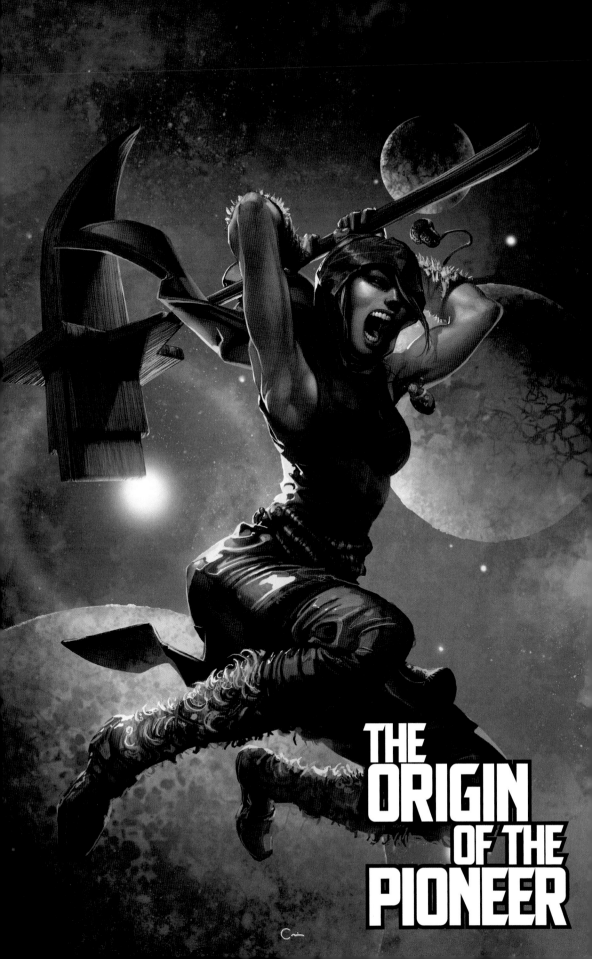

THE
ORIGIN
OF THE
PIONEER

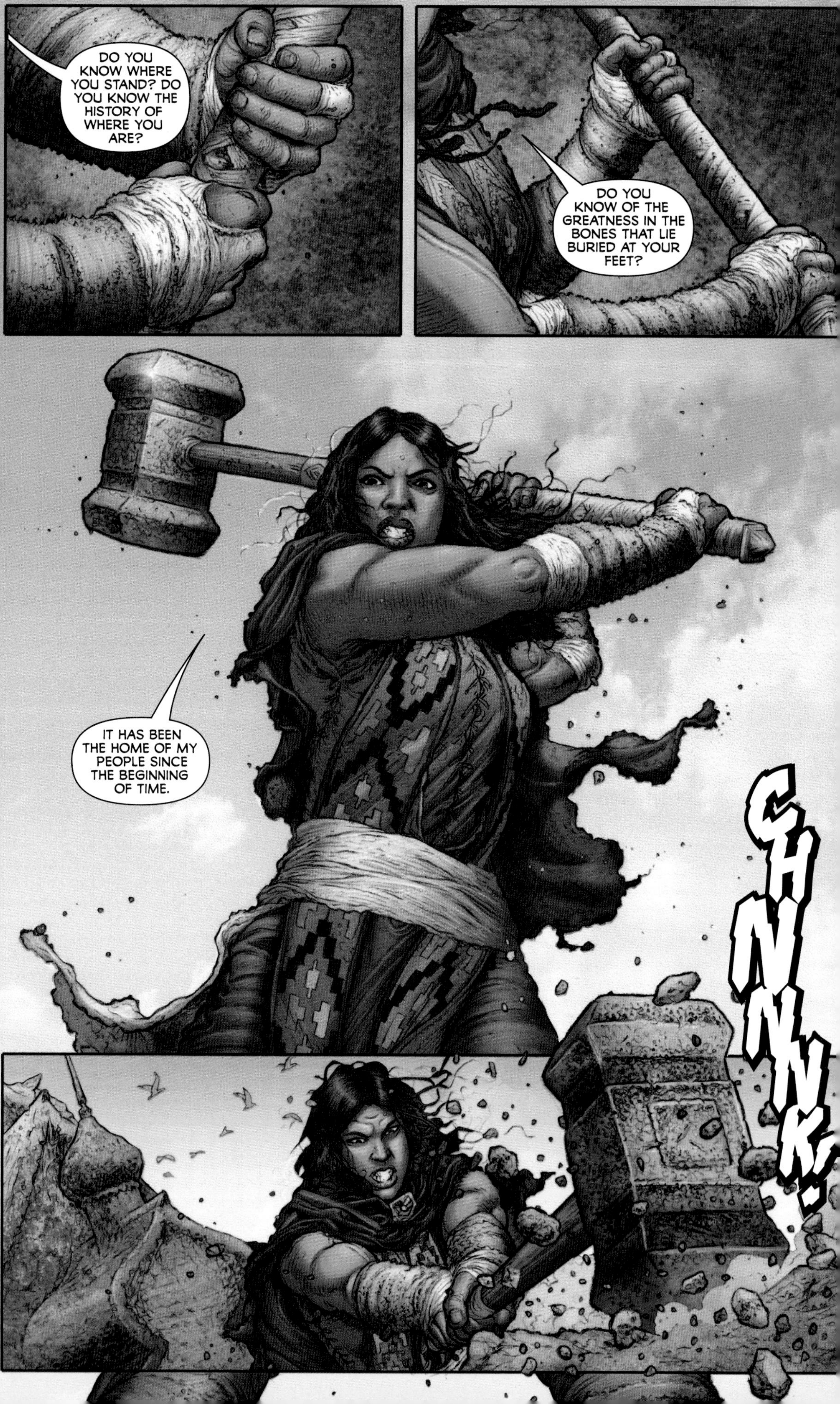
DO YOU KNOW WHERE YOU STAND? DO YOU KNOW THE HISTORY OF WHERE YOU ARE?
DO YOU KNOW OF THE GREATNESS IN THE BONES THAT LIE BURIED AT YOUR FEET?
IT HAS BEEN THE HOME OF MY PEOPLE SINCE THE BEGINNING OF TIME.
CHNNNK!

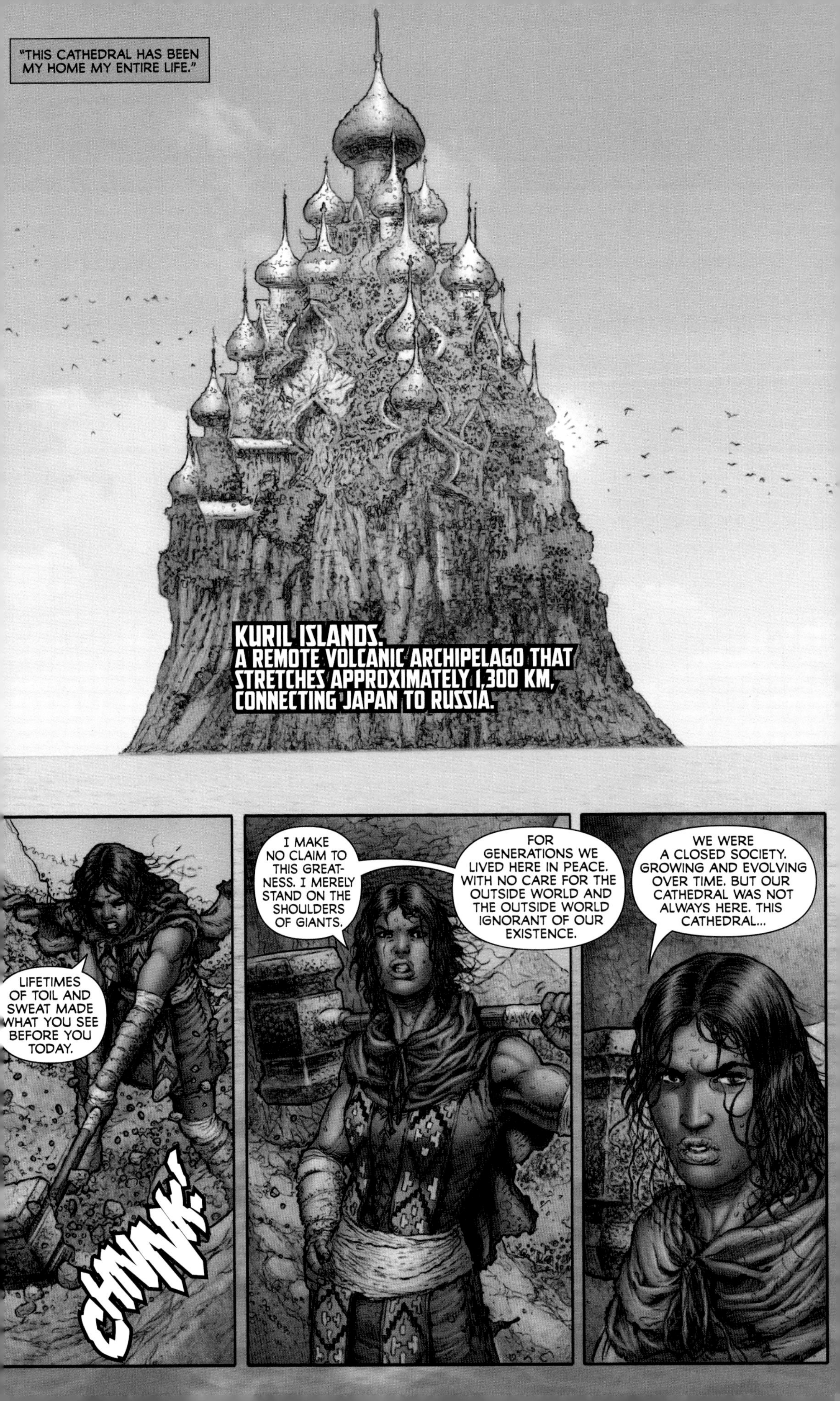
"THIS CATHEDRAL HAS BEEN MY HOME MY ENTIRE LIFE."
KURIL ISLANDS.
A REMOTE VOLCANIC ARCHIPELAGO THAT STRETCHES APPROXIMATELY 1,300 KM, CONNECTING JAPAN TO RUSSIA.
LIFETIMES OF TOIL AND SWEAT MADE WHAT YOU SEE BEFORE YOU TODAY.
CHINK!
I MAKE NO CLAIM TO THIS GREATNESS. I MERELY STAND ON THE SHOULDERS OF GIANTS.
FOR GENERATIONS WE LIVED HERE IN PEACE. WITH NO CARE FOR THE OUTSIDE WORLD AND THE OUTSIDE WORLD IGNORANT OF OUR EXISTENCE.
WE WERE A CLOSED SOCIETY. GROWING AND EVOLVING OVER TIME. BUT OUR CATHEDRAL WAS NOT ALWAYS HERE. THIS CATHEDRAL...

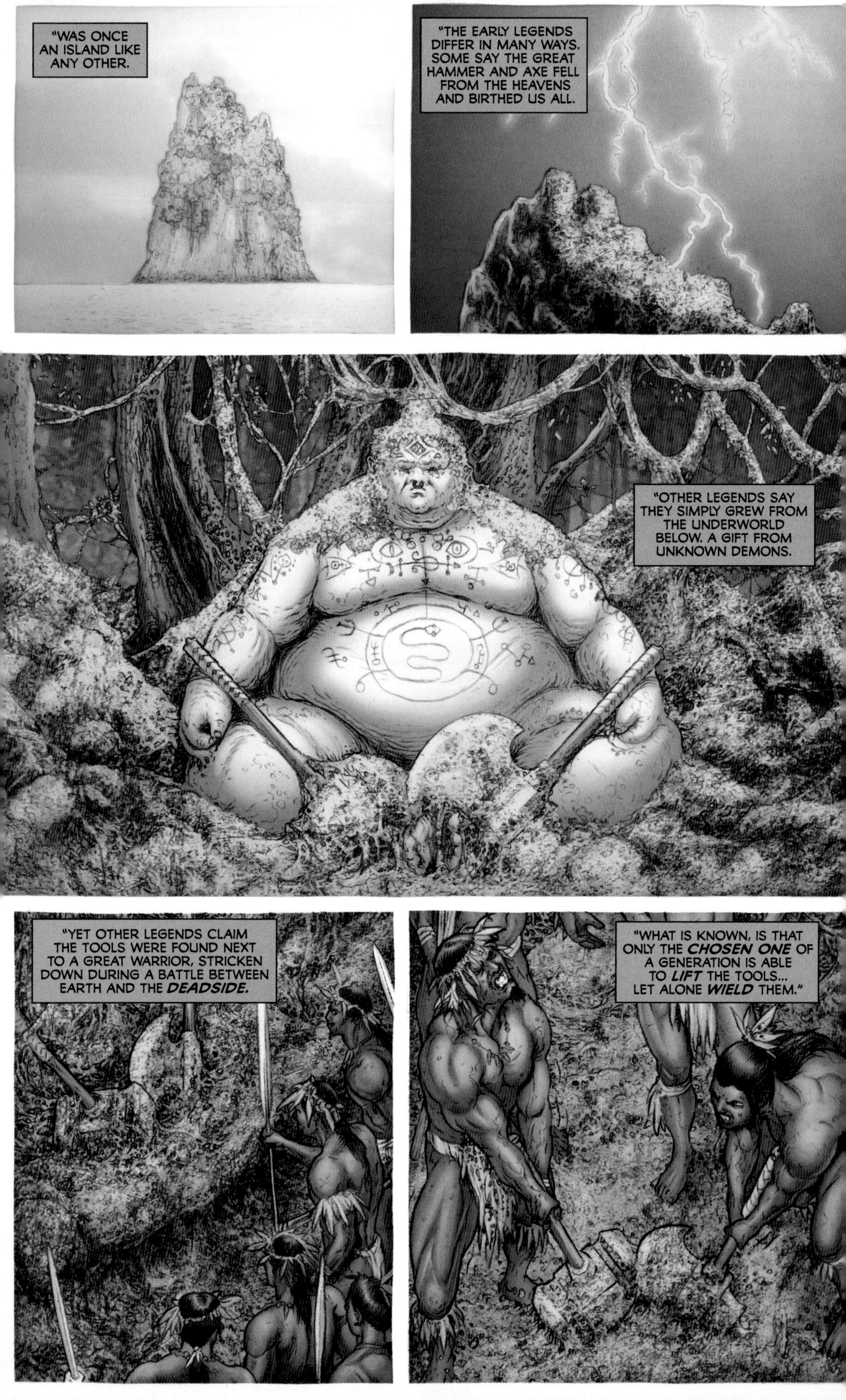
"WAS ONCE AN ISLAND LIKE ANY OTHER.
"THE EARLY LEGENDS DIFFER IN MANY WAYS. SOME SAY THE GREAT HAMMER AND AXE FELL FROM THE HEAVENS AND BIRTHED US ALL.
"OTHER LEGENDS SAY THEY SIMPLY GREW FROM THE UNDERWORLD BELOW. A GIFT FROM UNKNOWN DEMONS.
"YET OTHER LEGENDS CLAIM THE TOOLS WERE FOUND NEXT TO A GREAT WARRIOR, STRICKEN DOWN DURING A BATTLE BETWEEN EARTH AND THE ***DEADSIDE.***
"WHAT IS KNOWN, IS THAT ONLY THE ***CHOSEN ONE*** OF A GENERATION IS ABLE TO ***LIFT*** THE TOOLS... LET ALONE ***WIELD*** THEM."

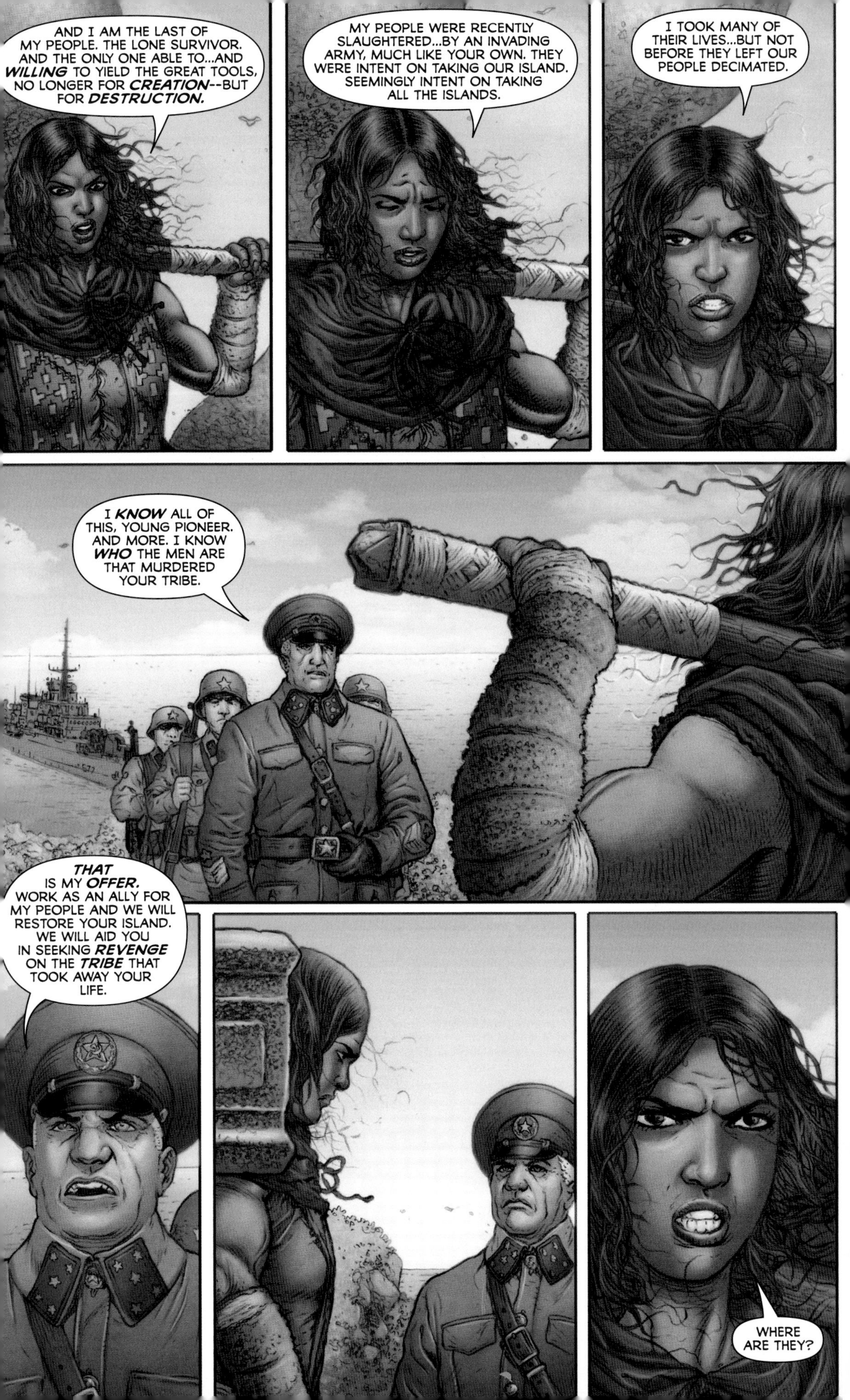
AND I AM THE LAST OF MY PEOPLE. THE LONE SURVIVOR. AND THE ONLY ONE ABLE TO...AND ***WILLING*** TO YIELD THE GREAT TOOLS, NO LONGER FOR ***CREATION***--BUT FOR ***DESTRUCTION.***
MY PEOPLE WERE RECENTLY SLAUGHTERED...BY AN INVADING ARMY, MUCH LIKE YOUR OWN. THEY WERE INTENT ON TAKING OUR ISLAND. SEEMINGLY INTENT ON TAKING ALL THE ISLANDS.
I TOOK MANY OF THEIR LIVES...BUT NOT BEFORE THEY LEFT OUR PEOPLE DECIMATED.
I ***KNOW*** ALL OF THIS, YOUNG PIONEER. AND MORE. I KNOW ***WHO*** THE MEN ARE THAT MURDERED YOUR TRIBE.
THAT IS MY ***OFFER.*** WORK AS AN ALLY FOR MY PEOPLE AND WE WILL RESTORE YOUR ISLAND. WE WILL AID YOU IN SEEKING ***REVENGE*** ON THE ***TRIBE*** THAT TOOK AWAY YOUR LIFE.
WHERE ARE THEY?

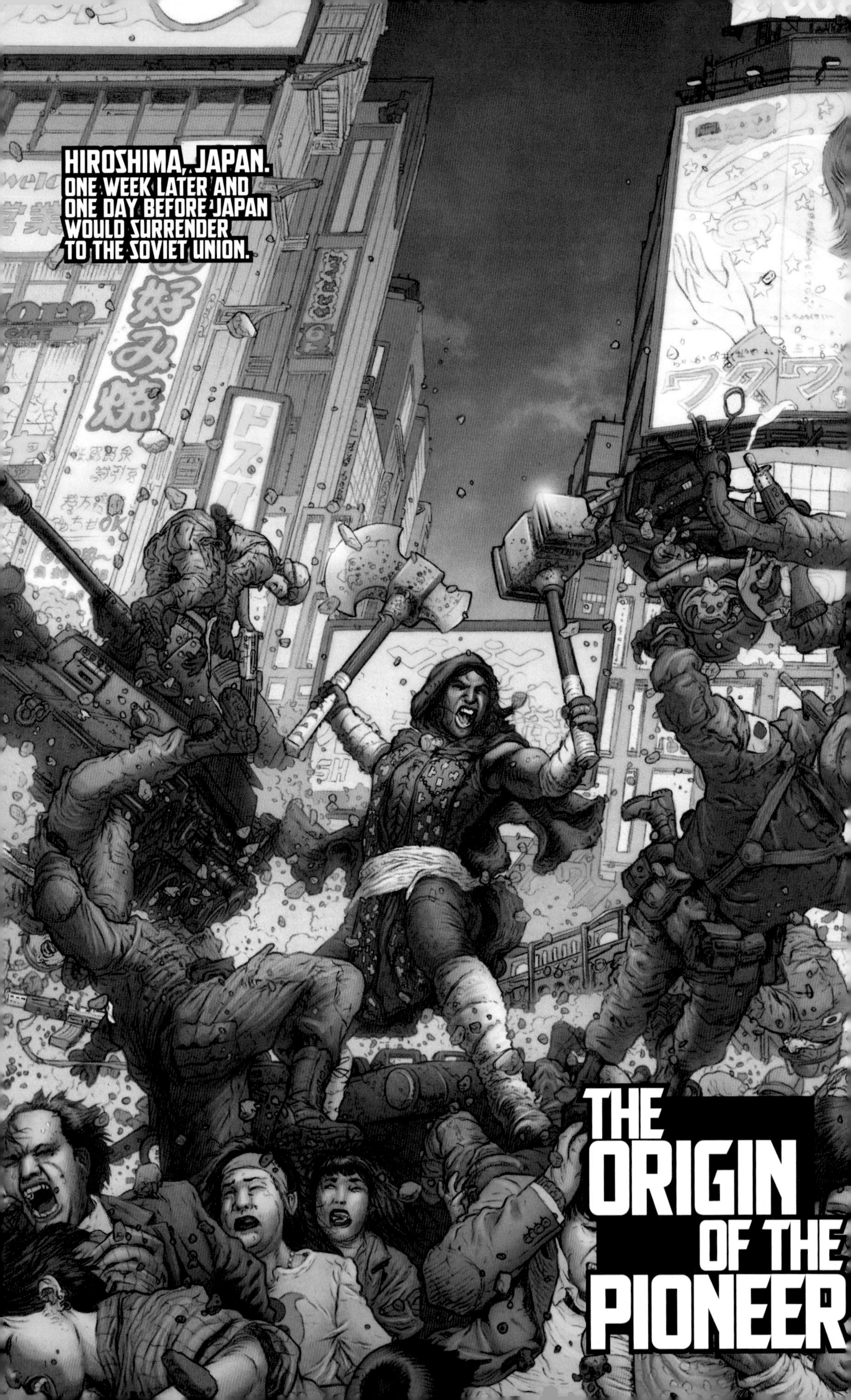
HIROSHIMA, JAPAN.
ONE WEEK LATER AND ONE DAY BEFORE JAPAN WOULD SURRENDER TO THE SOVIET UNION.
THE ORIGIN OF THE PIONEER

GALLERY

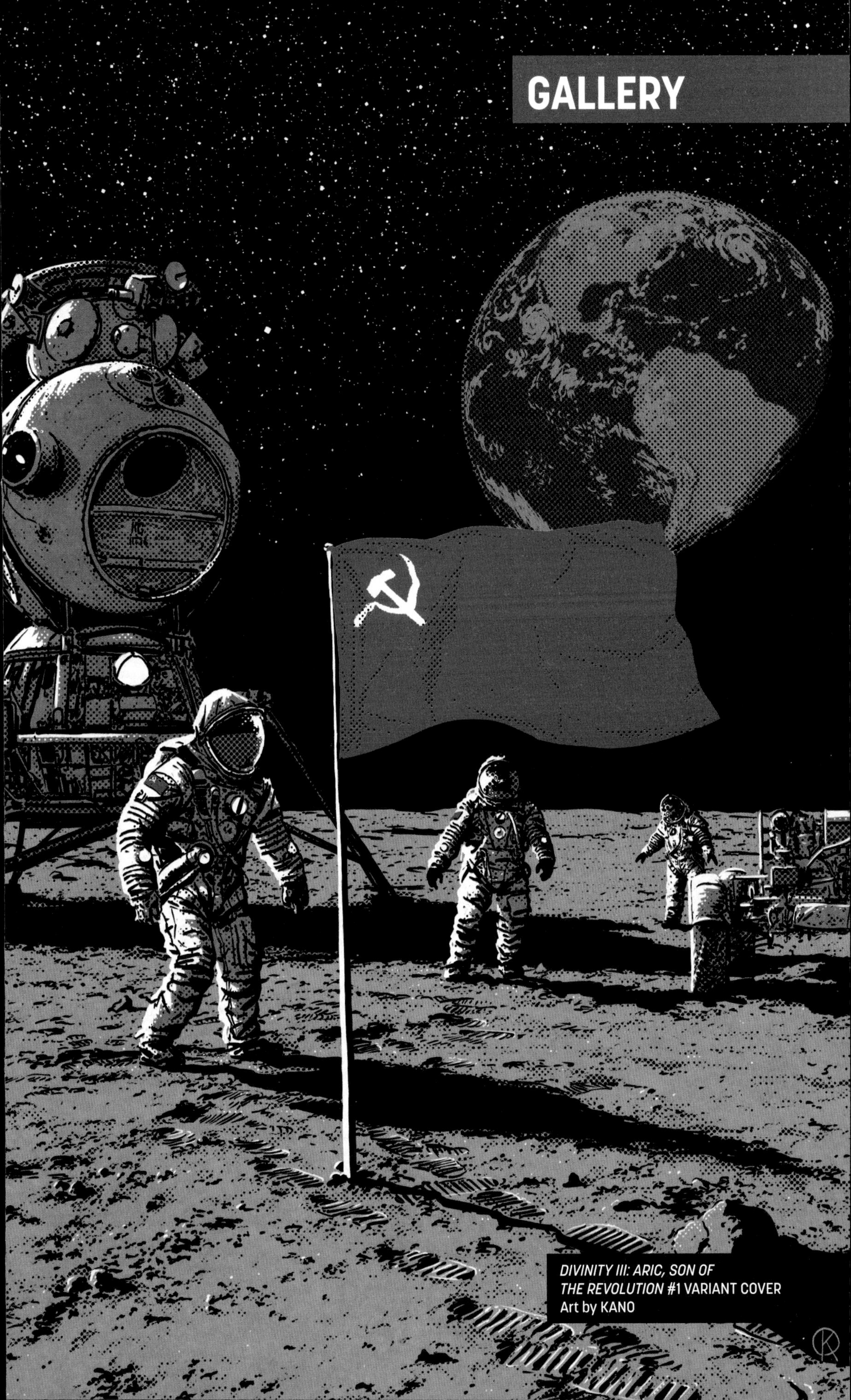

DIVINITY III: ARIC, SON OF THE REVOLUTION #1 VARIANT COVER
Art by KANO

DIVINITY III: KOMANDAR BLOODSHOT #1 COVER B
Art by RYAN BODENHEIM

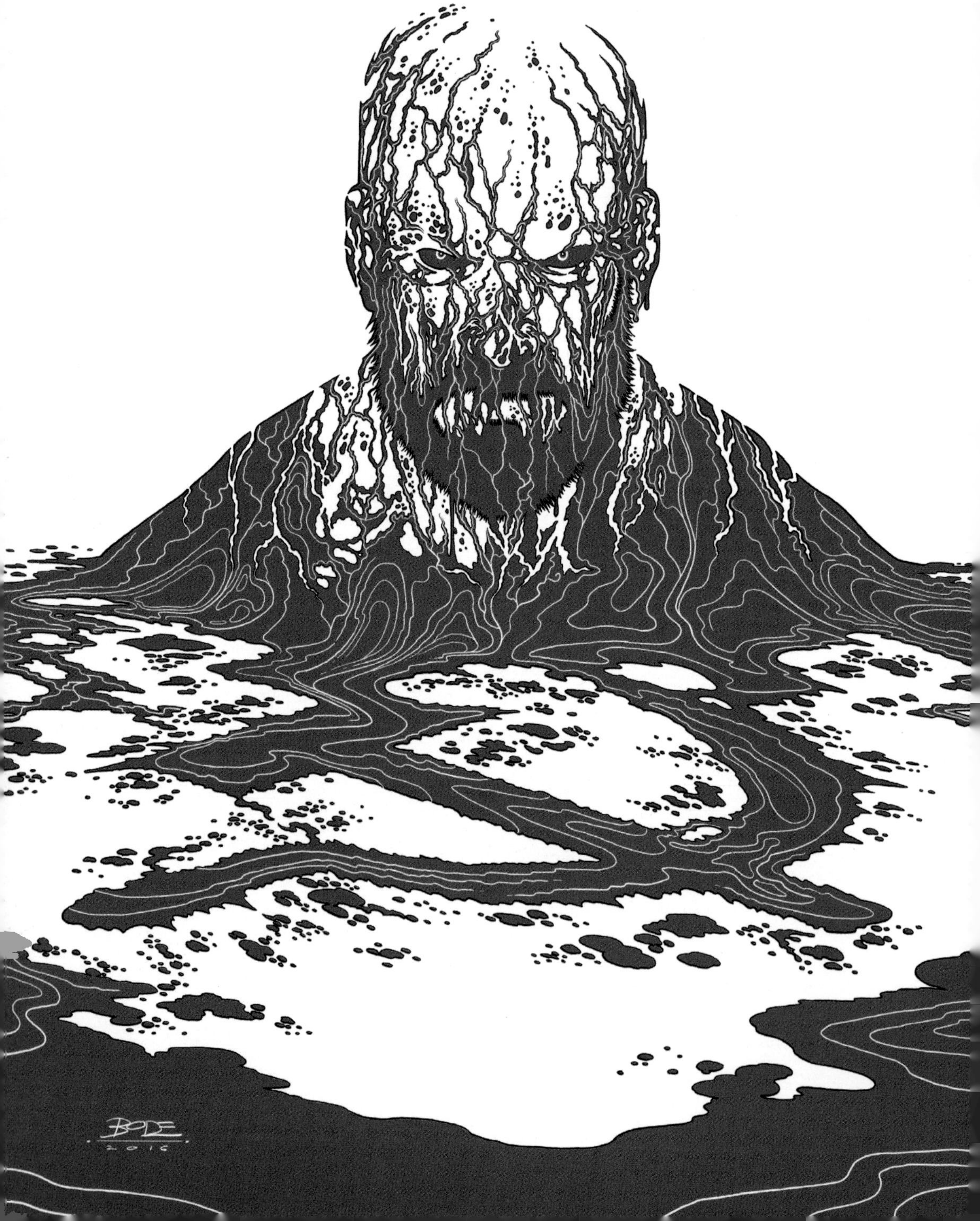
BODE
2016

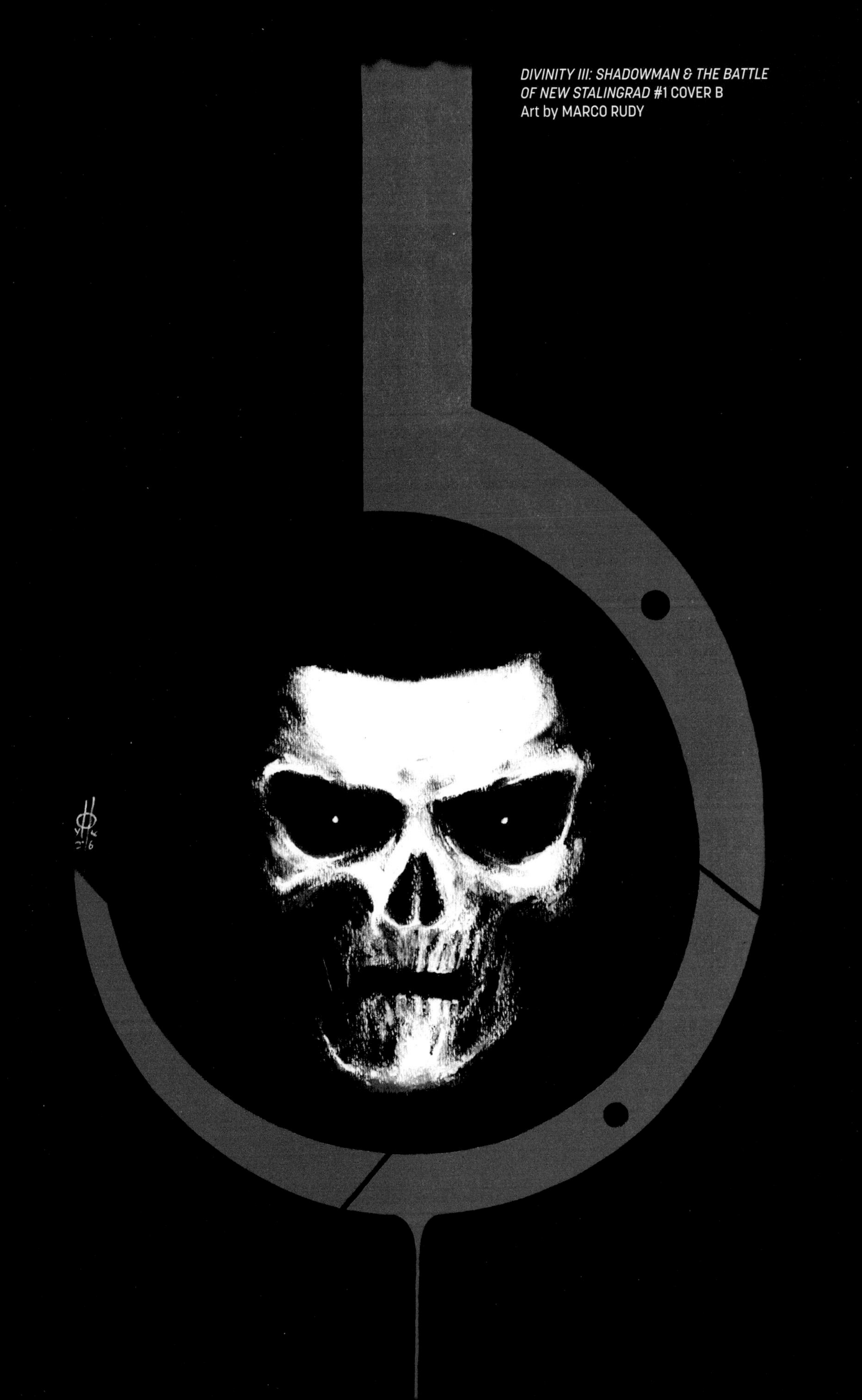

DIVINITY III: SHADOWMAN & THE BATTLE OF NEW STALINGRAD #1 COVER B
Art by MARCO RUDY

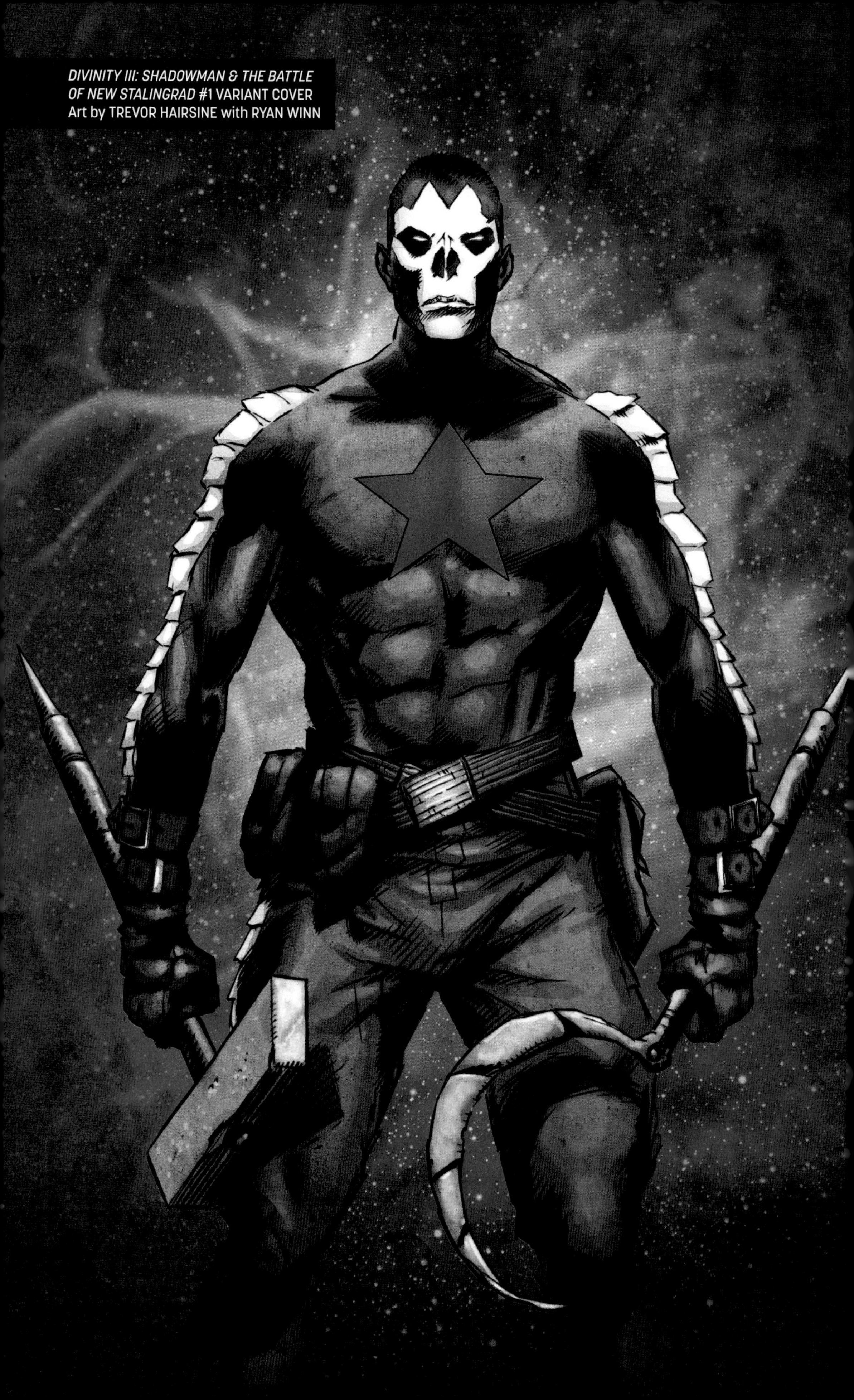

DIVINITY III: SHADOWMAN & THE BATTLE OF NEW STALINGRAD #1 VARIANT COVER
Art by TREVOR HAIRSINE with RYAN WINN

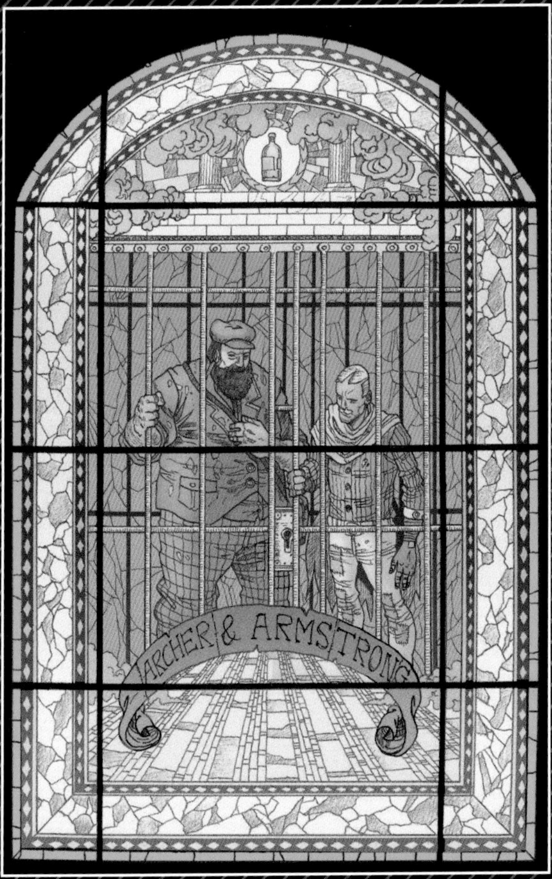
ARCHER & ARMSTRONG

DIVINITY III: ESCAPE FROM GULAG 396 #1 COVER C
Art by ANDRÉS GUINALDO

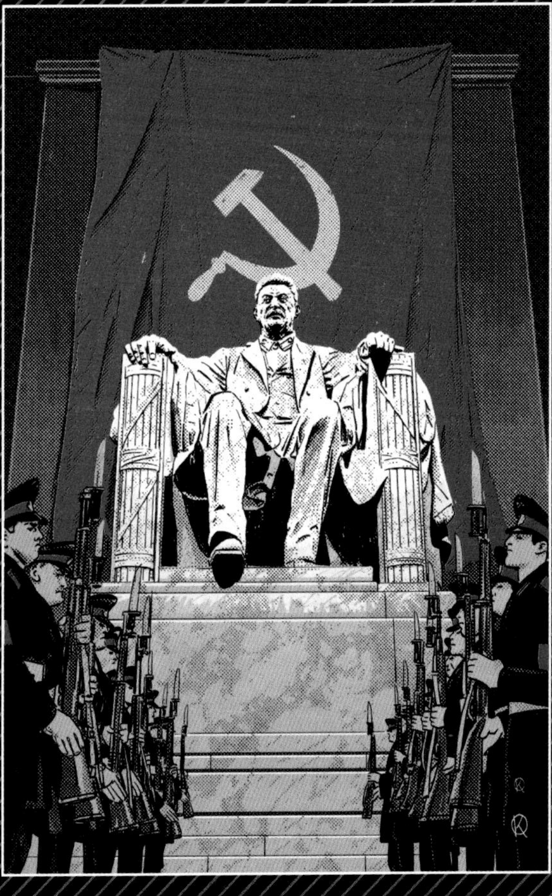

DIVINITY III: ESCAPE FROM GULAG 396 #1
VARIANT COVER
Art by KANO

DIVINITY III: KOMANDAR BLOODSHOT #1,
"The Origin of the Red Legend," p. 1
Art by JUAN JOSÉ RYP

DIVINITY III: KOMANDAR BLOODSHOT #1,
"The Origin of the Red Legend," p. 4
Art by JUAN JOSÉ RYP

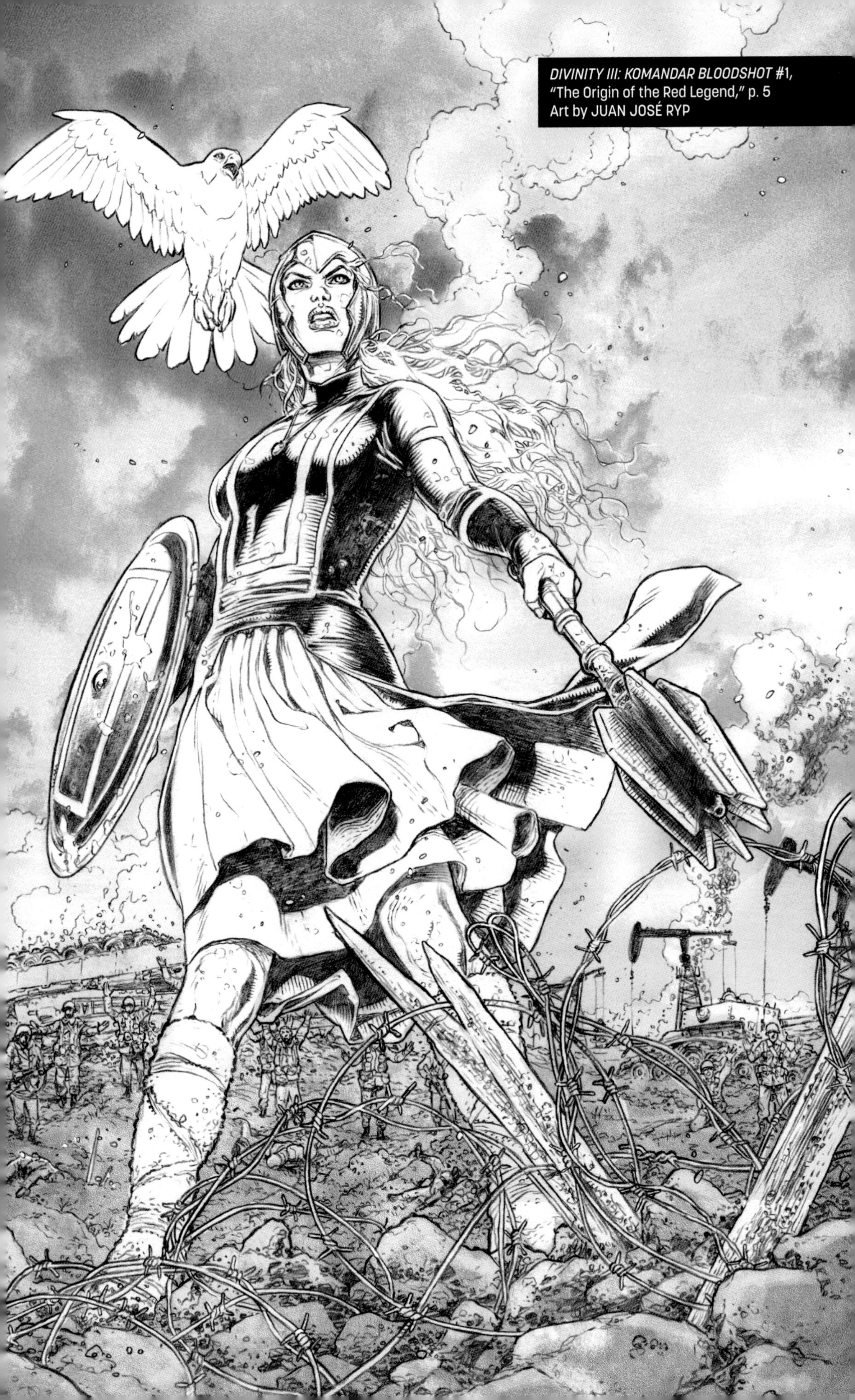

DIVINITY III: KOMANDAR BLOODSHOT #1,
"The Origin of the Red Legend," p. 5
Art by JUAN JOSÉ RYP

DIVINITY III: ARIC, SON OF THE REVOLUTION #1, p.1
Art by CAFU

DIVINITY III: ARIC, SON OF THE REVOLUTION #1, p. 2
Art by CAFU

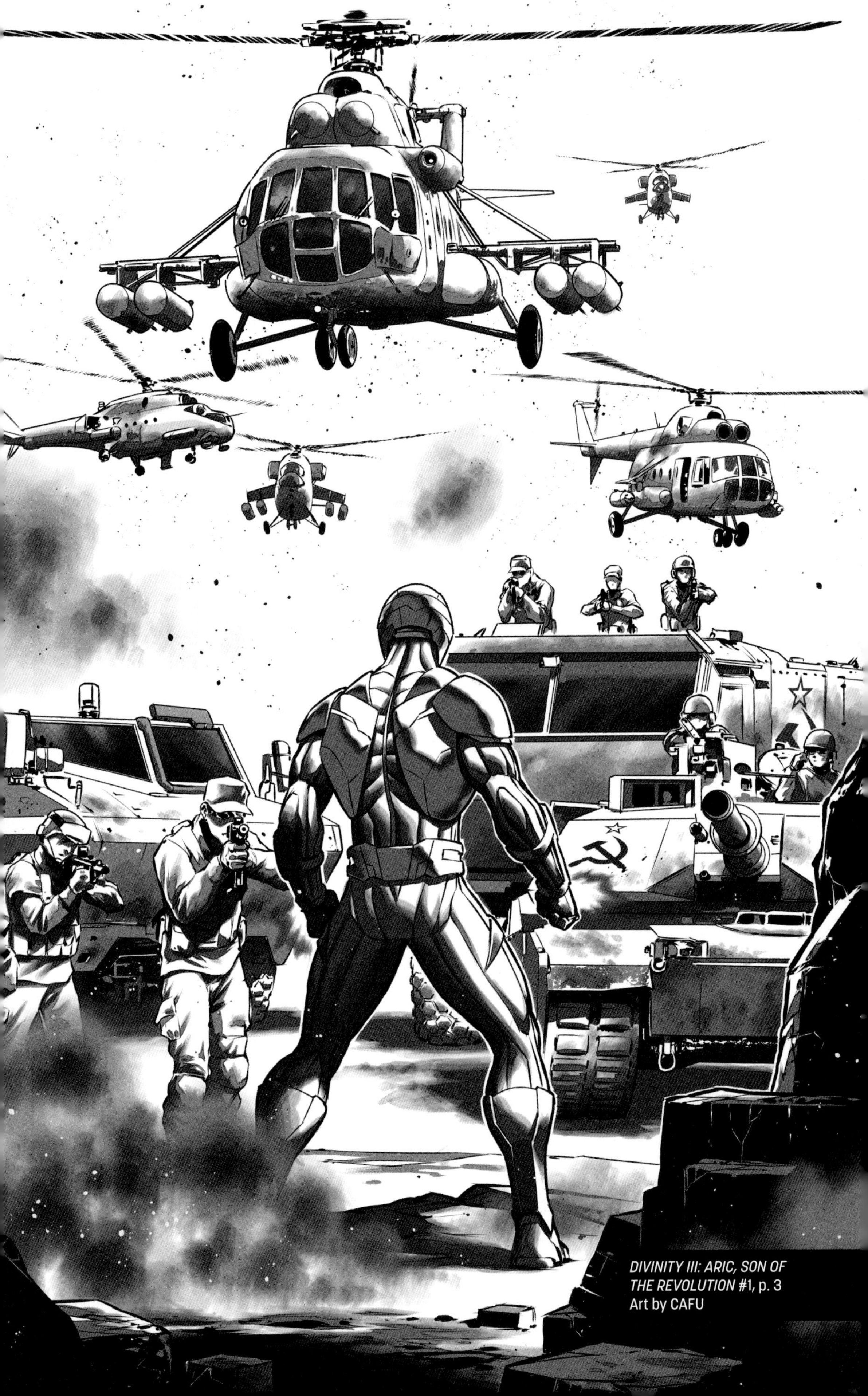

DIVINITY III: ARIC, SON OF THE REVOLUTION #1, p. 3
Art by CAFU

DIVINITY III: ARIC, SON OF THE REVOLUTION #1,
"The Origin of Kostiy, the Deathless," p. 2
Art by JUAN JOSÉ RYP

DIVINITY III: ARIC, SON OF THE REVOLUTION #1,
"The Origin of Kostiy, the Deathless," p. 3
Art by JUAN JOSÉ RYP

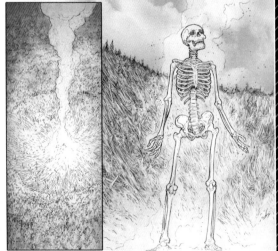

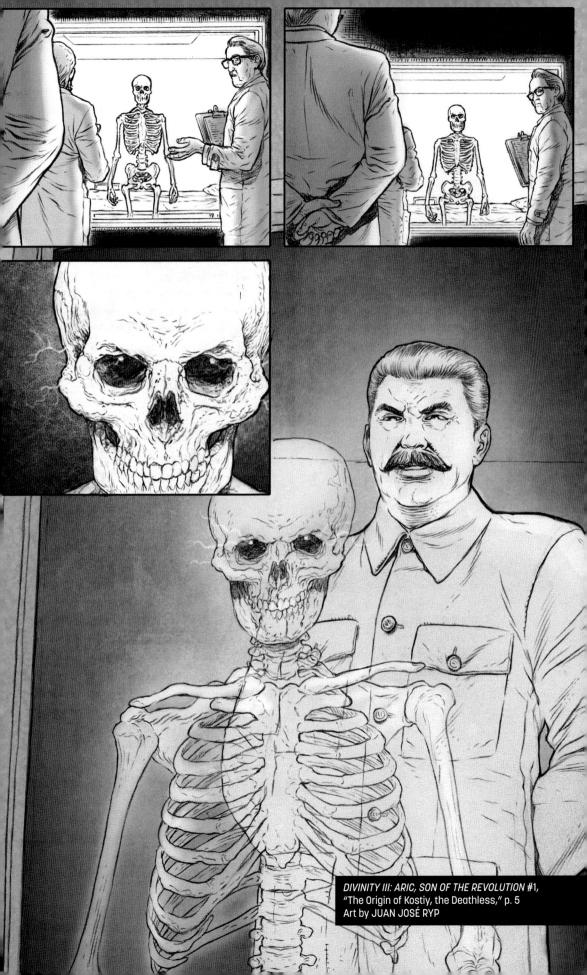

DIVINITY III: ARIC, SON OF THE REVOLUTION #1,
"The Origin of Kostiy, the Deathless," p. 5
Art by JUAN JOSÉ RYP

DIVINITY III: SHADOWMAN & THE BATTLE OF NEW STALINGRAD #1, "The Origin of Baba Yaga," p. 2
Art by JUAN JOSÉ RYP

DIVINITY III: SHADOWMAN & THE BATTLE OF NEW STALINGRAD #1, "The Origin of Baba Yaga," p. 5
Art by JUAN JOSÉ RYP

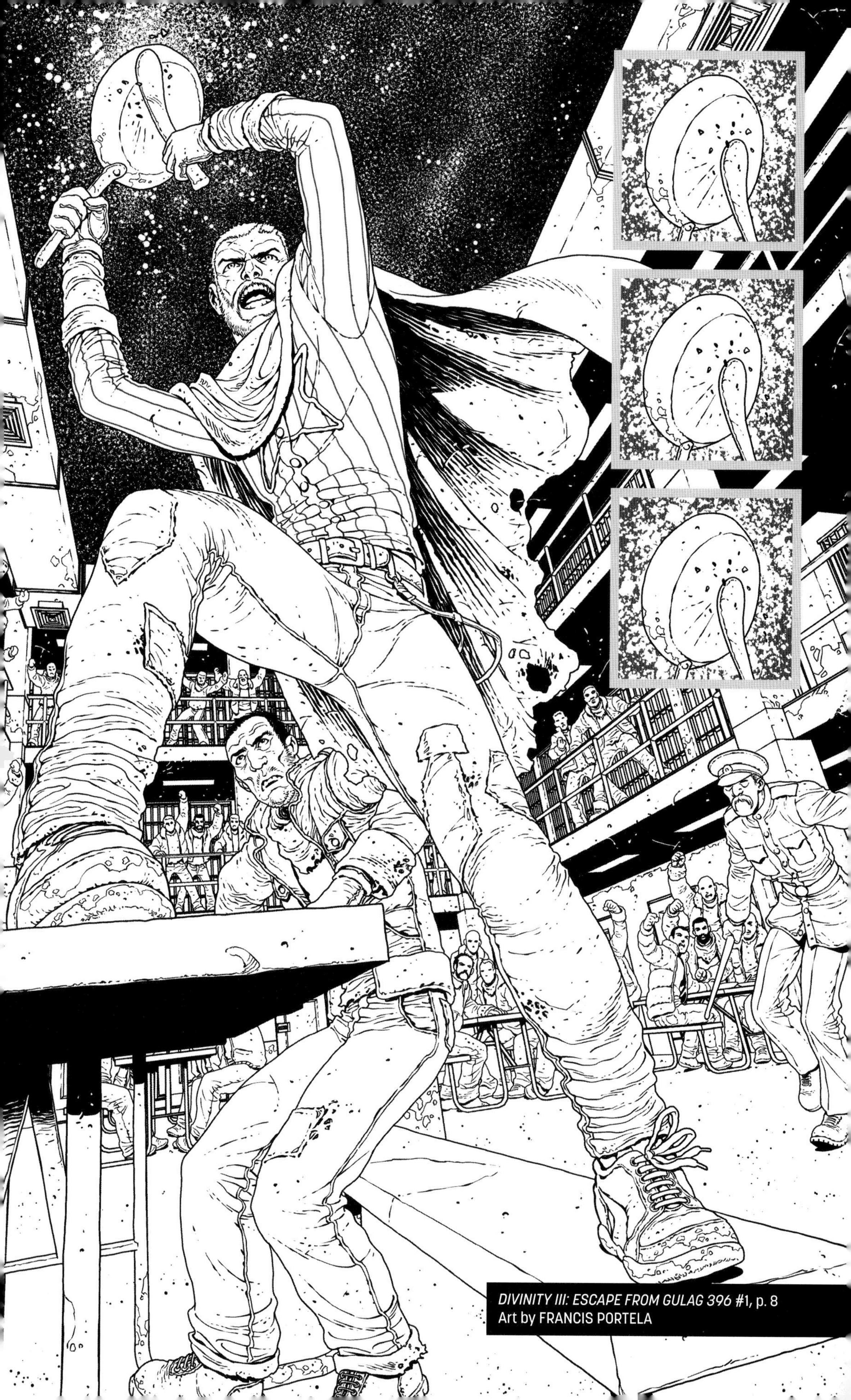

DIVINITY III: ESCAPE FROM GULAG 396 #1, p. 8
Art by FRANCIS PORTELA

EXPLORE THE VALIANT UNIVERSE

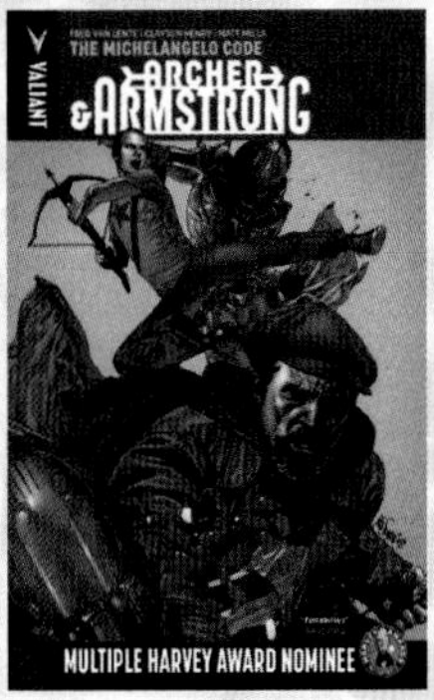
VALIANT
THE MICHELANGELO CODE
ARCHER & ARMSTRONG
MULTIPLE HARVEY AWARD NOMINEE

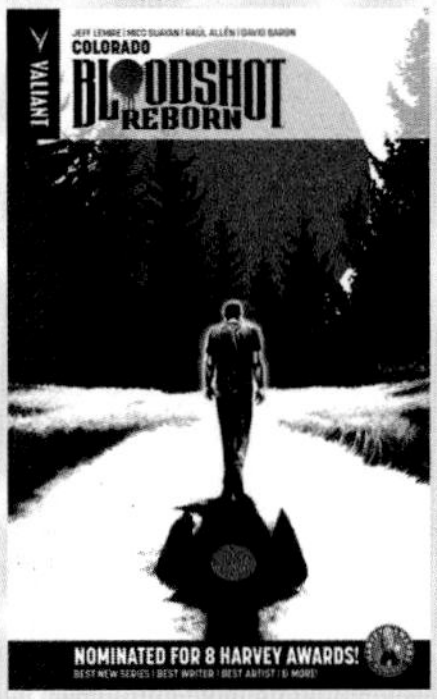
VALIANT
COLORADO
BLOODSHOT REBORN
NOMINATED FOR 8 HARVEY AWARDS!

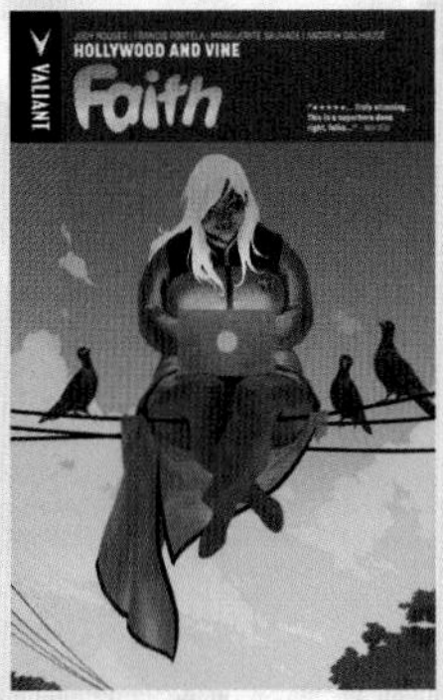
VALIANT
HOLLYWOOD AND VINE
Faith

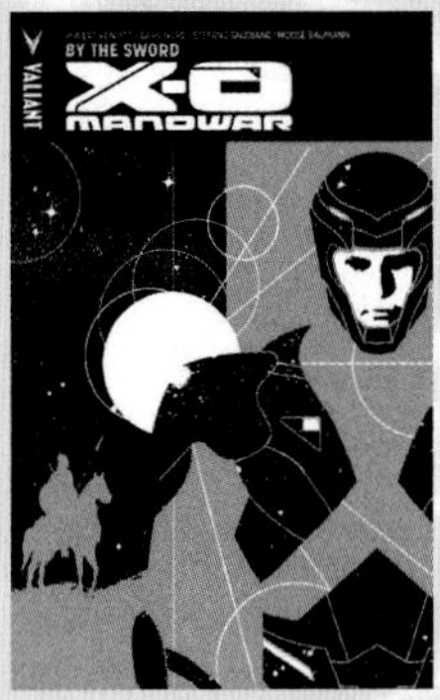
VALIANT
BY THE SWORD
X-O MANOWAR

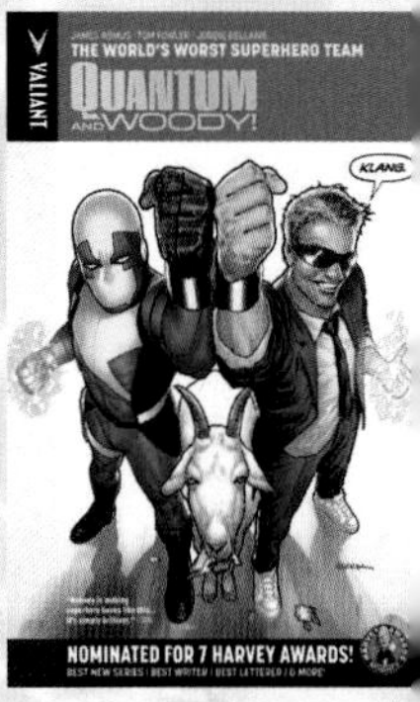
VALIANT
THE WORLD'S WORST SUPERHERO TEAM
QUANTUM AND WOODY!
KLANG
NOMINATED FOR 7 HARVEY AWARDS!

4001 A.D.

4001 A.D.
ISBN: 9781682151433

4001 A.D.: Beyond New Japan
ISBN: 9781682151464

Rai Vol 4: 4001 A.D.
ISBN: 9781682151471

A&A: THE ADVENTURES OF ARCHER AND ARMSTRONG

Volume 1: In the Bag
ISBN: 9781682151495

Volume 2: Romance and Road Trips
ISBN: 9781682151716

ARCHER & ARMSTRONG

Volume 1: The Michelangelo Code
ISBN: 9780979640988

Volume 2: Wrath of the Eternal Warrior
ISBN: 9781939346049

Volume 3: Far Faraway
ISBN: 9781939346148

Volume 4: Sect Civil War
ISBN: 9781939346254

Volume 5: Mission: Improbable
ISBN: 9781939346353

Volume 6: American Wasteland
ISBN: 9781939346421

Volume 7: The One Percent and Other Tales
ISBN: 9781939346537

ARMOR HUNTERS

Armor Hunters
ISBN: 9781939346452

Armor Hunters: Bloodshot
ISBN: 9781939346469

Armor Hunters: Harbinger
ISBN: 9781939346506

Unity Vol. 3: Armor Hunters
ISBN: 9781939346445

X-O Manowar Vol. 7: Armor Hunters
ISBN: 9781939346476

BLOODSHOT

Volume 1: Setting the World on Fire
ISBN: 9780979640964

Volume 2: The Rise and the Fall
ISBN: 9781939346032

Volume 3: Harbinger Wars
ISBN: 9781939346124

Volume 4: H.A.R.D. Corps
ISBN: 9781939346193

Volume 5: Get Some!
ISBN: 9781939346315

Volume 6: The Glitch and Other Tales
ISBN: 9781939346711

BLOODSHOT REBORN

Volume 1: Colorado
ISBN: 9781939346674

Volume 2: The Hunt
ISBN: 9781939346827

Volume 3: The Analog Man
ISBN: 9781682151334

Volume 4: Bloodshot Island
ISBN: 9781682151952

BLOODSHOT U.S.A.

ISBN: 9781682151952

BOOK OF DEATH

Book of Death
ISBN: 9781939346971

Book of Death: The Fall of the Valiant Universe
ISBN: 9781939346988

BRITANNIA

Volume 1
ISBN: 9781682151853

DEAD DROP

ISBN: 9781939346858

THE DEATH-DEFYING DOCTOR MIRAGE

Volume 1
ISBN: 9781939346490

Volume 2: Second Lives
ISBN: 9781682151297

THE DELINQUENTS

ISBN: 9781939346513

DIVINITY

Volume 1
ISBN: 9781939346766

Volume 2
ISBN: 9781682151518

Volume 3
ISBN: 9781682151914

ETERNAL WARRIOR

Volume 1: Sword of the Wild
ISBN: 9781939346209

Volume 2: Eternal Emperor
ISBN: 9781939346292

Volume 3: Days of Steel
ISBN: 9781939346742

WRATH OF THE ETERNAL WARRIOR

Volume 1: Risen
ISBN: 9781682151235

Volume 2: Labyrinth
ISBN: 9781682151594

Volume 3: Deal With a Devil
ISBN: 9781682151976

FAITH

Faith Vol 1: Hollywood and Vine
ISBN: 9781682151402

Faith Vol 2: California Scheming
ISBN: 9781682151631

GENERATION ZERO

Volume 1: We Are the Future
ISBN: 9781682151754

HARBINGER

Volume 1: Omega Rising
ISBN: 9780979640957

Volume 2: Renegades
ISBN: 9781939346025

Volume 3: Harbinger Wars
ISBN: 9781939346117

Volume 4: Perfect Day
ISBN: 9781939346155

Volume 5: Death of a Renegade
ISBN: 9781939346339

Volume 6: Omegas
ISBN: 9781939346384

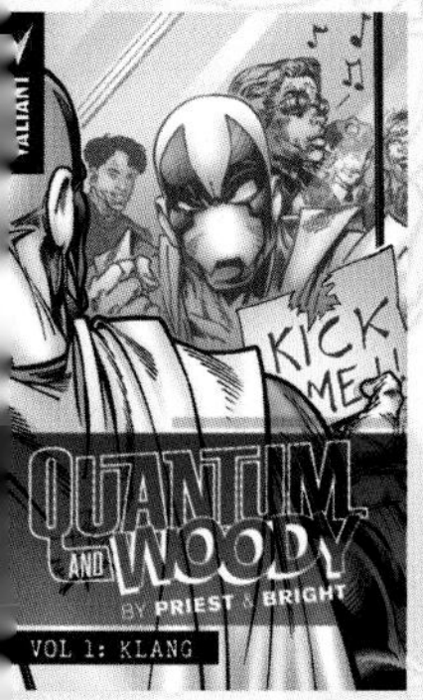
VALIANT
KICK ME
QUANTUM AND WOODY
BY PRIEST & BRIGHT
VOL 1: KLANG

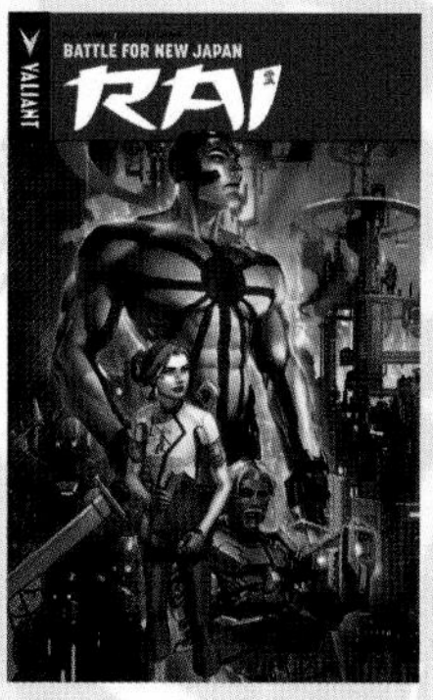
VALIANT
BATTLE FOR NEW JAPAN
RAI

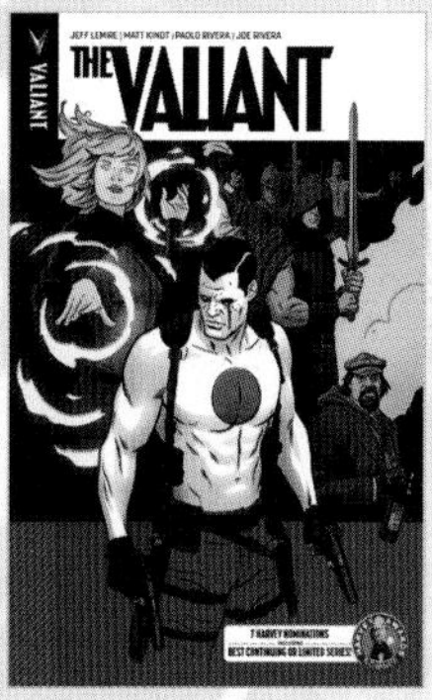
VALIANT
THE VALIANT

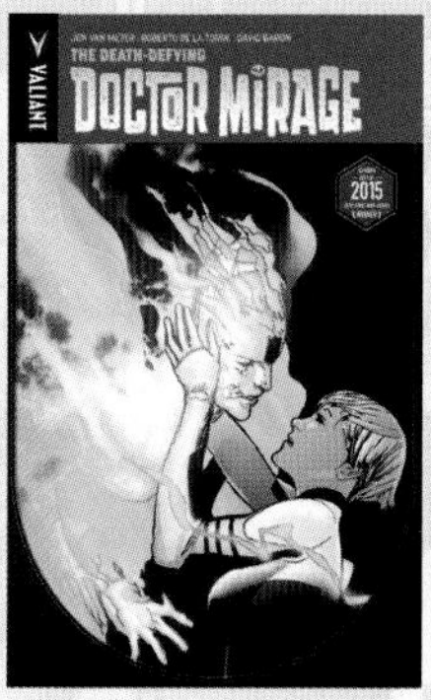
VALIANT
THE DEATH-DEFYING
DOCTOR MIRAGE

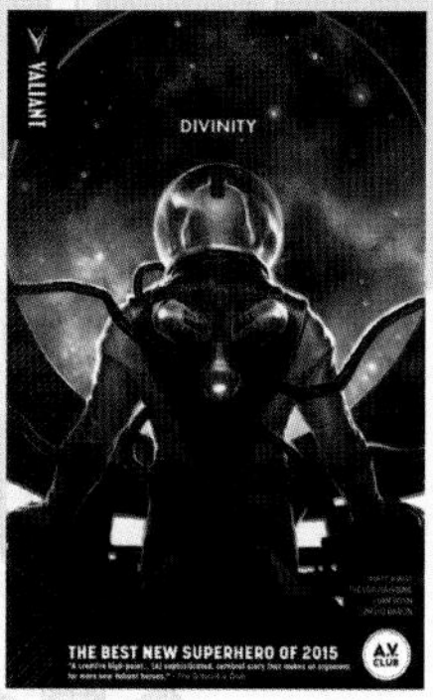
VALIANT
DIVINITY
THE BEST NEW SUPERHERO OF 2015

ARBINGER RENEGADE

olume 1: The Judgment of Solomon
SBN: 9781682151693

ARBINGER WARS

arbinger Wars
SBN: 9781939346094

loodshot Vol. 3: Harbinger Wars
SBN: 9781939346124

arbinger Vol. 3: Harbinger Wars
SBN: 9781939346117

MPERIUM

olume 1: Collecting Monsters
SBN: 9781939346759

olume 2: Broken Angels
SBN: 9781939346896

olume 3: The Vine Imperative
SBN: 9781682151112

olume 4: Stormbreak
SBN: 9781682151372

INJAK

olume 1: Weaponeer
SBN: 9781939346667

olume 2: The Shadow Wars
SBN: 9781939346940

olume 3: Operation: Deadside
SBN: 9781682151259

olume 4: The Siege of King's Castle
SBN: 9781682151617

olume 5: The Fist & The Steel
SBN: 9781682151792

UANTUM AND WOODY

olume 1: The World's Worst Superhero Team
SBN: 9781939346186

olume 2: In Security
SBN: 9781939346230

olume 3: Crooked Pasts, Present Tense
SBN: 9781939346391

olume 4: Quantum and Woody Must Die!
SBN: 9781939346629

UANTUM AND WOODY Y PRIEST & BRIGHT

olume 1: Klang
SBN: 9781939346780

Volume 2: Switch
ISBN: 9781939346803

Volume 3: And So...
ISBN: 9781939346865

Volume 4: Q2 - The Return
ISBN: 9781682151099

RAI

Volume 1: Welcome to New Japan
ISBN: 9781939346414

Volume 2: Battle for New Japan
ISBN: 9781939346612

Volume 3: The Orphan
ISBN: 9781939346841

Rai Vol 4: 4001 A.D.
ISBN: 9781682151471

SHADOWMAN

Volume 1: Birth Rites
ISBN: 9781939346001

Volume 2: Darque Reckoning
ISBN: 9781939346056

Volume 3: Deadside Blues
ISBN: 9781939346162

Volume 4: Fear, Blood, And Shadows
ISBN: 9781939346278

Volume 5: End Times
ISBN: 9781939346377

SHADOWMAN BY ENNIS & WOOD

ISBN: 9781682151358

IVAR, TIMEWALKER

Volume 1: Making History
ISBN: 9781939346636

Volume 2: Breaking History
ISBN: 9781939346834

Volume 3: Ending History
ISBN: 9781939346995

UNITY

Volume 1: To Kill a King
ISBN: 9781939346261

Volume 2: Trapped by Webnet
ISBN: 9781939346346

Volume 3: Armor Hunters
ISBN: 9781939346445

Volume 4: The United
ISBN: 9781939346544

Volume 5: Homefront
ISBN: 9781939346797

Volume 6: The War-Monger
ISBN: 9781939346902

Volume 7: Revenge of the Armor Hunters
ISBN: 9781682151136

THE VALIANT

ISBN: 9781939346605

VALIANT ZEROES AND ORIGINS

ISBN: 9781939346582

X-O MANOWAR

Volume 1: By the Sword
ISBN: 9780979640940

Volume 2: Enter Ninjak
ISBN: 9780979640995

Volume 3: Planet Death
ISBN: 9781939346087

Volume 4: Homecoming
ISBN: 9781939346179

Volume 5: At War With Unity
ISBN: 9781939346247

Volume 6: Prelude to Armor Hunters
ISBN: 9781939346407

Volume 7: Armor Hunters
ISBN: 9781939346476

Volume 8: Enter: Armorines
ISBN: 9781939346551

Volume 9: Dead Hand
ISBN: 9781939346650

Volume 10: Exodus
ISBN: 9781939346933

Volume 11: The Kill List
ISBN: 9781682151273

Volume 12: Long Live the King
ISBN: 9781682151655

Volume 13: Succession and Other Tales
ISBN: 9781682151754

VALIANT
HARBINGER
DELUXE EDITION 2

VALIANT
ROBERT VENDITTI MATT KINDT JOSHUA DYSART JOE HARRIS ROBERT GILL
DOUG BRAITHWAITE DIEGO BERNARD TREVOR HAIRSINE STEPHEN SEGOVIA
ARMOR HUNTERS
DELUXE EDITION

VALIANT
VALIANT MASTERS
JIM SHOOTER | DAVID LAPHAM
CHILDREN OF THE EIGHTH DAY
HARBINGER

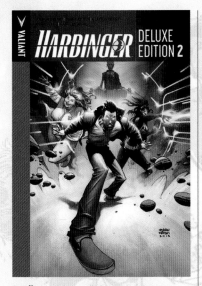

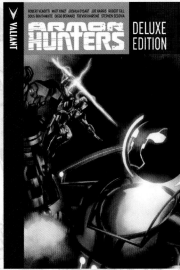

Omnibuses

Archer & Armstrong: The Complete Classic Omnibus
ISBN: 9781939346872
Collecting ARCHER & ARMSTRONG (1992) #0-26, ETERNAL WARRIOR (1992) #25 along with ARCHER & ARMSTRONG: THE FORMATION OF THE SECT.

Quantum and Woody: The Complete Classic Omnibus
ISBN: 9781939346360
Collecting QUANTUM AND WOODY (1997) #0, 1-21 and #32, THE GOAT: H.A.E.D.U.S. #1, and X-O MANOWAR (1996) #16

X-O Manowar Classic Omnibus Vol. 1
ISBN: 9781939346308
Collecting X-O MANOWAR (1992) #0-30, ARMORINES #0, X-O DATABASE #1, as well as material from SECRETS OF THE VALIANT UNIVERSE #1

Deluxe Editions

Archer & Armstrong Deluxe Edition Book 1
ISBN: 9781939346223
Collecting ARCHER & ARMSTRONG #0-13

Archer & Armstrong Deluxe Edition Book 2
ISBN: 9781939346957
Collecting ARCHER & ARMSTRONG #14-25, ARCHER & ARMSTRONG: ARCHER #0 and BLOODSHOT AND H.A.R.D. CORPS #20-21.

Armor Hunters Deluxe Edition
ISBN: 9781939346728
Collecting Armor Hunters #1-4, Armor Hunters: Aftermath #1, Armor Hunters: Bloodshot #1-3, Armor Hunters: Harbinger #1-3, Unity #8-11, and X-O MANOWAR #23-29

Bloodshot Deluxe Edition Book 1
ISBN: 9781939346216
Collecting BLOODSHOT #1-13

Bloodshot Deluxe Edition Book 2
ISBN: 9781939346810
Collecting BLOODSHOT AND H.A.R.D. CORPS #14-23, BLOODSHOT #24-25, BLOODSHOT #0, BLOODSHOT AND H.A.R.D. CORPS: H.A.R.D. CORPS #0, along with ARCHER & ARMSTRONG #18-19

Bloodshot Reborn Deluxe Edition Book 1
ISBN: 978-1-68215-155-6
Collecting BLOODSHOT REBORN #1-13

Book of Death Deluxe Edition
ISBN: 9781682151150
Collecting BOOK OF DEATH #1-4, BOOK OF DEATH: THE FALL OF BLOODSHOT #1, BOOK OF DEATH: THE FALL OF NINJAK #1, BOOK OF DEATH: THE FALL OF HARBINGER #1, and BOOK OF DEATH: THE FALL OF X-O MANOWAR #1.

The Death-Defying Doctor Mirage Deluxe Edition
ISBN: 978-1-68215-153-2
Collecting THE DEATH-DEFYING DR. MIRAGE #1-5 and THE DEATH-DEFYING DR. MIRAGE: SECOND LIVES #1-4

Divinity Deluxe Edition
ISBN: 97819393460993
Collecting DIVNITY #1-4

Faith: Hollywood & Vine Deluxe Edition
ISBN: 978-1-68215-201-0
Collecting FAITH #1-4 and HARBINGER: FAITH #0

Harbinger Deluxe Edition Book 1
ISBN: 9781939346131
Collecting HARBINGER #0-14

Harbinger Deluxe Edition Book 2
ISBN: 9781939346773
Collecting HARBINGER #15-25, HARBINGER: OMEGAS #1-3, and HARBINGER: BLEEDING MONK #0

Harbinger Wars Deluxe Edition
ISBN: 9781939346322
Collecting HARBINGER WARS #1-4, HARBINGER #11-14, and BLOODSHOT #10-13

Ivar, Timewalker Deluxe Edition Book 1
ISBN: 9781682151198
Collecting IVAR, TIMEWALKER #1-12

Ninjak Deluxe Edition Book 1
ISBN: 978-1-68215-157-0
Collecting NINJAK #1-13

Quantum and Woody Deluxe Edition Book 1
ISBN: 9781939346681
Collecting QUANTUM AND WOODY #1-12 and QUANTUM AND WOODY: THE GOAT #0

Q2: The Return of Quantum and Woody Deluxe Edition
ISBN: 9781939346568
Collecting Q2: THE RETURN OF QUANTUM AND WOODY #1-5

Rai Deluxe Edition Book 1
ISBN: 9781682151174
Collecting RAI #1-12, along with material from R #1 PLUS EDITION and RAI #5 PLUS EDITION

Shadowman Deluxe Edition Book 1
ISBN: 9781939346438
Collecting SHADOWMAN #0-10

Shadowman Deluxe Edition Book 2
ISBN: 9781682151075
Collecting SHADOWMAN #11-16, SHADOWMAN #13X, SHADOWMAN: END TIMES #1-3 and PUNK MAMBO #0

Unity Deluxe Edition Book 1
ISBN: 9781939346575
Collecting UNITY #0-14

The Valiant Deluxe Edition
ISBN: 97819393460986
Collecting THE VALIANT #1-4

X-O Manowar Deluxe Edition Book 1
ISBN: 9781939346100
Collecting X-O MANOWAR #1-14

X-O Manowar Deluxe Edition Book 2
ISBN: 9781939346520
Collecting X-O MANOWAR #15-22, and UNITY #1-

X-O Manowar Deluxe Edition Book 3
ISBN: 9781682151310
Collecting X-O MANOWAR #23-29 and ARMOR HUNTERS #1-4.

Valiant Masters

Bloodshot Vol. 1 - Blood of the Machine
ISBN: 9780979640933

H.A.R.D. Corps Vol. 1 - Search and Destroy
ISBN: 9781939346285

Harbinger Vol. 1 - Children of the Eighth Day
ISBN: 9781939346483

Ninjak Vol. 1 - Black Water
ISBN: 9780979640971

Rai Vol. 1 - From Honor to Strength
ISBN: 9781939346070

Shadowman Vol. 1 - Spirits Within
ISBN: 9781939346018

VALIANT
DIVINITY
MATT KINDT
TREVOR HAIRSINE
RYAN WINN
DAVID BARON
THE BEST NEW SUPERHERO OF 2015
"A creative high-point... [A] sophisticated, cerebral story that makes an argument for more new Valiant heroes." - The Onion/A.V. Club
A.V. CLUB

Divinity Vol. 1

VALIANT
DIVINITY II

Divinity Vol. 2

BROKEN ANGELS
インペリアム
IMPERIUM

Imperium Vol. 2: Broken Angels
(OPTIONAL)

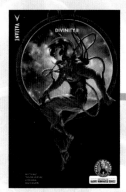

VALIANT
DIVINITY III

Divinity III: Heroes of the Glorious Stalinverse
(OPTIONAL)

VALIANT
DIVINITY III
ONE OF THE BEST SERIES OF 2016

Divinity Vol. 3 : Stalinverse

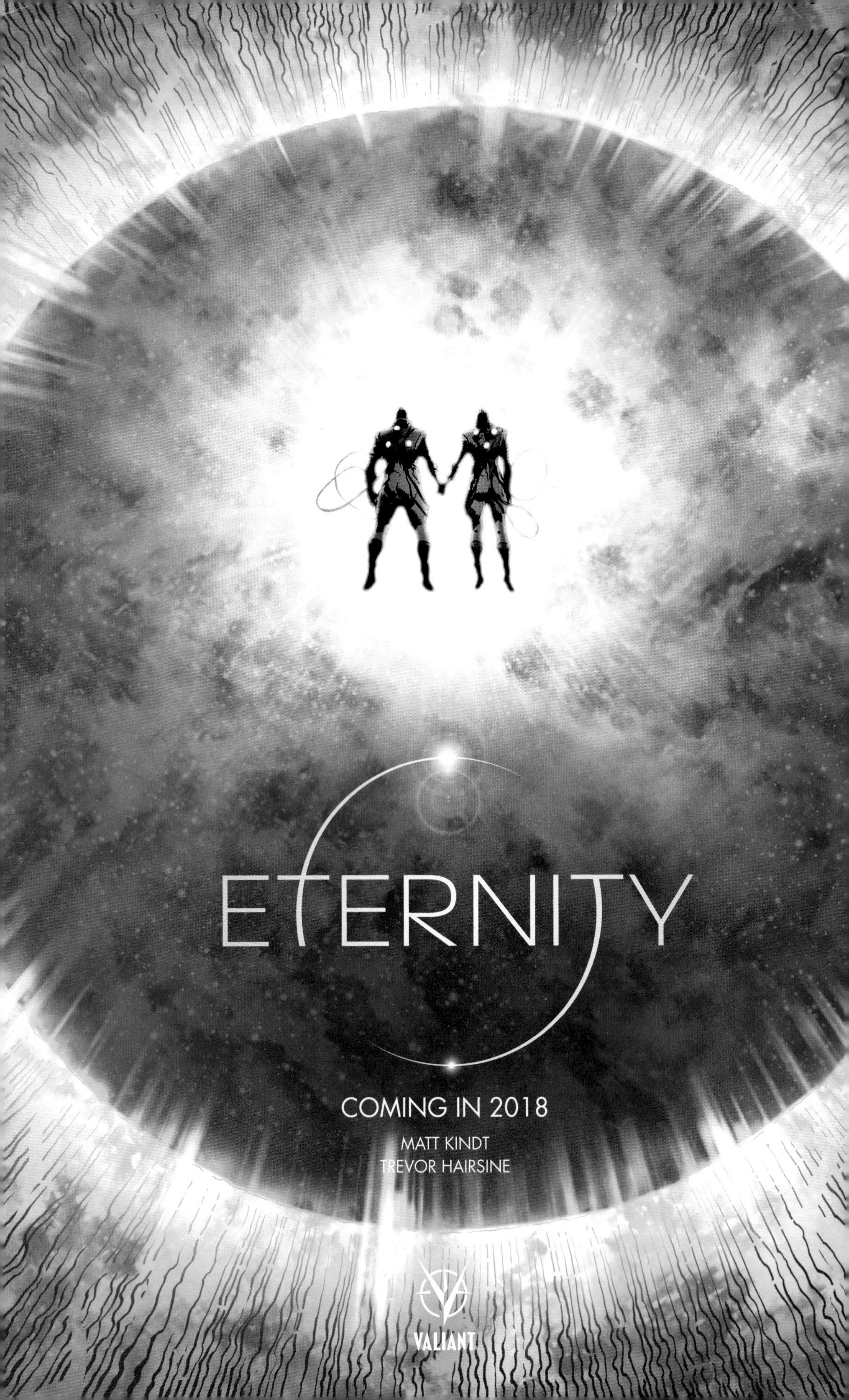
ETERNITY
COMING IN 2018
MATT KINDT
TREVOR HAIRSINE
VALIANT